NERO

THE MAN BEHIND THE MYTH

NERO

THE MAN BEHIND THE MYTH

RICHARD HOLLAND

SUTTON PUBLISHING

This book was first published in 2000 by
Sutton Publishing Limited · Phoenix Mill
Thrupp · Stroud · Gloucestershire · GL5 2BU

This paperback edition first published in 2002

British Library Cataloguing in Publication Data
A catalogue record for this book is available from the British
Library.

ISBN 0 7509 2876 X

Typeset in 10.5/12.5pt Plantin.
Typesetting and origination by
Sutton Publishing Limited.
Printed in Great Britain by
J.H. Haynes & Co. Ltd, Sparkford.

CONTENTS

PREFACE

The man who called himself 'Saviour of the World' knew he was about to die. Great crowds had hailed him as the 'Son of God' when he entered the capital city in triumph, riding slowly through packed streets while the common people cheered and strewed his path with flowers. But now everything had changed. With terrifying suddenness the rulers of the city and the temple turned against him. They hated and feared the reforms he spoke of, his unconventional behaviour, the way he preferred to eat with sinners, his dramatic appearances in front of superstitious crowds who believed he might be the promised Messiah – above all, they hated him for the way he had singled out so many members of their own privileged caste for personal warnings of wrath to come.

Now, deserted by all but a few followers – men drawn from the humblest ranks of society – he went out beyond the city walls, under cover of night, after a last supper. He hoped to be allowed to escape his fate. But a messenger brought news that he had just been condemned as a public enemy by the rulers and the chief priests. If captured, he would be dragged in front of a court composed of his bitterest enemies and sentenced to a horrifying death. He would be stripped naked in a prescribed ritual of cruelty and humiliation under the jeers of the very mob who had so recently fawned at his feet. Then the Roman executioners would clamp his neck to a cross-tree, make him stagger under it through the public streets and flog him with heavy rods. Only when pronounced dead would his broken body be removed for disposal.

But this particular 'Son of God'[1] cheated the law and the executioners. As the first of the soldiers galloped up to his hiding place at dawn he cut his throat with a knife and bled to death in the arms of a centurion who vainly tried to stem the flow. For this was Nero, Emperor of Rome, last of the aristocratic Julio–Claudian line that had ruled for a hundred years since the fall of the Republic, and his death was to plunge his vast empire into civil war and chaos.

The point at issue here is not that Nero can stand comparison in any metaphysical sense with Jesus of Nazareth, whose last days on earth showed such striking similarities with his own. The young Emperor was much too human for that! Most of the academic scholars now pursuing the quest for the 'historical Jesus' agree that the New Testament, in its original Greek form, is chiefly the creation of people who never met Jesus but who wrote about him some twenty-five or more years after his death. It is not just an interesting coincidence that the myth of Nero as archetypal sadistic monster is chiefly the creation of people who never met him but who wrote about him some fifty or more years after his death.

In both cases the various authors were partisans – for Jesus in one case, against Nero in the other. They were not historians in the modern sense of being disinterested scholars concerned only to establish the truth about the past. They did not necessarily tell direct lies, but they were often happy enough to treat hearsay as fact or invent words to put in people's mouths to represent the gist of what they believed those people were likely to have said. Such unscientific methods were recognized in the ancient world – especially in the absence of verbatim reporting – as being natural to the art of rhetoric, the purpose of which is not simply to inform but to persuade.

The quest for the historical Jesus,[2] launched to free him from later rhetorical and theological accretions, has become an academic growth industry, from its roots in the eighteenth-century Enlightenment. By contrast, the quest for the historical Nero has scarcely begun. While there has been scepticism about many of the details recorded by the three main ancient authorities – Tacitus, Suetonius and Dio Cassius – the general picture of him as both a monstrous tyrant and a pretentious buffoon remains largely unchallenged. This book is an attempt to demonstrate that the 'facts' of Nero's life, so far as they can be extrapolated from the written record, do not justify the rhetoric that continues to sustain the myth of the monster.

There are other parallels between the earthly careers of Jesus and Nero.[3] Both men were in their early thirties when they died, although Jesus' crucifixion had taken place about forty years earlier in the Roman province of Judaea. It is even probable that during his lifetime more people believed that Nero might be the Messiah than those who entertained similar beliefs about Jesus in his lifetime. Messianic prophecies abounded in the Near East at that time and Nero had much greater public exposure. Astrologers are said to have forecast a future for him as King of Jerusalem.

It is in the way that posterity has perceived them that their chief differences lie. To a billion Christians throughout the world today Jesus is the Christ, the eternally living Son of God, in whose name all mankind may hope for salvation. Nero is remembered as the tyrant who murdered his mother, who 'fiddled while Rome burned' and who threw Christians to the lions in his arena. He has been identified as the Beast of the Apocalypse, bearing the number 666, as recorded in the Book of Revelation. In modern times his most enthusiastic and inventive disciple has been the Marquis de Sade, who exclaimed in prayer: 'O Nero! Let me venerate your memory!'[4]

This book will not try to whitewash Nero, much less venerate his memory, but it will attempt to rescue him from Hollywood kitsch and the hostile spin-doctoring that began before his body was cold and has continued to the present day. It will also try to show that he was more of a liberator than an oppressor, that his policy amounted to 'make love, not war', and that he became – through his own drive and ability – the first mass-market pop star in recorded history.[5] Unlike his militaristic predecessors, he never led an army nor even troubled to visit any of the legions guarding his frontiers, although he loved to dress up in uniform on state occasions. He preferred to write poetry, play music, sing to an audience, act classical roles on the stage, compete in chariot races, dine with philosophers rather than generals and amuse himself and his friends for hours on end with lots of food, drink and sex.

To Roman traditionalists, all those activities were associated with Greeks and with decadence. They believed, not without justification, that Nero's favourite activities lowered his dignity and that of the state. He believed he was enhancing Rome's reputation by his magnificent lifestyle and by his artistic achievements and patronage. The evidence that the common people loved him is overwhelming. They flocked to his games and concerts, and they ate and drank their fill at his huge, free-for-all street parties. Nero's problems arose chiefly from the natural antagonism of the old ruling class. Politically, they would have preferred a return to the days of the Republic, when their ancestors had taken turns to share power. Most of them were realistic enough to acknowledge that this ambition was an impossible dream. But if they had to be ruled by an emperor, they wanted a competent military leader who would conform to the unwritten rules of the *mos majorum* – the traditional moral ways of the worthiest Romans.

This hallowed and instinctively understood code of conduct was deemed to include the traditions of dead ancestors as well as the opinions of living contemporaries. In its plural form, *mores majorum*, one can see how close it is linguistically to the modern English 'moral majority'; it is not, of course, its precise equivalent in meaning, but can serve as useful shorthand to indicate the area where Nero chiefly disappointed his most influential subjects. The Roman moral majority, deeply resentful of his Hellenizing ways, plotted to kill him once it became clear he was determined to follow a professional artistic career as a singer and actor. After his death, an official policy of *damnatio memoriae* ensured that little that was favourable to him survived in the written record.

Two millennia later, we apparently remain prisoners of the traditional way of assessing the relative merits of Nero and, for instance, Julius Caesar, the charismatic precursor of all the emperors. Caesar continues to enjoy the adulation of posterity as a result of his glittering career of military conquests, although he was rightly accused in his own day of war crimes. The fact that he had no more excuse for invading Gaul than Hitler had for invading Poland in 1939 is conveniently overlooked, along with the fate of the hundreds of thousands of Gallic and Germanic tribesmen whom he slaughtered or sold into slavery, often with their women and children, too. Far from denying his responsibility for these serial bloodbaths, he writes about each of them in a frank, matter-of-fact way, as if taking professional pride in a job well done.[6]

How much longer are we to go on admiring Caesar for helping to create the grandeur that was Rome out of the genocide that was Gaul, while we continue to revile Nero – a man who spent his adult life trying to persuade his people to embrace and enjoy the blessings of Greek civilization? Caesar did not even have Nero's excuse, as head of state, that he was having to take hard decisions in the national interest. At the time of the rape of Gaul, Caesar was a power-hungry ex-consul who, by political manipulation and bribery, had managed to secure a five-year command of some Roman legions and used them ruthlessly for his personal aggrandizement, ignoring any senatorial protests. Nero, by contrast, was forced to become Emperor at the age of sixteen for the most potent of dynastic reasons: had he not done so, he and his mother would inevitably have faced death.

Nero certainly punished 'Christians' in the aftermath of the Great Fire of Rome, but the historical evidence (as set out in Chapter Eleven) is confusing and open to widely differing interpretations. During his reign of more than thirteen years he also executed or forced to suicide about thirty named people who plotted to kill him, or whom he had good reason to suspect of having done so. There were no doubt some others in that category (the record is incomplete for about the last two years of the reign), but no government, whether monarchical or democratically elected, can be expected to tolerate assassination as a form of political opposition. The same fate befell three adult male members of his family (his brother-in-law and two cousins), who may or may not have been guilty of conspiracy but who were potentially dangerous rivals. His worst personal crimes –

although both had political dimensions – were the murder of his mother Agrippina (herself a murderess) and of his first wife Octavia, whom he had been compelled to marry while still a child. He is also accused of murdering his thirteen-year-old step-brother Britannicus after sodomizing him, but I attempt to show (in Chapter Five) that both those accusations are false.

In total, this is not a good record, but neither is it especially bad for an absolute ruler, who effectively held the power of life and death over all his subjects. It must take a very special person indeed, who, on acquiring supreme power, refrains from using it to protect himself. Perhaps no such person has ever existed. The warlike Constantine the Great, the 'first Christian emperor' (baptized on his death-bed so that he might go straight to Heaven!), killed large numbers of people, including his wife and son; but that aspect of his career is rarely emphasized. Nero's immediate predecessor, Claudius – portrayed as a delightfully sympathetic character by Sir Derek Jacobi in the television adaptation of Robert Graves' *I Claudius* – was an active sadist who loved to watch executions as well as gladiatorial combats, and tortured many victims in his private chambers.[7]

Claudius' earliest extant biographer, Suetonius, tells us that in the course of Claudius' own 13-year reign no fewer than 35 senators and 300 knights (*equites*) were summarily disposed of either by execution, murder or written invitations to take their own lives.[8] It is as if, at the height of the British Empire, Queen Victoria had been in the habit of slaughtering each year a good two dozen assorted peers and bishops, judges and generals, mill-owners and MPs and knights of the shires, at an average rate of about one a fortnight. And that, of course, would have been after torturing, in pursuit of evidence and therefore of justification, their entire household staffs from the butler down to the youngest scullery maid and boot-boy.

So why is Nero still singled out as being arguably the biggest villain of all time? One reason, of course, is that he persecuted Christians, while his second wife, Poppaea, protected the Jews.[9] Some contemporary historians wrote favourably about him but their work has not survived, and he himself left no memoirs, letters or essays. We know of a few half-lines of his poetry only because other writers quoted them. Our most important source, the *Annals* of Tacitus, survived the depredations of antiquity in an incomplete manuscript, from which the first nine and the last two years of Nero's life are missing. Suetonius' *Life* of Nero is largely a series of disconnected anecdotes, most of which cannot be dated to a particular year. Dio Cassius' *History* was written a century after the works of Tacitus and Suetonius, and the part dealing with Nero's reign comes down to us in a summary made by Byzantine monks in the Middle Ages. (See Appendix One.)

But the problem is wider than this. Although it has been obvious for some years that most of his later biographers were drinking from a poisoned well, classical historians have been reluctant to embark on a radical reassessment of Nero's life and character. In a few cases this is no doubt due to beliefs that individuals scarcely matter in the context of the rise and fall of great empires. But in the main, academic writers have been wary, for understandable professional reasons, of venturing beyond the received written sources in a field where, in the comparatively recent past, great scholars have demonstrated formidable erudition.[10] 'The sources may lie, but without the sources we are nothing' is how Jás Elsner and Jamie Masters succinctly express the problem in their introduction to *Reflections of Nero* (Duckworth, 1994), a collection of essays by modern scholars at English and American universities. The two editors acknowledge the need for 'a more sympathetic reappraisal of Nero', but feel that a comprehensive retelling of his story would be very hard to achieve by traditional scholarly methods.[11] The task is plainly not for the faint-hearted, but in my view it is both possible and necessary, which is why I have had the temerity to step into a field so closely guarded by career specialists. The book is intended for the general reader, although I have tried to indicate both in the text and through end-notes wherever it challenges the ancient sources, and also to draw attention to some of the recent secondary literature on the early empire. All translations are my own, except in such obvious instances as well-known passages from the Bible. Exceptions are indicated in the notes.

Depending on one's perspective, the Roman Empire may be deemed to have declined and fallen at least three times – in the West, at Byzantium and in central Europe – but it has continued to lead a ghostly existence in the hearts and minds of those in each generation who succumb to the lure of its dangerous glamour. It was not until the twentieth century that the Kaiser and the Czar lost their titles (derived from the name 'Caesar') in the furnace of a world war that their imperial rivalries had helped to provoke. Mussolini then tried and failed, ludicrously, to resurrect the Roman Empire in its original heartlands of Italy and its Mediterranean neighbours. Since the Second World War a new Treaty of Rome has already reunited to some degree much of the territory that Nero ruled over, and may yet eventually eclipse his *imperium* in geographical scope and untrammelled power.

The importance of discovering the truth behind the myths that still obscure general awareness of the realities of ancient Rome needs no further emphasis. To professional historians, of course, Augustus is the key figure. Among the wider public only two names really resonate – those of Julius Caesar and Nero. Of those two, only Nero ruled the Augustan Empire. So long as we recognize the bias in the ancient texts, treat them with common sense and set them in the context of the other evidence of their times – social, cultural, archaeological, literary and artistic – it becomes possible to encounter Nero imaginatively as a man, not a monster; as a great populist, not a clown; as misguided aesthete rather than evil Antichrist.

Nero was excessive in everything he did. Because he was the most powerful man in the world he pushed his personal freedom to the limits. He revelled in inventive choices, not all of them good or sensible. After his death people talked of a Second Coming, something else he had in common with Jesus. Spurious, born-again Neros sprang up from time to time in odd spots around the Mediterranean to create brief disturbances of the *Pax Romana*. But the hostile myth-makers were at work on his case, and they transformed him from the people's favourite into a bogeyman to frighten children.

An attempt to set the record straight begins here.

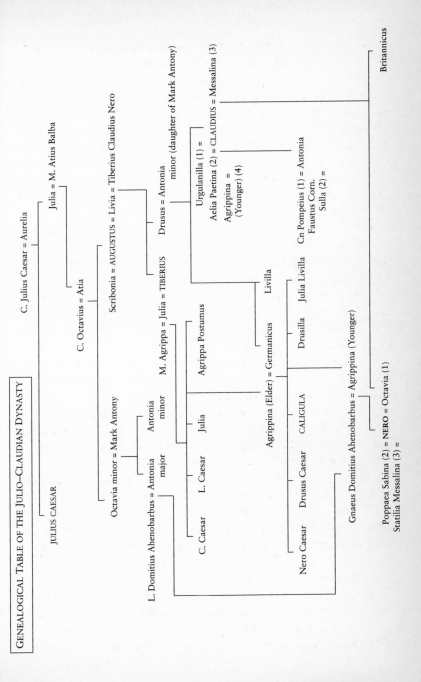

GENEALOGICAL TABLE OF THE JULIO-CLAUDIAN DYNASTY

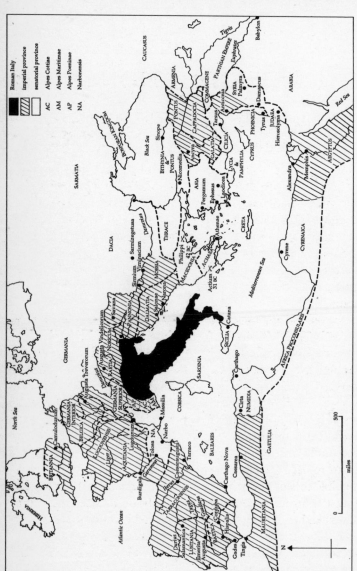

Map of the Roman Empire at the time of Nero.

INTRODUCTION

BIRTH OF AN EMPIRE

Nero was only the fifth in the long line of men who ruled the Roman Empire from its foundation by Julius Caesar's great-nephew Augustus in the last decades before the Christian era. The city itself had been founded by Romulus, according to legend, more than 800 years before Nero's reign. Archaeological remains show that the area of the original seven hills was inhabited for centuries before Romulus; and Virgil's great poem, the *Aeneid*, celebrates the belief that the first Romans were descended from Trojans who fled from Troy when the Greeks sacked it after the ten-year siege.

The historian Livy collected together all the early legends of Rome's heroic past – from the period when the people were ruled by kings and during the later Republic, lasting nearly 500 years, when annual magistrates provided the main examples of heroism. He wove them into a coherent but romanticized account which, by Nero's day, had become required reading for every upper-class schoolboy. The young emperor was therefore the inheritor of a grand tradition of antique republican 'virtue' as well as the fundamentally anti-Republican power structure that Augustus devised to replace it. The tension between these two apparently incompatible sets of notions and procedures ensured that the task of ruling the Empire could never simply be a case of issuing commands and expecting them to be obeyed without question.

Under Augustus' slowly evolving new constitution, an emperor had all the legal powers he needed to be able to rule as an absolute monarch; but unless he respected republican forms he would inevitably encounter the hostility of the great families whose ancestors had taken it in turns to be ruling magistrates at a time when consuls were the true heads of state. That hostility often surfaced as murder or attempted murder. Of Nero's predecessors, Julius Caesar and Caligula were stabbed to death by republican conspirators, Claudius was poisoned for dynastic reasons and Augustus and Tiberius were lucky to survive assassination plots. They became so suspicious of possible rivals that, over the years, they virtually exterminated the direct bloodlines of their own imperial clan.

Julius Caesar had fought his way to supreme power without becoming 'emperor' in a Neronian sense.[1] He was, rather, the military and political adventurer who effectively destroyed the Roman Republic by leading part of his legionary army from Gaul against their own capital city, which submitted without a fight. The civil war that followed was fought in other parts of the Empire, where republican leaders had fled to serve under Pompey's banner. After Pompey's defeat and death, Caesar 'forgave' most of his remaining senatorial opponents in return for their promise of co-operation. A group led by Brutus and Cassius broke the promise by murdering him at the base of Pompey's statue in Rome on the Ides of March, 44 BC.

Caesar's heir was an eighteen-year-old student, Octavian, from an obscure Italian family. The news of the assassination took almost a fortnight to reach him in Greece, where he was improving his knowledge of Greek language and literature. His late father had counted himself honoured, as a *novus homo* (new man), to have been elected to the Senate in a junior position. But Octavian's mother, Atia, was the daughter of Caesar's sister Julia; without that tenuous connection to the great general, the world would probably never have heard of 'Augustus' – the name that Octavian later adopted. In the event, the inheritance of his great-uncle's fortune enabled him to recruit his own army by the time he was nineteen.[2]

The senatorial conservatives assumed that they could overawe this untried youth and use him as a pawn in their opposition to Mark Antony, Caesar's chief lieutenant, who believed that he, not Octavian, should have been the heir. But Octavian first fought against Antony on behalf of the Senate, then joined forces with him. Together they ordered the execution of 300 senators and 2,000 knights in a wave of proscriptions that crushed and cowed the Republicans, although some of those on the death-lists managed to escape. Octavian had no intention of risking being stabbed to death by Republican zealots in a re-run of the Ides of March.

Where Caesar had spared the lives of his senatorial enemies but treated them with calculated contempt, Octavian killed them *en masse* and then treated the surviving senators with exaggerated respect. On a famous occasion Caesar had remained seated, like any eastern potentate, when almost the entire Senate called on him in a body to offer him unprecedented dictatorial powers (they had little choice at the time). By contrast, Octavian, even after he became the Emperor Augustus, always made a point of rising politely to his feet whenever a consul entered the room. Effectively, he exercised the powers of a king while pretending to defer to the senior magistrates, whose appointment he controlled.

This system of institutionalized hypocrisy, which historians call the Principate after the title that Augustus took, *Princeps* (first man), worked more efficiently than the old Republican system. That had relied on the election each year of two consuls and a range of lesser magistrates – who divided power among themselves and held office for only twelve months at a time – and the appointment of ex-magistrates as provincial governors and legionary commanders. There was no permanent civil service, so continuity of control and administration was impossible. It was an apallingly inefficient way to run an empire, which was the first (and only) one ever to encompass the entire Mediterranean world, from the Atlantic eastwards to the River Euphrates, as well as huge areas to the north, bounded roughly by the Rhine, and stretching as far south as the Sudanese frontier.

At first, Augustus effectively ruled the western half of these domains, while Antony controlled the East, with its fabled riches. But at the epoch-making sea battle at Actium in 31 BC he smashed and scattered the forces of Antony and Cleopatra, driving them to suicide. For the next forty-five years he was sole ruler. It would be difficult to overestimate the importance of this long time-span for the survival of his system. In that era, average life expectancy was no more than about thirty years, taking into account that half of all babies are estimated to have died before they could walk.[3] This would have meant that by the time Tiberius succeeded Augustus there was scarcely anybody left who had been an adult before Caesar crossed the Rubicon, and who therefore had direct experience of the genuine Republic in action.

Augustus' success, less flamboyant than Caesar's but more lasting, has inclined modern historians to portray him as a typical 'great man', a Napoleonic figure embodying everything the old Roman oligarchy approved of in a leader: courage, dignity, self-discipline, high moral standards, manly virtue, truthfulness, fidelity – expressed on public occasions in weighty oratory and with a stern, unbending manner. In reality, Augustus was a hypocrite of genius, a liar, a coward, an adulterer and a mass murderer.[4] To get away with all this, he needed the skills of a great actor as well as those of a master politician. He was as much the Godfather of the nation as its *Pater Patriae* (father of the fatherland), never leaving home without his sinister escort of hired killers, and making a series of offers to the *Senatus Populusque Romanus* that they could not refuse. He raised humbug to the level of great art, and his reward from posterity has been the elevation of his adopted name to a byword for all that is august and noble in a human being.

Nothing, of course, can detract from Augustus' achievement in creating and passing on to his many successors a framework of government and society that, in spite of its inherent contradictions, was to last for centuries. There is a sense in which his empire formed the common bedrock out of which so many of the future nations of Europe were carved. His system, when operated by an intelligent *Princeps* capable of acquiring sufficient personal prestige, minimized the risks of civil war while maximizing the prospects for peace over huge areas of the known civilized world. Augustus himself greatly expanded the Empire through war, in particular pushing its boundaries northwards to the defensible line of the Danube, but he instructed his adopted son and successor, Tiberius, to consolidate what had already been won rather than seek to acquire even more territories. Tiberius tried to follow this command, but both Caligula and Claudius disregarded it in their search for glory.[5] It was Nero who most effectively resumed the peace policy.

The ferocious civil war that followed the death of Nero marked the first great test of the durability of Augustus' imperial foundations. The Empire could easily have collapsed. It remains something of a mystery why it did not, in fact, split into two or more separate parts. That it held together, against the odds, is chiefly a tribute to Augustus' political genius, but it also demonstrates an overwhelming desire not to lose the benefits of the long peace that Nero, in particular, had so carefully nurtured. It was thanks to that peace, indeed, that St Paul had been able to make his successful missionary journeys to Europe from Asia in Nero's reign, spreading the Gospel to the Gentiles, whose later Catholic leaders would take over Nero's old imperial title of *Pontifex Maximus* (highest priest) of Rome, while reviling him as the cruellest of persecutors.

The evidence, however, suggests that Nero was less cruel than any of his predecessors, and probably had no taste for cruelty at all. On being presented with his first set of execution warrants to sign as Emperor, he exclaimed: 'I wish I'd never learnt to write.'[6] And he courted unpopularity with the Roman mob by trying to soften the rules of gladiatorial combat, so that fewer of them – and preferably none at all – were killed.[7] This vain attempt was made in the context of Nero's ambition to introduce Greek games in place of traditional Roman ones, but that is no reason for assuming that his motives were not also genuinely humanitarian. His former tutor and chief early mentor, the philosopher Seneca, hated the slaughter of the arenas for obvious moral reasons that, unfortunately, were shared by only a few of his contemporaries. The underlying problem was that theirs was a hierarchical society in which 'human rights', as a universal concept, simply had no place. The only rights they recognized were legal and traditional, and those varied according to one's position within the hierarchy.

Senators who chafed under imperial restriction and mourned their lost 'freedom' were not talking about democracy but of what they thought of as their immemorial right to compete within their own exclusive circle for the great offices of state, which they could use to enrich themselves and their families. They believed that their fathers and grandfathers had gained an empire by the valour of their arms and the favour of the gods, and that this empire had been fraudulently taken away from them by a tyrant, who maintained his power with the help of their social inferiors. Such modern notions as the one written into the American Constitution, declaring the right of all people to life, liberty and the pursuit of happiness, would have been regarded by them with moral disapproval as well as astonishment. They were, after all, slave owners on a colossal scale,[8] who crucified any who revolted, taking the view that there were plenty more where those came from. With some honorable exceptions, including Nero, they evidently enjoyed watching other people suffer and die – to such an extent that they institutionalized the spectacle in the form of public 'games', which included feeding live criminals to jungle beasts.

The emperors themselves provided some notable examples of sadism, but they generally protected their millions of subjects in the far-flung provinces from the worst rapacity of the Roman elite. This imperial policy was based less on altruism than on sound reasons of state; they wanted peaceful citizens who paid their taxes without too much argument and were prepared to go on doing so year after year, decade after decade, while they continued to enjoy the protection afforded by the *Pax Romana*. By contrast, the former Republic's proconsuls, appointed to rule a particular province for only one year, had no direct long-term interest in the welfare of its inhabitants, having probably waited more than half a lifetime for this one brief opportunity of enriching themselves and their families before they returned to private life.

Those appointed under the emperors as governors and procurators often served longer and were subject to tighter controls; like the colonial administrators sent out from Britain in the days when the sun never set on their empire, they were expected to keep the peace and try not to upset the natives. That is why a certain imperial procurator, Pontius Pilate, was prepared to crucify an apparently well-meaning but politically naive Jewish rabbi from Galilee rather than risk serious mass rioting in Jerusalem, which would damage property, threaten many lives, including his own, disrupt commerce and might require troop reinforcements to put down. On the other hand, if Jesus, like St Paul, had been a Roman citizen, Pilate would scarcely have risked crucifying him. Instead, the soldiers who, in the event, diced for his garments, would quite likely have been detailed by Pilate to hurry him out of town in disguise with a warning not to show his face in Jerusalem again.

The essential point here is that the men who presided over the courts, from the Emperor downwards, were not disposed to decide cases on the basis of natural justice but preferred to rely on the letter of the law. This was not because of cynicism. A deep respect for the law and for the rule of law is one of Rome's great legacies to us. Abstract ideas of justice are difficult to define, vary from society to society and from age to age, and require the judgment of Solomon to impose successfully. The practical Romans considered that a well-drafted law should be something that an appellant could point to with confidence, and a judge could uphold without fear of reproof. But it is vital to remember that their laws did not apply equally to all. There was one law for slaves and quite another for their masters. As we have seen from the contrasted cases of Jesus of Nazareth and Paul of Tarsus, there were different laws for the free citizens of Rome and for free non-citizens.

There were differences, too, in theory if not always in practice, in the permitted activities of the two highest groups in the state: the senatorial order and the equestrian order of knights. Senators were not supposed to soil their hands with trade, but as this had not applied to agriculture in the distant past when they were small farmers, they happily moved with the times by supplying the market with surplus crops and livestock from their vast estates, many of which were now run by organized slave-gangs. Most of the original peasants had been displaced by these landowners, often because, while serving with the legions, they had been unable to prevent their families from starving except by allowing the ancestral acres to be bought up, thereby additionally swelling the ranks of the urban mob in Rome. This was the very rabble sneered at by both ancient and modern writers for dependence on 'bread and circuses', which cheered Nero on against his aristocratic enemies, whom they hated as corrupt land-grabbers.[9]

Even lower than the free-loading mob were the enormous numbers of slaves who had no effective protection against cruel masters. By Nero's time it was of doubtful legality to kill one's slave deliberately without a good reason, or abandon a sick old slave by the roadside to die; but if one of them succumbed after a beating it was nobody's business to go to court to prove that the death had been intended.[10] On the other hand, if a slave killed his (or her) master, then every other slave in the household – men, women and children – would be put to death by the state.

In Nero's reign the city prefect, Pedanius Secundus, who among his various duties was effectively a police chief, was murdered by one of his 400 slaves. An emotional Roman mob demonstrated in the streets against the law taking its course. The issue was hotly debated in the Senate, with arguments on both sides, but eventually they voted overwhelmingly for the execution of all 400 on the grounds that if they were to make an exception, even just this once, then no law-abiding slave owner would ever be able to sleep easy in his bed again. Nero did not challenge the Senate's verdict, but refused a further demand to exile Pedanius' former slaves as well. The executioners were sent in under military protection, the mob melted away and the sentence was carried out to the last childish throat.[11]

The ancient Romans have been praised in modern times for the great number of slaves whom they 'freed', as compared with those many other societies where slaves almost invariably died in their chains, metaphorical or real. We know that the manumission rate was high, not least because the Emperor and Senate from time to time fretted over the numbers given liberty, and tried to think of ways of slowing down the process. However, many of those manumissions were paid for with money that the slaves themselves had accumulated over the years. Some masters did allow them meagre earnings, which after ten or fifteen years might amount to a worthwhile sum. Making them buy their freedom with some or all of it sounds more like profitable business than paternalistic care.

The word 'freedom' here must be treated with caution. A freed slave still owed duties to his former owner. These might not necessarily be onerous but often were.[12] Slaves who worked on the big ranches (*latifundia*) or down the mines, or who for other reasons were not likely to be personally known to the individual who owned them, were much less likely to be freed – and in the mines, especially, death rates were high. Slaves could not serve as soldiers; but gladiators were usually slaves (or convicted criminals) and therefore almost inevitably doomed to unfortunate ends.[13] The link between sadism and sex needs no emphasis, but it cannot have been any consolation to a dying gladiator to know that his agonized last cries were stimulating the debased crowd in the arena, and that some who had watched the slaughter would already be in the embrace of one of the many prostitutes who worked the shadowy corridors behind the terraces, and who were mostly slaves themselves.

The best prospect for a slave was to be directly owned by the Emperor. Those who were literate could rise to astonishingly high levels in the imperial civil sevice, where even senators might find it prudent to defer to them in some measure.[14] This paradoxical situation was largely due to traditional Roman attitudes to paid employment. A free-born citizen took the view that to be employed, except for instance as a soldier, could reduce his status to an unacceptable level of servility, especially if he had to work under direct orders in his employer's household, even if that employer happened to be the Emperor. When, therefore, a secretariat began to develop with the growth of empire, each emperor was obliged to choose mainly from among his personal retinue of slaves and ex-slaves for people to do the work that in modern states would be carried out by senior civil servants or government ministers.

Those chosen would, of course, be 'freed' before advancing to the upper levels of the bureaucracy; and it is these despised freedmen, acting as secretaries of state with immense powers of patronage and opportunities for graft, whom the ancient historians typically criciticize for insolence to their social betters, as if that was infinitely more important than the value of their services to the Empire. Later, however, free citizens, especially knights, came to realize what opportunities they had been missing, and flocked from all over the Empire to join the civil service.[15]

In the final analysis, the Emperor's power rested on the army. By Nero's reign the number of legions had been reduced to about twenty-nine, almost entirely stationed in frontier areas. A legion at full strength numbered 6,000 men, but usually managed with 5,000 to 5,500. They were supported in most areas by roughly equal numbers of auxiliaries, strong in cavalry, recruited from non-citizen subject peoples, who served for less pay and fewer privileges. In addition, the elite Praetorian Guard protected the city of Rome and the person of the Emperor. At least once a year, every soldier in the empire took an oath of loyalty to the Emperor and his family, but not to the Senate.[16]

Nero personally appointed all governors of provinces in which legions were based. Other governors were generally appointed by the Senate, usually by drawing lots from a restricted list of candidates approved by the Emperor. Egypt was a special case because of its wealth and strategic importance. No senator was allowed to set foot there without the Emperor's specific permission, which seems to have been rarely given, and the province was run by an equestrian prefect. The largest concentrations of Nero's troops were up to eight legions guarding the Rhine, and the fluctuating numbers in the general area of Syria and Armenia, confronting the Parthian Empire. The Parthians were Rome's only neighbours who could expect to fight them on reasonably equal terms. Their empire stretched eastwards from the Euphrates to the Indus, as well as north to the Caspian Sea and south to the Persian Gulf; they, too, needed to maintain frontier armies, especially to repulse frequent attempted incursions by Asian nomads, and protect their trade routes to China. Rome actually needed a strong and friendly Parthia as a buffer state, but that consideration never stopped glory-seeking militarists from dreaming of conquering it.[17]

Such, in brief, is the social, administrative and strategic background to Nero's reign. At first he left the running of his Empire to others, who were obviously better qualified than a boy of sixteen, and he deserves some credit for acknowledging this. But events were to force him, little by little, to assume control himself. His mature imperial policy was to maintain peace and harmony within the frontiers, restricting military activity to a necessary minimum, preferring diplomacy to war. His domestic policy, by the end, was to avoid assassination by any means, while keeping the people happy and trying to raise their sights to what he considered to be the best things of life – music, poetry, the visual arts and erotic delights.[18]

Nero's was an age, too, of spiritual yearnings and gross superstition. Placatory blood-sacrifices of animals and birds formed part of the routine of the state and of individuals. Almost everyone believed that if their homes were struck by lightning, this signalled the personal anger of a god. The early Christian missionaries were outnumbered by those of other religions, notably the proselytizing worshippers of the goddess Isis, who also promised her followers immortality, and even had a district of Rome (Isis and Serapis) named after her. The rituals of another important cult, identified as that of Bacchus, are preserved in the excavated 'Villa of the Mysteries' at Pompeii, where mural paintings depict a woman initiate receiving a token whipping on her bare back before being admitted to the fold. The Eleusinian Mysteries, near Athens, had a sufficiently potent reputation to prompt Nero himself – as a matricide – to withdraw from their sacred precincts when a priest warned all unpurified sinners to leave or risk divine vengeance.[19]

In the main part of this book, an attempt will be made to expose some of the fraudulent testimony against Nero, which is all too often expressed by the ancient writers as innuendo and is therefore doubly difficult to rebut. As an example, consider their outrageous treatment of another prominent victim – Messalina, the Emperor Claudius' third wife, and mother of Nero's rival Britannicus. Tacitus emphasizes her scandalous sexual immorality, which may in truth amount to little more than understandable adultery at the expense of a man who was 48 when he married her, and she a virgin of fourteen. But the satirist Juvenal asserts that, while Empress, she used to slip out of the palace at night in disguise to ply her trade as a prostitute, standing bare-breasted in the doorway of a pavement cubicle, ready and eager to embrace all comers to feed her insatiable lust.[20]

What may have occurred – if, indeed, it is possible to dignify this puerile canard with a rational explanation – is that Juvenal, or his informant, conflated two quite different aspects of the various mystery religions that had spread to Rome from Greece and the Near East. First, Messalina undoubtedly took part in an illicit 'wedding' ceremony and some sort of Bacchanalian revel while Claudius was out of town. She seems to have played the part of the sacred bride to her aristocratic boy-friend's role as the god Dionysus or one of his votaries. They dressed up in animal skins and capered about. Whatever the full truth of the matter – and Tacitus lavishes his considerable descriptive powers on these scenes – Messalina, who was still only about twenty-three, and her lover were executed without trial. Secondly, moralists had long denounced the reported Eastern cultic practices of sacred prostitution, whereby (at least in fable) a woman dedicates a night to the gods by going to a temple and awaiting the attentions of a 'stranger', who (hopefully) will be a god in disguise. Augustus himself was rumoured by the credulous to owe his conception to an encounter between his mother and Apollo, while Julius Caesar prided himself on being descended from Venus.

By the early third century AD, Juvenal's story had been modified to make it marginally more plausible. Dio Cassius tells us that Messalina acted as a prostitute, not out in the street but in the comfort of her palace, and that she forced other noble ladies of the court to do the same.[21] Ultimately, in the television adaptation of *I Claudius* – which ends as Nero's reign begins – Messalina is seen winning a contest at the imperial court against a professional prostitute to see how many men each woman can satisfy, one after the other, on a sort of production-line system. Such is the staying power of malicious invention over reality.

It is also the measure of the task facing anyone trying to overturn the prejudice of two millennia that long ago achieved mythic status for Nero as the most loathsome Roman of them all. Before his death, most writers had carefully followed the line laid down by courtiers of the Julio–Claudian dynasty, praising fulsomely whichever member of the family happened to be in power at the time. Afterwards, the last four of those emperors were transformed into 'hate' figures, with varying degrees of justification. Tiberius, in spite of his outstanding achievements as a general and a statesman, was damned to posterity as a reclusive pederast who liked to swim naked with equally naked little boys – despite the fact that Roman males never wore swimming costumes when taking their daily communal baths.[22] Caligula has gone down in history as a homicidal maniac, and Claudius is caricatured as a slobbering dim-wit. But it is Nero, in particular, whose reputation has been buried under mounds of literary and ecclesiastical manure, and who most deserves to be dug out.

ONE

PRINCE AND PAUPER

The little prince who was to become the Emperor Nero had to endure a series of psychological shocks in infancy. First, his mother was banished for treason and left to rot on a prison island 40 miles off the Italian coast. He remained behind to celebrate his second birthday in the care of his sick but notoriously brutal father. Nobody wanted to know them; the Romans had learnt it was unhealthy to have friends who were too close to a convicted traitor. Then his father died, his inheritance was seized by his wicked uncle, and he was sent as a pauper to live with an aunt.

It sounds like the beginning of one of those fairy tales by the aptly named Brothers Grimm. And, indeed, as if by the wave of a magic wand, his wicked uncle, the Emperor Caligula, came to an unfortunate end, and his mother and his wealth were returned to him. Suddenly, at the age of three, everyone loved him again – except for an evil empress. But then the empress vanished, too; and the new Emperor Claudius married his mother and later adopted him as his son and heir. It must have seemed to be the perfect story-book ending. But, unfortunately, they didn't manage to live happily ever after.

What the fairy tales leave out of the account are the traumatic effects upon their princely heroes of the unpleasant things that happen to them before the magic wand is waved. How do you explain to a toddler, not yet two years of age, what has happened to his absent mother, especially when nobody knows how long she'll be away or if she will ever come back? And in this particular case there was an ominous precedent. The mother of Nero's mother (both were named Agrippina) had been banished to just such a prison island by an earlier emperor, Tiberius, and had starved to death four years before Nero was born.

The boy, whose name at birth was Lucius Domitius Ahenobarbus – he acquired the name of Nero later – is unlikely to have had much sympathy from his father, Gnaeus Domitius Ahenobarbus, who came from a long line of red-bearded, hard-drinking, devil-may-care aristocrats whom it was dangerous to cross. Gnaeus Domitius was said to have killed one of his ex-slaves in a drinking argument, gouged out the eye of a knight who criticized him in the Forum, and to have run his carriage wheels deliberately and fatally over a boy who annoyed him.[1] No doubt he told Nero that he had to be brave if he wanted to grow up to be a soldier.

That, in fact, was exactly the sort of answer the Romans would have wanted and expected. For if there was one thing that united patricians and plebs it was reverence for the memory of the soldier-prince Germanicus, who was Nero's maternal grandfather. We shall never understand the unique place that the boy occupied in the hearts and minds of his future subjects, or the extravagant hopes they placed in him, unless we grasp the significance of this heritage. For them, Germanicus was the man who should have been Emperor instead of Tiberius. In their opinion he was the greatest soldier Rome had produced since Julius Caesar and Mark Antony, whose mingled family blood ran in his veins.

At the head of eight legions, Germanicus had fought in the thick of many battles, pursuing his dream of conquering Germany. But just when it seemed that one more push would add to the Empire the entire region between the Rhine and the Elbe, Tiberius ordered him back to Rome and abandoned the campaign. What made matters doubly frustrating was that, on genealogical grounds, Germanicus had a much better claim to rule the Empire than Tiberius, who had joined the royal family merely by adoption after his mother, Livia, married Augustus. By contrast, Germanicus, on his mother's side, was the grandson of Mark Antony and Augustus' sister, Octavia; his father was Tiberius' warlike brother Drusus, the first to add the name 'Germanicus' to his *nomen* in recognition of his Rhine victories.

This was a starry but dangerous pedigree for the younger Germanicus.[2] The Emperor Tiberius was his uncle as well as his adoptive father, the future Emperor Claudius was his brother, Caligula was his son, and Nero, of course, was to be his grandson. He compounded the danger by marrying Agrippina the Elder, daughter of Augustus' most senior general, Marcus Agrippa, and grand-daughter of the divine Augustus himself, through his tearaway daughter Julia. The elder Agrippina (the one who starved to death in prison) had nine children by Germanicus; the six who reached adulthood included Caligula and Agrippina the Younger, Nero's mother.

This tragic family became the target of any politician who wanted to ingratiate himself with the Emperor Tiberius, who had been forced by Augustus to adopt Germanicus in preference to his own son Drusus. They managed well enough while Germanicus lived. But he died, in suspicious circumstances, two years after celebrating his 'triumph' over Germany. By that time he was on a diplomatic and military mission in the East, which was being frustrated at every turn by a senatorial enemy who was in Tiberius' pocket. Thousands of travellers before and since have died from drinking untreated water in the Near East, but Germanicus was convinced he had been poisoned and asked his wife, on his deathbed, to see that he was avenged.

Whatever the truth of the matter, she turned her mourning into a focus for every discontent that until then had been festering beneath the surface of the oppressive Tiberian regime. Bearing her husband's ashes before her in an urn, as though emblematic of martyrdom, the elder Agrippina, still only thirty-three, boarded a ship at Antioch and sailed in winter around Greece to the island of Corcyra (Corfu). There, according to Tacitus, she spent a few days recuperating from her devastating misery. The true reasons for this detour, of course, was to arrange for a suitable reception in Italy, just across the water. When her ship finally came in sight of the port of Brundisium (modern Brindisi), the wharfs and rooftops were overflowing with a sea of humanity, come to pay homage, weep with her and indirectly attack the government.[3]

Tiberius sent two cohorts of the Praetorian Guard to escort the ashes back to Rome. It proved a slow and solemn procession, and the effect was stupendous. At every town and village on the route, crowds lined the way, pressing forward to gain a glimpse of this woman of legendary courage and beauty. Everyone knew the story of how she had defied the vengeful Germans by holding open the one bridge left spanning the Rhine to save a retreating legion of her husband's army, standing on the creaking timbers like Horatius, her tiny son Caligula at her side, welcoming back each weary soldier as they trooped by to safety.

Caligula (the name means 'little boots', after the military pair made for him as an infant in the legionary camp) was with her again now, a boy of seven, as she made her highly publicized way through the Italian countryside. So was his four-year-old sister Agrippina. What must these children have thought as they followed their father's urn? Wherever they stopped, crowds of people dressed in black or grey and wailing in the ritual grief of mourning burnt incense at makeshift altars and offered up animal sacrifices. On the approach to Rome, the senators and a great part of the population came out to salute the cortège and follow it for the final miles, the soldiers marching slowly with arms reversed and carrying blank, funereal standards. Those exhausted royal children could never, for the rest of their lives, have doubted the strength of popular feeling for their parents – or their own importance.

A conspicuous absentee on this occasion was the Emperor himself, who simply stayed indoors and did not bother to invent an excuse. As the mass mourning continued even after the ashes had been placed in Augustus' Mausoleum, Tiberius issued a worried statement. He reluctantly acknowledged that no Roman had ever been so lamented before, but called on the people to be calm, show moderation and return to their normal lives. Tacitus, whose loathing and contempt for Tiberius, Caligula, Claudius and Nero runs like a dark thread through the tapestry of his prose, displays Germanicus as a shining figure of Roman manhood, whose service was basely undervalued and whose loyalty and bravery were betrayed. He even compares him with

Alexander the Great, whose exploits he might have matched if his freedom of action had been equal to his genius. These are lofty claims – but are they true? Alas, the handsome and dashing Germanicus seems to have been a hero with hollow legs.[4]

During two-and-a-half seasons of campaigning with his huge army, he lost large numbers of his own men and gained not an inch of new territory; after every aggressive expedition he led his troops out of the war zone to spend the winters in the comparative safety of permanent quarters on the Roman side of the Rhine, leaving the Germans to re-occupy any land they had retreated from. He was lucky to extricate his forces from an ambush sprung by his wily adversary Arminius, and on a later occasion his plan to achieve victory by sailing an armada of small ships up German rivers was turned to near-disaster by a storm. In the ensuing chaos he and his crew were washed up as fugitives in enemy territory, and some of his surviving troops had to be ransomed from as far away as Britain (not then part of the Empire), where they had been blown across the North Sea.

None of this seemed to bother Germanicus' devoted admirers back home. What mattered to them was that he demonstrated the might of Rome by a fearful slaughter of 'barbarians' – including the immolation of women and children in burning villages – and that he brought back the standards of the three legions virtually wiped out by Arminius some six or seven years earlier when trapped in the Teutoburg Forest, in what is now Lower Saxony. That had been one of the worst disasters in the history of Roman arms. Varus, the defeated general that day, fell on his sword, and it was reported that Augustus could be heard afterwards, pacing up and down his house near the Forum, crying out: 'Varus! Varus! Give me back my legions!'[5]

Tiberius, who had plenty of personal experience fighting Germans, had no wish to suffer an equal loss. He was accused of jealousy of his nephew's achievements, but his primary motive in recalling Germanicus from the front line was surely straightforward prudence. No doubt he thought that his ambitious young general had been given his chance and had squandered it. There were serious problems elsewhere in the

Empire, and in any case Tiberius' inclination was always to follow, where practicable, the guidelines laid down by Augustus, whose general view was that the frontiers were already difficult enough to man and ought not to be expanded unwisely.

After Germanicus' death, Tiberius found the widow Agrippina the Elder such a difficult character that he became vulnerable to self-seeking enemies of the royal family. He allowed himself to be persuaded by the notorious Sejanus,[6] effectively his chief minister for home affairs, that Agrippina and her growing sons were too dangerous to remain at liberty. The two older boys were arrested on trumped-up charges and packed off to prison. Luckily for Caligula, the third son, he was considered too young to be a threat. Tiberius did not apparently accuse the revered Agrippina of any actual crime; instead, he sent an astonishing letter to the Senate, complaining that she was insubordinate and 'arrogant at the mouth' (*adrogantiam oris*). It was enough to secure her banishment.[7]

The later overthrow of Sejanus did not save Agrippina, who by that time had been so brutally treated – a centurion had smashed her in the face, blinding her in one eye – that no reconciliation was possible. Her eldest son was already dead, and she herself starved to death in AD 33 after four years in exile and nearly fourteen years as a widow. It is not known whether she deliberately refused food. Her second son, Drusus Julius, was certainly executed by starvation; it is recorded that he kept himself alive for a last wretched day or two by eating the stuffing of his mattress.

It is anybody's guess why Tiberius allowed Caligula to survive. Perhaps the old Emperor derived a grim satisfaction from watching the young man's struggle to be sycophantic to him every day in the hothouse atmosphere of the imperial court, which by then had been transferred to the Isle of Capri in the Bay of Naples. It took another four years, after the death of his mother, for Caligula to succeed to the purple, and during all that time he can never once have betrayed his true feelings. When the mask finally came off, he allowed those feelings unrestrained expression, killing with every refinement of sadism those who offended him, often enough with an accompanying joke. He became noted for his wit almost as much as for his cruelty.

Caligula was the first Emperor apparently to believe himself to be a god,[8] as distinct from simply being hailed as one by his subjects. As absolute ruler, he certainly considered himself above all merely human laws. The Senate slavishly cleared his path at his accession by voting him the unprecedented legal power to do anything he wished. The formula reported by Suetonius is *ius arbitriumque omnium rerum*, 'law and decision-making over all things'.[9] Although Augustus and Tiberius were no doubt able to exercise such power in a crisis, it was only on a *de facto* basis, not *de jure*. Augustus had taken many years to accumulate his range of powers, and Tiberius was careful to follow his precedents wherever possible. Both men also had the advantage of outstanding *auctoritas* by the time they came to use them. Caligula was given supreme power all at once at the age of twenty-four, when he had no experience of either civil or military command.

After a promising early start, while he felt his way forward, his reign is notable for its descent into unconcealed tyranny – and for gross personal behaviour. The belief is almost universal that he had an incestuous relationship with his favourite sister, Julia Drusilla, in the tradition of the Pharaohs of Egypt, a country that interested him because of its close connection with his ancestor Mark Antony. Suetonius records that he also went to bed with Nero's mother Agrippina and with his third sister, Julia Livilla.[10] Nobody suspects, however, that he might have been Nero's father, because the baby inherited the reddish hair of his forbears, whose *cognomen* Ahenobarbus means 'bronze beard'.

Tiberius had chosen Gnaeus Domitius Ahenobarbus from a wide range of possible suitors to marry the younger Agrippina, and Nero was their first and only child, born after nine years of marriage. He was conceived at a time when Gnaeus Domitius was facing arrest for treason, having apparently involved himself in one or other of the endless plots against the ageing, absentee Emperor. He was lucky that Tiberius died before he could be brought to trial; he escaped execution to be thrust immediately into the limelight as the new Emperor Caligula's brother-in-law and, nine months later, father of a new potential heir of the Julio–Claudian line.

Nero was born on 15 December AD 37 as the sun rose over Antium (Anzio), an upmarket seaside resort south of Rome where the royal family had a sumptuous villa. Its golden rays fell on the emerging baby, an auspicious occurrence which, thirty years later, took material shape as a 120-ft high gilded statue of Nero as the Sun God Helios, which he commissioned to stand outside his new palace. Gnaeus Domitius, unaware of this future glory for his son, seems to have been a less-than-proud father. As his friends crowded around to congratulate him on the birth, he is reported to have said: 'Anything born to me and Agrippina has got to be ghastly – and a public misfortune (*detestabile et malo publico*).'[11]

This sounds suspiciously like the invention of an enemy long after the event, intended to prove that Nero was fated to be a monster; but it does coincide with the fact that the baby was born feet-first, which the Romans considered to be unlucky, and not only for the mother while giving birth. We have no information about the first eighteen months of Nero's life, which we must presume were spent cheerfully enough in his parents' home among all the luxury and state that money and pride could pay for. But then we hear that Agrippina had to go North, by imperial invitation, obviously leaving the child behind her.

Caligula had decided to carry out an extensive inspection of the Rhine army, perhaps combining pleasure with business by revisiting the scenes of his childhood on the German frontier.[12] He invited not only Agrippina but also their sister Julia Livilla and their brother-in-law Marcus Aemilius Lepidus. It might sound like a happy family excursion, prompted by nostalgia, but it ended in stark tragedy. Somewhere along the way, possibly before they had even left Italy, the Emperor got wind of a conspiracy involving Gaetulicus, Governor of Upper Germany, and Lepidus himself, who was the widower of Drusilla, Caligula's sister-lover, who had died the previous year. If his information was correct – and most authorities believe it was – it would seem that he narrowly escaped stumbling into a murderous trap.

Gaetulicus controlled four legions, and Lepidus had the family qualifications to make him a reasonably acceptable successor as Emperor. While Drusilla was still alive, Caligula had shown Lepidus sufficient marks of honour to propel him to the forefront of the political stage, but the Emperor ought not to have expected love and loyalty from a man whose wife he had reputedly abused. The plot would have had the virtues of simplicity and surprise. Had they succeeded in assassinating Caligula so far from his court, they could have marched to Rome at the head of Gaetulicus' legions to ensure Lepidus' acceptance by both the Senate and the Praetorian Guard.

Without wasting much time investigating the charges fully, Caligula had both Lepidus and Gaetulicus executed on the spot. The question then arose of whether Agrippina and Julia Livilla had conspired with them. The Emperor produced letters from both women that, he claimed, proved they were guilty. We do not know when the letters were written, who they were addressed to or what they said. It scarcely seems likely that two such sophisticated women would have implicated themselves by writing incriminating letters that might be intercepted; so it may well be that they were forced to write them in order to save their lives, by providing him with documentary evidence to justify his actions against those who were apparently his nearest and dearest.

Both sisters were banished, like their mother and their two elder brothers before them. Agrippina suffered the further punishment of being forced to carry the ashes of Lepidus back to Rome. It was a macabre restaging of the journey that the elder Agrippina had made with their father's ashes nearly twenty years earlier. But in this case there were no crowds of weeping mourners and political allies, and when the urn finally reached Rome, the Senate refused the remains a proper burial. Agrippina went to her prison island with the further shame hanging over her of Caligula's accusation that she had committed adultery with Lepidus.

Was she allowed to see little Nero for a last embrace before she left? We do not know. But Gnaeus Domitius would have been anxious to distance himself and their son from her if they wished to survive. It may well be that by the time Agrippina passed through Rome as a prisoner, father and son had already left the city. That would certainly have been the safest course for both of them, if only on the principle of 'out of sight, out of mind'. If he had ostentatiously insisted on meeting his wife, there would have been a danger that Caligula, already thought to be mad, would take it as an indication that the supposedly wronged husband did not believe her to be guilty of either treason or adultery.[13]

Meanwhile, the personal exile of Nero continued – the exile from his mother. It would be futile – and perhaps even ludicrous – to attempt to reconstruct from hints in unreliable ancient documents, written, 1900 years ago in a dead language, the precise psychological state of a Roman infant not yet two years old and born into a society radically different from our own. However, there is overwhelming research to support the contention that a long separation from the mother has a harmful effect on children of that age,[14] whatever society they live in, whether in ancient Rome or modern Manhattan. The bewildered longing that cannot be satisfied must inevitably be repressed. The child, at an unconscious level, protects itself against unbearable emotional deprivation by various strategies, founded on mistrust, which persist into adult life and make it hard to maintain genuinely close personal relationships.

Of course, it may be countered that, for all we know, Agrippina handed Nero over to a wet-nurse on day one, and only ever bestowed an occasional peck on his cheek during sporadic visits to the nursery. In those circumstances, the baby would have bonded with his nurse. But the written evidence suggests strongly that Agrippina, who knew full well the importance of her charge, became the dominating mother of a dominated boy – and that this phase did not end until after Nero had become Emperor. It is scarcely conceivable that a mother can achieve such emotional control over a lively teenager without intense bonding at a much earlier stage of life. Nero, to be sure, broke his dependency on her in the most definitive way imaginable; but it is perhaps significant that he continued to prefer older, strong-willed women as confidantes – and lovers – while spurning his child-wife. As an adult, as we shall see, he displayed masochistic tendencies (see Appendix Two) and seemed to need constant reassurance from the people surrounding him, even if they were blatantly sycophantic.

Nero lost his father the year after his mother was taken away. The ancient sources agree that Gnaeus Domitius died of dropsy, but modern medicine knows that this is not a disease in itself but a symptom of something else, usually a weak heart or faulty kidneys. The body starts to fill up with surplus water and, lacking diuretic pills to aid its removal, the victim becomes heavy and shambling, with puffy ankles and blistered legs. It must have been debilitating to endure and painful to watch. Whether his son was there at the end is not known. At some stage Nero was sent to the house of his father's sister, Domitia Lepida, with whom the dropsical Gnaeus Domitius had been accused, late in Tiberius' reign, of incest – a charge of more than usual implausibility.

Aunt Lepida, according to Suetonius, handed him over to be brought up by 'a dancer and a barber'. These would almost certainly have been household slaves, or ex-slaves, and were presumably male, as Suetonius uses the masculine form *saltator* for dancer, instead of the feminine *saltatrice*; and *tonsor* is also a masculine noun. He describes the upbringing as *paene inops atque egens*, which carries a range of possible meanings from 'almost destitute' to 'rather poor and helpless'.[15] Whatever meaning Suetonius intended, it does not appear that life at his aunt's home was very happy for the infant Nero, who was still only two years old. Nor could she, any more than her brother, give the boy any reassurances about his exiled mother, whom, for all she knew, he would never see again.

Meanwhile, Caligula was rapidly alienating those who had once been his most powerful supporters. He had already outraged the army, during his visit to the Rhine, by apparently trying to decimate one of the legions which, twenty-four years earlier, had temporarily rebelled against his father Germanicus over pay and conditions of service. Decimation was a terrible punishment: every soldier in the legion would have had to draw lots to select the 10 per cent who would be clubbed to death. It had been imposed very rarely in the past, for cowardice in face of the enemy. In this case there would have been few, if any, individual soldiers remaining from the time of Germanicus. Fortunately, Caligula himself seems to have shown cowardice by beating a hasty retreat from the military camp in question, once it appeared that the legion might rebel again rather than submit to the Emperor's mad scheme.

On returning to Rome after this exploit, Caligula embarked on a series of trials of prominent people, supposedly for treason, but, in any case, to enable him to seize their property. For by now the royal treasury was bare, thanks to his extravagance – in less than a year after becoming Emperor he had frittered away Tiberius' entire hoard of 27 million gold pieces, the savings of more than two decades. 'Let them hate me so long as they fear me!', he is reported to have said, as the treason trials and the confiscations multiplied. And he cheerfully filled his coffers with the proceeds of the auction of his banished sisters' jewellery, along with their furniture and slaves, forcing the bidders to pay excessively high prices in order to maintain their credit with him.[16]

Aunt Lepida probably calculated that she would be safe enough, because her daughter, Messalina, had just married Caligula's uncle, Claudius, the younger brother of Germanicus. Claudius owed his survival through several different 'reigns of terror' to his physical condition, which seemed to debar him from serious political activity. His head quivered as he limped along, dragging a defective right leg; he could not eat without slobbering, and his stammering speech gave the impression that he was mentally sub-normal. But his consummate grasp of political realities, which he demonstrated in his achievement and retention of power, shows him to have been highly intelligent. He also wrote a number of serious historical works, none of which, unfortunately, has survived. It appears likely that Claudius suffered from comparatively mild cerebral palsy. Caligula liked to make fun of him in front of his courtiers, and Claudius was far too astute not to play up to him – occasional humiliation was part of the price of survival.

Nevertheless, Lepida would have been careful not to draw Caligula's attention to the sad little prince in her care, because the Emperor had recently married a young wife who might at any time present him with a son. She knew more than enough about family history to realize that Nero's life would be doubly in danger from perceived rivalry with a direct heir. Caligula had already disposed of Tiberius' grandson, Tiberius Gemellus, for a similar reason and as his reign progressed it became clear that he did not need any reason for murder, if his whim prompted him to it. At dinner one night with two consuls, he suddenly burst into peals of laughter. When they asked him what the joke was, he replied that he had just realized he could have their throats cut, simply by giving a nod.

For Caligula was as capricious as he was cruel. He sent for three elderly senators in the middle of the night, knowing they would be fearing the worst as they were escorted by guards to a row of seats in front of an empty stage in a palace room. There was a burst of music, and Caligula rushed on stage in a flowing cloak to perform a song-and-dance number, before vanishing as suddenly as he had come.[17] This points up an essential difference between Caligula and Nero in their attitude to dressing up and playing a part on stage. For Caligula it was no more than an amusement – if, in this particular case, one with a characteristically macabre touch.

It also shows that there must have been previous amateur theatricals at the palace in which members of the ruling family participated – the stage would scarcely have been set up just for an elaborate practical joke to make three old senators tremble. But the stage was private, not public. An emperor was entitled to let his hair down at home, out of the public gaze; he was, after all, a human being, even if superstitious foreigners wanted to claim him for a god. But he could not perform like that in public without forfeiting his *dignitas*, thereby demonstrating his unfitness to rule. The Roman establishment knew the value of keeping up appearances. Behaving as Nero was to do invited derision from men whose chief motivation was the will to power.

Caligula's offence, by contrast, was not that he sang and danced on his private stage that night but that he treated the three senators as butts of his humour, whereas the Augustan system crucially required that he treat them with respect. Another of Suetonius' stories shows even more clearly how Caligula could make bitter enemies of the very men whose support he needed. He is reported to have held beauty contests at palace dinners to which he invited the wives of noblemen as contestants; after slowly examining them in front of their tight-lipped husbands, as if they were dishes on the sweet trolley, he would take the 'winner' off to a private room, while the feast continued in his absence. Some time later the two would return, dishevelled, to the table, where he would comment on the finer points of the lady's anatomy and give a frank assessment of her abilities as a lover.[18]

The list of Caligula's tortures and other cruelties is horrifying.[19] They came to an end in January AD 41 when a group of officers of the Praetorian Guard, with some senatorial backing, ran him through with their swords during an interval at the theatre. The man who had wished the Romans had only one neck so that he could slice it in half more easily, had reigned for less than four years. He was twenty-eight years old. The assassins also killed his wife and their baby daughter. For his surviving sisters, Agrippina and Julia Livilla, it marked a reprieve from the executioner's sword that had been hanging over their heads in prison for more than a year. For Nero it meant a joyful reunion with his long-lost mother. There was also a huge rise in status and wealth for him, as Claudius restored his confiscated estates.

With Caligula out of the way, the three-year-old boy was now the only living male descendant of both Augustus and Germanicus. Whoever controlled him might one day control the Empire. Claudius was over fifty years of age, in deteriorating health and without a son of his own. His young wife Messalina, however, had already given Claudius a daughter, and at the date of her husband's accession she was eight months pregnant. If the imminently expected baby turned out to be a boy, that would alter all the calculations. Rome and its empire of 50 million people would face the prospect of a murderously disputed battle for the succession – but this time waged by women, on behalf of their sons.

The Principate, however, was not an entirely hereditary system; there could have been no serious question, at that stage of its constitutional development, of a small child ruling the vast Roman Empire through a regent. Much would depend, therefore, on how long Claudius would live. In the event, this apparently imponderable factor would turn out to be strangely convenient for Nero and his scheming mother.

TWO

THE ASSASSINS CALL

Claudius seized power in the wake of Caligula's assassination by disregarding the constitutional fictions so carefully respected by Augustus. His opportunistic coup shocked the Senate, which had not even considered him as a possible contender. He marked out a route to the throne for any potential successor to follow, and lived in fear throughout the thirteen years of his reign that someone might try to topple him by the same means. That is why, from the beginning, he set out deliberately to minimize his role in the plot that brought him to power, by encouraging the belief that the outcome was due to a series of chance events over which he had no control.[1]

Luck obviously played a part. But in Claudius' case it was combined with some degree of advance knowledge of what might happen. His rivals all enjoyed higher reputations than his own and thought they would get greater public support. Their mistake was to suppose that senators, rather than soldiers, would determine the outcome. While it will never be possible to establish the precise motives and moves of all the participants in the assassination crisis, especially as the relevant chapters in Tacitus' *Annals* are missing, we can nevertheless piece together a coherent account by concentrating on what Claudius is reported to have done, rather than what he is supposed to have thought – or wanted people to think.

The killing of Caligula took place on the final day of festival games in honour of the divine Augustus. They were held before an invited audience of several thousand people in a temporary wooden 'theatre' on the Palatine Hill.[2] This prefabricated structure had been erected on an open space outside the palace and the adjacent Temple of Apollo, one of the most striking buildings in ancient Rome, covered with external statuary in imitation of Greek originals. A group of seats at one side of the auditorium was reserved for Caligula and his special guests. From this restricted area, a corridor led towards a palace door. Before taking his seat for the morning session, the Emperor sacrificed a flamingo at Apollo's altar; he stabbed the bird himself, spattering his toga with a few drops of blood.

The assassins, mostly officers of the Praetorian Guard, were on duty in the corridor between the theatre and the palace. It proved to be a long, nerve-racking wait. Caligula had had a stomach upset the previous night, and so, against their expectations, he did not get up to return to the palace for lunch. One of the senatorial conspirators, who was sitting close to the Emperor, rose from his seat, intending to urge the waiting assassins to enter the theatre and kill him there and then. But Caligula grabbed his toga and told him to sit down again.[3] It was well into the afternoon before a buzz of activity from the direction of the imperial seats indicated to the assassins in the corridor that Caligula was at last about to come their way.

But when the theatre door opened it was not the Emperor who stepped out, but Claudius, closely followed by Nero's uncle, Marcus Vinicius, and a billionaire senator, Valerius Asiaticus.[4] The three of them hurried past the assassins along the main corridor to the palace. We can assume that the Praetorian officers were surprised by the appearance of this trio instead of the Emperor, because Josephus, the Jewish historian who recorded these events, tells us that they briefly wondered whether to block their path but decided not to do so. We know that the assassination had been carefully planned, and that therefore the plotters would presumably have allowed for the contingency of someone other than the Emperor emerging first into the corridor, if that had been at all likely.

Anyone who pushed in front of the homicidal egomaniac Caligula would have needed a better reason than wanting to get to lunch, however long it had been delayed. The obvious explanation is that Claudius and his two companions knew in advance what was going to happen. Either they were active participants in the plot or they were aware of the conspiracy and were making sure they were not in the vicinity when it was carried out. Josephus' proffered explanation for why the assassins let them pass unhindered – that they did not want to inconvenience such dignified individuals – is naive, to say the least.

In the light of what was to happen later, it is clear that some of the conspirators intended to murder Claudius along with Caligula. If Nero had been in the palace they would, logically, have murdered him, too, as their object was to end the hereditary transfer of power by wiping out the imperial dynasty. They were evidently prepared to let Claudius go at that early stage for fear of alerting Caligula, their main target, which would have risked total disaster for themselves and their cause.

When Caligula emerged from the auditorium he did not follow Claudius all the way to the palace, but turned aside into another corridor, where some dancers were assembled, and stopped to talk to them. A Praetorian tribune, Cassius Chaerea,[5] stepped smartly forward to ask him to announce the password of the day, which it was his duty to request. As the Emperor paused to think of a reply, Chaerea slashed him across the throat with his sword. Other officers crowded around to finish him off as he lay bleeding on the ground.

Mayhem broke out. Caligula's heavily armed German bodyguards,[6] trailing behind their master in the crowd of theatre spectators who had followed him, went on a murderous rampage along the corridors. They cut down suspects who crossed their path, including at least three senators. Meanwhile, a small breakaway group of the assassins, under a Praetorian officer named Lupus (meaning 'wolf'), rushed into the palace. They stabbed the Empress Caesonia[7] to death. A centurion picked up her baby daughter, Drusilla, and dashed her brains out against a wall. They failed to find Claudius and went away. His hiding place was discovered by another Praetorian named Gratus (meaning 'grateful'), who initiated his rescue.

Claudius was no doubt grateful, too – but scarcely surprised – that his supporters were rallying to him. He and they already knew he was the best-qualified man for the suddenly vacant position. Gratus took him to a large group of Praetorians who were milling about in the Palatine area, uncertain about who was in charge now that Caligula was dead. They carried him at a run to their barracks nearly 2 miles away, just outside the city wall. People who saw them may have thought he was being taken to execution – which would help to explain the later story, obviously encouraged by Claudius himself, that he had been kidnapped against his will and forced to become Emperor in order to avoid civil strife.

Once he reached the barracks, Claudius made sure that the vast majority of the Praetorians, under their two commanding prefects, were on his side. One of the prefects, Marcus Arrecinus Clemens, had been aware of the plot and turned a blind eye to it. He did not, however, approve the killing of anyone but Caligula. With Clemens' support, Claudius now followed the example of Julius Caesar ninety years earlier: he bypassed the Senate and was acclaimed as ruler by the troops. The price was a bribe of 15,000 sesterces for each guardsman, equivalent to five years' pay.[8] He thus effectively bought the Roman Empire for himself by virtue of his family connections, his access to funds and his inside information, which allowed him to outmanoeuvre all other rivals.

Meanwhile, during the bloody confusion on the Palatine, which had culminated in the German bodyguards placing a row of severed heads on Apollo's altar, the two consuls had called out the Urban Cohorts[9] to restore order and protect the senators and others from further attack. These 4 cohorts, in total at least 2,000 armed men, were under separate command from the much larger and better-paid Praetorian Guard, to whom they would normally have been expected to defer. In the absence of most of the Praetorians with Claudius at their barracks, except for the group led by the chief assassin Cassius Chaerea, the consuls summoned an emergency meeting of the Senate, guarded by the Urban Cohorts, on the more easily defended Capitol Hill,[10] on the opposite side of the forum to the Palatine.

Here, in the massive and ancient Temple of Jupiter, Sentius Saturninus, one of the consuls, submitted his name as a candidate for the vacant position of Princeps and made a speech praising the assassins. The only other nominated candidates among those known to have been actually present at the meeting were Marcus Vinicius and Valerius Asiaticus – the very men who had left the theatre with Claudius, just ahead of Caligula. Vinicius was Caligula's brother-in-law through his marriage to Agrippina's exiled sister Julia Livilla. That was a close enough relationship to the imperial dynasty to make him the most immediately credible of the three candidates. He had probably felt he had little to lose and everything to gain by conspiring against Caligula, given the taint of his wife's exile for treason; and he must have been living in fear of the knock on the door in the middle of the night that would mark the arrival of one of the tyrant's execution squads.

Valerius Asiaticus, the second of Claudius' companions, was undoubtedly part of the conspiracy. After the assassination, but before the Senate met, he spoke to a crowd in the Forum. Challenged to name those who had killed the Emperor Caligula, he replied: 'I wish I had!' Although Tacitus' direct narrative of these events has not survived, his account of the arrest and suicide of Asiaticus six years later – for allegedly plotting against Claudius – includes a reference to him as the main initiator or organizer (*praecipium auctorem*) behind the assassination of Caligula.[11] Is it not stretching credulity too far to assume that these three individuals – Claudius, Vinicius and Asiaticus – just happened by chance to emerge from the theatre together at precisely the right moment to avoid getting mixed up in a messy assassination, while at the same time staying close enough to the action to be in a position to take advantage of it?

Vinicius may well have been counting on Claudius' support in the Senate, believing that physical disability would rule out the personal candidature of the older man. As for Claudius himself, it is certainly arguable that he was no more than a lucky opportunist who took his chance when it was unexpectedly offered to him. But how can one accept at face value the legend of his being merely a blundering innocent? Claudius had lived in the rambling palace complex all his life and must have known every hiding place in the disparate group of linked buildings.[12] If the 'wolf' failed to find him it was because Claudius did not wish to be found. If his Praetorian allies succeeded where the 'wolf' had failed, it was no doubt because he wanted them to.

When the Senate learnt that Claudius had been hailed as Emperor by the Praetorians, they sent a deputation to the barracks to try to persuade him to put himself under senatorial protection. By now, darkness had fallen. Claudius had no hesitation in calling their bluff, but he did not want to risk starting a civil war by ordering the Praetorians up to the Capitol to enforce his will. He temporized by pretending that his guards would not let him go. In order to make sure that senior senators understood the true position, he employed his friend Julius Agrippa[13] – grandson of the Salome who performed the dance of the seven veils before King Herod – as a confidential go-between. By next morning, all opposition had collapsed, bringing to an ignominious end the adjourned Senate debate over which of their number would succeed Caligula. Now they voted obediently for Claudius, who executed a few Praetorian extremists, including Chaerea and Lupus. All the other surviving conspirators were unharmed.

Agrippina was to be the first to take advantage, on Nero's behalf, of Claudius' example of how to achieve supreme power. She was to add the further refinement of disposing of the incumbent Emperor chiefly by herself, without the need for an elaborate web of conspiracy, and therefore being able to hold up the announcement of his death until she was ready to put the rest of the programme into effect. But that was for the future. For the present, Agrippina found it prudent, after her arrival back on the mainland from her island prison, to remain as inconspicuous as possible. She must, of course, have gone to the imperial court, to thank her Uncle Claudius for his clemency – and was no doubt assiduous in offering her congratulations to him on the birth of his son, later to be known as Britannicus,[14] only three weeks into his reign. Claudius, for his part, would have wanted to see the three-year-old Nero, if only to assess the state of his health.

Agrippina would also have renewed her acquaintance with the new Empress Messalina, in whose mother's house Nero had been living in the care of the dancer and the barber. What she and Messalina said to each other is not recorded, but her subsequent actions show us that she had sniffed the political wind at court and scented danger, both for herself and Nero. Her urgent priority became a search for a powerful male for them to shelter behind – one who would also be a credible contender for the purple if Claudius should die while Britannicus was still a baby. First, she targeted Servius Sulpicius Galba, the patrician general who, some twenty-seven years later, would succeed Nero as emperor. He currently commanded part of the Rhine army, and his name is reported to have been put forward (almost certainly *in absentia*) as a candidate during the Senate's abortive debate.

Agrippina presumably met him when the new Emperor summoned him back to Rome for consultation. Galba's mother-in-law intervened aggressively to save her daughter's marriage – thereby preserving, perhaps, the course of history by a timely slap on the intruder's face.[15] Galba was a conservative of the deepest dye, who had a reputation as a military disciplinarian. He evidently thought a woman's place was on her knees and a son's on the field of battle. He was also bisexual. It is disturbing to imagine how his paternal authority would have mixed with Nero's artistic temperament.

Fortunately for the small boy, his mother settled instead upon Gaius Sallustius Passienus Crispus, a distinguished senator, noted for his quick wit as well as for great wealth.[16] When the incestuous Caligula asked him if he had slept with his own sister, Crispus replied disarmingly: 'Not yet!' The only problem for Agrippina was that he was already married to her sister-in-law, Domitia, elder sister of Domitia Lepida (who had cared for Nero in his mother's absence), and therefore also the aunt of the new Empress. Such a match would clearly need Claudius' approval. Perhaps more importantly, it would need at least the tolerant acquiescence of Messalina if the ambitious Agrippina were to have any chance of survival beyond the short-term. Whatever the state of family feelings and feudings may have been, the outcome was that Crispus abandoned his wife and married Agrippina to become Nero's step-father.

For the moment, therefore, Agrippina seems to have been reasonably safe. It was her sister Julia Livilla, wife of Marcus Vinicius, who fell victim to Messalina's jealousy. After only a few months of freedom, she was sent back to her prison island, never to return alive. The official reason was adultery with Lucius Annaeus Seneca, the celebrated orator and philosopher, who was later to play such an influential role in moulding Nero's career. In paying court to a princess of the imperial house, particularly a married one, Seneca, who was in his early forties, was aiming dangerously far above his station. He was a junior member of the Senate, having held the office of quaestor, and came from an equestrian family of Italian stock who had settled at Cordoba, where he was born, in what is now Andalusia in southern Spain.

Seneca's reputation as a public speaker, especially in the law courts, was sufficiently outstanding to have aroused the jealousy of Caligula, who is said to have refrained from killing him only because he had been told (incorrectly) that Seneca was suffering from a terminal illness. But it is as a writer of philosophical essays and verse tragedies that he has been chiefly remembered by posterity – to an extent almost of veneration during the Renaissance, when his prose works were felt to embody the moral wisdom of the classical world, and his plays strongly influenced the dramatists of Italy, France and England, including Marlowe and Shakespeare[17] and, later, Corneille and Racine.

This outstanding man nevertheless went on trial on a capital charge before the Roman Senate, and he avoided the death sentence only because of the personal intervention of Claudius. He was exiled to Corsica, where he was to remain for seven rusticated years, writing letters and treatises and verses, interspersed with pleas to be allowed to come back to Rome. That people should be on trial for their lives for adultery in a society notorious throughout recorded history for its sexual licence demonstrates once more the problem of gross inequality before the law.

Roman moralists (including Seneca) tended to regard adultery by a married woman as connected in some way with a more generalized corruption of the body politic. A man who could not

control his wife's desires, for example, was considered unfit to
have any role in controlling the state. In support of this and other
social theories, Augustus had introduced a wide range of moral
legislation, including a Draconian law against adultery, which
was aimed in particular at the aristocracy.[18] Augustus' own
daughter Julia paid the price for her many failures under this law,
and it continued to be used as a weapon against anyone close to
the imperial dignity.

Messalina's true motive for bringing the charge against Julia
Livilla, however, is conjectured to have been her suspicion that
Livilla was about to steal her husband. As Claudius' niece, the
seductive young woman had apparently been given the run of the
palace, and had used this privilege to flirt rather too intimately
with the Emperor. Once again, therefore, the ubiquitous Marcus
Vinicius found himself in the risky position of a man whose wife
has just been banished through imperial displeasure. Augustus'
laws prescribed severe penalties for a complaisant husband, and
the fact that he was not hauled up before a court shows that he
made no serious attempt to save his wife. Soldiers were sent to
ensure Livilla's demise, probably by starvation – fast becoming a
family tradition – but Vinicius lived on for another five years.

There is an interesting possibility that Nero may have spent a
year abroad when he was four or five years old, because his
stepfather Crispus was put in charge of the province of Asia. This
was not, of course, the vast continent that we know by that name
today, but the western (non-European) part of what is now
Turkey, encompassing the city of Pergamum and the
Mediterranean port of Ephesus, mainly inhabited by Greeks.
Would Crispus have left his new wife behind in Rome when he
took up his foreign appointment? Would Agrippina have
abandoned Nero once again in order to accompany her husband?
We simply do not know, because the historical record is
extremely sketchy for this period of Nero's life. However, it is not
unreasonable to assume that the boy may have travelled to Asia
in the entourage of a Roman proconsul, with all the display of
pomp and power over a subject people that that this implies.

The ruins of Graeco-Roman Ephesus, which survive to this

day, are among the most beautiful and evocative of their kind in existence. In Nero's day its architecture was famous throughout the Empire, especially for the gigantic Temple of Artemis-Diana, one of the seven wonders of the ancient world. This was the city where St Paul was to cause a riot by his preaching, within ten years of the governorship of Crispus, upsetting the silversmiths whose trade depended on the worship of the many breasted goddess, as reported by St Luke in Chapter 19 of the Acts of the Apostles.[19] Another decade later, Paul was to make his 'appeal to Caesar' after yet another riot, this time in Jerusalem. By that date 'Caesar' was the Emperor Nero, who had approved arrangements for his own worship as a god alongside Artemis in her Ephesian temple.

If Nero and Agrippina in fact went to Asia, they must have returned to Rome by AD 44, because Crispus had been appointed as a consul for part of that year.[20] It may have been during this period that, according to Suetonius, assassins came for Nero but were frightened away by a snake that emerged from his bed.[21] Some details of the story are plainly invented but the authenticity of the underlying attempt on Nero's life may have been rather less doubtful. Palace intrigue under Claudius seems to have been developing along the murderous lines common enough in the petty kingdoms of the Near East, where factions grew up around influential individuals below the level of the sovereign. For years after the alleged attempt on his life, Nero wore a gold bracelet incorporating part of the snake's skin, which the creature fortuitously shed before slithering away. The legendary hero Hercules, of course, wrestled with a snake as a baby in his cot, and the connection in the public mind of Nero, snake and nursery did the little prince no harm at all in a society where the worship of Hercules had achieved cult status.

Messalina gets the blame from Suetonius for sending in the assassins; and unquestionably she had a motive in wanting to clear the path to ultimate power for her own small son, Britannicus, by a pre-emptive strike. Unfortunately, we do not know the date of the snake incident, but we do know that when Nero was nine and Britannicus was six, a huge Roman crowd, which had assembled to watch the two youngsters perform on horseback in an ancient pageant,[22] gave much louder cheers for the red-haired grandson of Germanicus than for the son of Claudius and Messalina. Nero's outstanding popularity with the people was demonstrated early.

Agrippina became a widow for the second time in about 47. Some ancient sources suggest she may have poisoned Crispus; but that seems unlikely, not least because his death exposed her to the intensive scrutiny of Messalina. The Empress would not have forgotten what Agrippina had done to her Aunt Domitia, nor what Julia Livilla had apparently tried to do to her. We can be sure that Nero's mother behaved with impeccable propriety in the Emperor's company while Messalina was still alive. By this date the Empress had become as notorious for killing off her perceived opponents as she had long been for sexual infidelity. However, the large fortune that Agrippina inherited from Crispus put her in a position to buy political support in high places and she patiently built up a network of influential friends committed to Nero's interest.

Claudius' grasp of power had become more practised with the passage of time but not necessarily any firmer. The frequent trials attest to the strength of the opposition, in spite of his military triumph in AD 43 in adding south-east Britain to the Roman Empire, where Julius Caesar had failed. That was, in hindsight, something of a Pyrrhic victory. Rome derived no income from its conquest sufficient to compensate for the bottling up of several legions there for almost four centuries; and the Picts and the Scots – not to mention the Manx and the indomitable Irish – never accepted their sway. Prestige, however, was another matter. Claudius milked every available drop of it, although his generals had taken most of the physical risks before they invited him to cross the Channel to be in at the kill. After a mere sixteen days in Britain he returned to Rome to don the laurels of victory and bask in popular approval.[23]

Claudius needed it. The total of 35 senators and 300 knights who were killed or ordered to take their own lives during the course of his reign of more than 13 years indicate that the upper classes had never forgiven Claudius for seizing power in the way he did. The manner in which he delegated imperial responsibilities to some of his freedmen ensured that their hostility rankled on a daily basis. It became ever clearer that, in spite of his occasional fine words, the Senate had been reduced to impotence in all matters deemed important, not simply by the Emperor but by his wife and even his former slaves. His favoured freedmen grew rich by exploiting their offices for profit, and the ancient writers protest with every show of righteousness at the humiliation involved for gentlemen – who were, naturally, owners of slaves – to be obliged to defer to such servile underlings.

The leading imperial freedman, Narcissus, a man of Greek origin, was to play the main role in the downfall of Messalina, which occurred not long after Agrippina was widowed and therefore available for marriage. There is no direct evidence to show that Agrippina herself set the trap into which Messalina fell, but she was the chief beneficiary. The story is so bizarre that Tacitus, in telling it with a wealth of picturesque detail, emphasizes that he has derived it from both written and verbal accounts, thus implying that the events were the subject of common gossip long afterwards and that he may have spoken to people who were caught up in it.[24]

For about a year, Messalina had been in love with a personable and handsome aristocrat, Gaius Silius. He was a consul-designate and was therefore probably about thirty-five years old unless she had used her influence with her husband to obtain the honour for him earlier than the regulations allowed. Tacitus, stretching a point, calls him *iuventutis Romanae pulcherrimus* – 'the most beautiful of Roman youths'.[25] The Empress forced him to divorce his wife, Junia Silana, to ensure his faithfulness. As their relationship deepened, Gaius told her he wanted to marry her and was prepared to adopt her son Britannicus.

Did he mean his proposal to be taken seriously? It sounds like a lover's profession of hope rather than a statement of intent. Messalina initially declined his offer. But the more she thought about it, the more plausible and attractive the idea seemed. In the autumn of AD 48, while Claudius was away supervising construction works at the port of Ostia, about 15 miles from Rome, she 'married' her lover in a ceremony before witnesses. A crucial question, which cannot now be definitively settled, is whether the ceremony they went through made Gaius Silius and Messalina man and wife in any sense that would justify the accusation by Narcissus that Claudius had been divorced.

Whatever may have been going on in Messalina's head, it is arguable that the 'bridegroom' had his sights set on power. He was a patrician with five consuls in his family tree, and he himself was now due to be a sixth at the start of the new year, AD 49, only about two or three months away. His late father had commanded part of Germanicus' Rhine army, so he would have had reason to hope for support from the military as well as from his natural allies in the Senate. There has been much speculation over why, having 'married' Messalina, he did not immediately act to take control of the city in Claudius' absence. At least one of the two Praetorian Prefects, Lusius Geta, was a supporter of the Empress. Perhaps Gaius intended to wait until he actually became consul in January to make it easier to mount a successful coup.

His pledge to Messalina to adopt Britannicus must have meant – assuming that he was aiming at the Principate – that he intended to make the seven-year-old boy his official heir. That would have seriously prejudiced Nero's chances of ultimate succession in the event of Claudius' sudden death. Nero, not yet eleven, was still far too young to succeed his great-uncle directly, but it may be that the reason for his and Agrippina's survival, despite Messalina's supposed antagonism, was that Claudius was keeping him in reserve in case anything happened to the rather sickly Britannicus. On this reading, Nero was a valuable pawn, who at any time might need to be promoted in order to shore up the rocky Claudian regime. Messalina had not produced a second son. She may have begun to ration her visits to the Emperor's bed. Claudius took his two favourite concubines, Calpurnia and Cleopatra, with him to Ostia.

'Messalina avidly desired to get married on account of the sheer scale of the affront to morality – the ultimate sexual buzz for a voluptuary,' Tacitus writes. His description of the wedding day is spare and epigrammatic, yet it leaves an indelible impression: 'I realize it will seem fantastic how any mortal beings could have supposed themselves safe and secure in a city where everybody's business is known and nothing can be kept quiet – much less when it is the consul-designate and the Emperor's wife who get together on a prearranged day, before invited witnesses, as if for "marriage for the begetting of children"; when the woman listens to the soothsayers' pronouncements, wears a bridal veil and offers sacrifice before the gods; and when the couple recline at table with the wedding guests, embrace with a kiss, and finally spend the night together in the freedom of the conjugal act.'[26]

Narcissus, who controlled or had easy access to the regime's intelligence network, which fed the palace with reports on undesirable activities, decided to inform on Messalina and Gaius. He had become afraid of the Empress' appetite for judicial murder; her recent victims had included his close colleague, the freedman Polybius. Fearing that he might be next on her list, Narcissus left for Ostia after consulting two other highly placed freedmen, Pallas and Callistus, at a series of confidential meetings within the royal household. Pallas was a secret supporter of Agrippina, and could have been expected to pass on some of the information to her.

The two concubines were now drawn into the moves to destroy Messalina. Narcissus, who was plainly using them as buffers between himself and retribution in case he had misjudged Claudius' probable reaction, briefed Calpurnia on what to tell the Emperor, with Cleopatra standing by to back up every word. Narcissus, summoned in due course to the imperial presence to explain himself, immediately put his own spin on the news: 'Surely you know you're divorced!' he said. 'The people, the Senate and the Army have seen Gaius Silius' wedding. Act quickly – or this new husband rules the city!'[27] Other advisers who were called in confirmed the freedman's account, none more significantly than the Praetorian Prefect, Lusius Geta. Claudius, badly rattled, agreed to Narcissus' request to be put in control of the Praetorians for just one day to ensure they were given the necessary orders. 'But am I still Emperor?' he asked pathetically, over and over again.

Tacitus now switches the scene back to the Empress and her lover in Rome, and it is here that the Dionysian aspect of the 'wedding' story comes to the fore. 'But Messalina, more than ever, was living in the lap of profligate luxury. Autumn was in its prime, and she was celebrating make-believe rites of the vine harvest in her grounds. Feet were treading the grapes, wine vats were overflowing, women in animal skins were capering around as maenads in the ecstasies of ritual sacrifice. She herself, hair streaming, brandished the sacred thyrsus; beside her, wearing actors' buskins, stood Gaius Silius, tossing his ivy-wreathed head, while all about them rose the cries of the wanton chorus.' This famous description has been used to support a theory that the form of marriage that Messalina and Gaius went through was no more serious, from a legal and constitutional viewpoint, than these Bacchic revels in her palace garden, which were related in cultic terms to the earlier ceremony.[28]

It is an attractive idea, which would solve at a stroke the basic problem of implausibility in Tacitus' narrative: why should the lovers take such a gigantic risk by getting married without moving to secure their position? It also fits in with the long and sometimes turbulent history of the worship in Rome of the god of ecstasy and wine, whether under the name of Bacchus or Dionysus. As far back as 186 BC the Senate had banned the cult, but without lasting success. By Claudius' time the rites of Bacchus, if correctly performed, were popularly believed to confer the promise of a happy afterlife, without any need for his devotees to be morally irreproachable. That would certainly have suited Messalina. Tacitus, however, would have wanted his more sophisticated readers to pick up his references to a seminal literary text of Dionysian mysteries, the *Bacchae* of Euripides, written in about 407 BC.

The play is set in the palace grounds of King Pentheus of Thebes, who, like the Roman Senate, strongly disapproves of the worship of Dionysus and tries to stop it by force. To teach him his place in the order of the universe, Dionysus, the miracle-working son of Zeus, sends all the Theban women into an ecstatic frenzy in which they tear the king to pieces, eat his flesh and suck his blood. At the play's horrific climax, the king's mother comes on stage carrying her son's head on her thyrsus wand, believing it to be the head of a lion. Dionysus himself, an androgynous figure, is the main character, crowned with ivy, wearing the skin of a fawn, and tossing his long hair. At the touch of his sacred thyrsus the very earth spouts wine. The intended identification of Gaius Silius with Dionysus in Tacitus' account seems plain.

Messalina's revels ended abruptly, as a messenger brought news that Claudius was on his way back to Rome from Ostia, seeking revenge. The boisterous party broke up in confusion. Gaius sidled off to the Forum, hoping to pretend that for him, at least, it was business as usual. Messalina, deserted by all but three companions, walked to the outskirts of Rome and hitched a ride along the Ostia Road on a rubbish cart. She managed to get within pleading distance of Claudius' carriage after it came in sight towards her, but Narcissus shouted her down and distracted the Emperor with a prepared list of all Messalina's previous lovers. Narcissus also prevented young Britannicus and his sister Octavia from reaching their father, whom he led to the Silius mansion to show him the wide range of Claudius' possessions that had been transferred there from the palace.

The Emperor, hitherto apprehensive and uncertain, now became enraged. He stormed off to the Praetorian barracks where Gaius and some of his associates had already been brought. They were paraded for judgment on a platform, where at least one of them protested that he had just been flogged, and drew back his clothes to display the marks of the whip.[29] As consul designate, Gaius would presumably not have received quite such degrading treatment, but he must have been severely man-handled, because he offered no defence at all, and pleaded for a quick death. This favour was promptly granted by Claudius, to him and to several others, including another senator, all without trial.

After the slaughter, the Emperor went back to his palace for dinner, where he said that 'the poor woman' must be brought before him in the morning to defend herself. Narcissus, knowing he would not long survive a reconciliation between Emperor and Empress, sent a senior Praetorian officer to kill Messalina if she had not yet already killed herself. The officer found her in her ornamental gardens, some distance from the palace complex, in a state of nervous exhaustion. She was with her mother, Nero's former mother-substitute Domitia Lepida, who was trying to persuade her to face death with dignity. But as Messalina proved quite unable to stab herself as directed, the officer ran her through with his sword.

Claudius was still dining when news of her death was brought to him. He called for more wine and went on with the meal. Perhaps his fuddled brain could not recall whether or not he had given the order to kill her. If so, that was taking absent-mindedness rather too far. More likely, he was dissembling. 'During the days which followed he gave no sign of hatred or delight, anger or sadness, nor indeed any human emotion – not even when he witnessed the glee of her accusers or the sorrow of his children.'[30] The Senate ordered the removal of Messalina's statues from public places and her name from prayers, effectively designating her a non-person. The stage was now set for Agrippina's ascent to unprecedented heights of power – unprecedented, that is, for a woman. Nero was to rise in her long shadow.

THREE

THE DOMINANT MOTHER

The palace was convulsed by the execution of Messalina. Claudius had to come to terms with the infidelity of his wife and the hatred of his children, for killing their mother. But chiefly he was unnerved by the threat to his power from a younger generation. The atmosphere must have been deadly, with many of his courtiers and slaves in daily fear for their lives. It cannot have taken Narcissus long to work out that, in spite of the public honours to be voted to him for 'saving' the Emperor, he could scarcely expect to outlive him by more than a few days. Britannicus, if old enough to succeed his father, would surely execute Narcissus as a point of honour, to avenge his mother. So would the husband of Octavia, whoever he might turn out to be, if marriage to Claudius' daughter – still only about nine years old – proved the key to power.

In these circumstances it might have been supposed that Narcissus would throw in his lot with Agrippina and Nero, to thwart a purely Claudian succession. He did not do so. Instead, he compounded his error by openly opposing Agrippina's attempt to marry Claudius. It may be that the freedman had already incurred Agrippina's enmity. In any case, she had her own agent in the royal household in the person of Marcus Antonius Pallas, another Greek ex-slave, who had worked his way up to be the Emperor's secretary, *a rationibus*, effectively in day-to-day charge of the imperial finances.[1] It was a position of immense influence and trust, as well as of obvious opportunities for personal gain. Pallas had been careful to stay on the sidelines while Narcissus destroyed Messalina. Now he was free to campaign on Agrippina's behalf.

Tacitus gives us a fascinating glimpse of Pallas and Narcissus meeting behind closed doors with a third senior freedman, Callistus, supposedly to decide who should be next to marry Claudius, as his fourth wife. Initially the Emperor wanted to do without another empress; Suetonius reveals that he had told his faithful Praetorians he 'would not refuse death' from their swords if he was stupid enough to get married again. Tacitus, however, describes a scene in which each of the three ex-slaves puts forward a different contender, confident that their master can be nudged to the altar for a fourth attempt.

Pallas, of course, was backing Agrippina. Callistus also had a strong candidate: Lollia Paulina, the stupendously rich and still attractive former wife of Caligula, who had divorced her in order to marry Caesonia. But Narcissus nominated a hopeless outsider, Aelia Paetina, whom Claudius himself had already divorced – she had been his third wife – in order to marry Messalina.[2] Agrippina demonstrated her opinion of the relative threats posed by each of these apparent rivals by making it her business, after becoming empress, to arrange for the death of Lollia Paulina, but to leave the matronly Aelia Paetina (mother of Antonia) in peaceful obscurity.

Although Agrippina was a twice-married mother of thirty-three, she was a slim and elegant woman, judging from a sculptured relief of her from Aphrodisias, Asia Minor, made when she was nearly forty. She appears to be at least as tall as Claudius and Nero, who are seen beside her. She wears a thin, high-bodiced robe, which emphasizes her perfectly proportioned breasts. Her hair is in a triple row of tight ringlets above her forehead, while two thin plaits fall to a shapely neck from behind slightly prominent ears. A straight nose, firm chin and an expression of calm dignity, complete the impression of an ideal, possibly idealized, Roman matron, still just in the prime of life. Pliny the Elder says she had doubled canine teeth on her upper right jaw. That would presumably have resulted in a slight swelling of her cheek, but it is not shown by the sculptor. Dio states unequivocally that she was beautiful.

Tacitus sketches her taking advantage of her relationship as the

Emperor's niece to seduce him with feminine wiles, allowing him liberties little by little until he can no longer resist her. Claudius, for his part, is shown as a lecherous old fool who finds it impossible to live without daily doses of marital sex. Neither of these descriptions fits the underlying realities of the situation.[3] The Emperor could have sex, if he chose, with any combination of his many concubines at any hour of the day or night. Agrippina, although very attractive, could not hope to compete with a replenishable supply of young women, some of whom would have been half her age or even less. In any case, at this stage of her life, Nero's mother was driven almost exclusively by the will to power, while Claudius had become increasingly concerned about threats to his rule. We can be quite certain that his decision to marry Agrippina was taken primarily for political reasons, to shore up his unpopular regime.

It is difficult to think of any plausible option that might have been open to Claudius that would have benefited him more. By marrying Agrippina he would return the Julian blood-line to the mainstream of the dynasty. By adopting Nero he would settle the succession to almost everybody's approval while removing a major incentive for senatorial opponents to assassinate him. If he could also arrange for Nero to marry his daughter Octavia when she reached an appropriate age – and twelve or thirteen was considered quite acceptable in ancient Rome – then he would further concentrate power within the family. Britannicus, of course, would be the theoretical loser; but he suffered from epilepsy, and there were doubts about his general physical condition and his level of intelligence. Claudius no doubt felt that, if he himself were to go the way of Caligula, then his son would probably have his throat cut, too.

Of course, Tacitus is right to say that Agrippina would have taken every possible advantage of her family ties with the Emperor, but their private meetings in the palace before their marriage were not for her to exercise her supposed sexual skills but to argue a severely practical case for a new dynastic partnership, to rival that of Augustus and Livia. The pair faced two serious obstacles, both far more important than the outraged feelings of the seven-year-old Britannicus. First, it was held to be incestuous for an uncle to marry his niece. Secondly, Octavia was already betrothed, to a young aristocrat who might be only one heartbeat away from the Principate if Claudius should suddenly die – the praetor Lucius Junius Silanus, one of three brothers who were all, like Nero, the great-great-grandsons of Augustus. No doubt it was at Agrippina's insistence that she and Claudius tackled the problem of Silanus first.

In Agrippina's Machiavellian universe, Silanus posed a more urgent threat to Nero's chances, both of assuming power in the future and hanging on to his life in the present, than did the existence of Britannicus; if he were to become Emperor, Silanus would be advised not to leave her son alive as a probable focus for discontent. There is no evidence, however, that Silanus was other than a perfectly upright young man, whose only fault lay in his family connections and his link with Princess Octavia. He was only a boy when originally betrothed to her and when Claudius associated him with triumphal honours, presumably those for his partial conquest of Britain in AD 43. His descent from Augustus was entirely on the distaff side. He was the grandson of Agrippina's Aunt Julia, through his mother Aemilia Lepida; thus, his great-grandparents were Marcus Agrippa and Augustus' daughter Julia, whom Tiberius later married and divorced before becoming Emperor.

Claudius had already killed off one son-in-law, a descendant of the great Pompey, allegedly caught *in flagrante* with a boyfriend. Whatever the strength of their respective motives, Claudius and Agrippina decided to call on the services of the pliable senator Lucius Vitellius[4] to destroy Silanus. The senator, whose son Aulus was destined to become the short-lived Emperor Vitellius in AD 69 – the so-called 'Year of Four Emperors' – had made his career by anticipating the desires of the most powerful in the land, and doing whatever they wanted. He had begged Messalina for one of her shoes, which he carried about inside his toga, taking it out from time to time, in public, to give it a kiss. Such adulation was revealed as a hollow sham when she suddenly lost her power; Vitellius travelled in the coach that carried Claudius and Narcissus from Ostia to Rome on the day of her fatal revels, and plainly did nothing to help her.

Now Vitellius stood up in the Senate, in his role as official Censor, and accused young Lucius Silanus of committing incest with his sister, Junia Calvina, who until recently had been Vitellius' own daughter-in-law. It was not, apparently, an entirely implausible charge. Silanus was known to be very close to Junia, and evidently showed some embarrassment in defending himself. He was expelled from the Senate and simultaneously stripped of his position as praetor,[5] with only one day to go before the expiry of his term of office.

Next, Vitellius organized a campaign to set aside the law forbidding a man to marry his brother's daughter. This was apparently considered less offensive to public morality than for a man to wed the daughter of his sister. It was not felt appropriate for the Emperor to demean himself by asking the Senate for permission; instead, senators were to be persuaded to plead with Claudius to marry the daughter of his brother Germanicus for the good of the state. This strategy may have been Agrippina's first contribution to Claudius' political rehabilitation. Softening up the potential opposition in advance was to be the hallmark of her mature style as empress. She liked the votes to be safely counted before the question was put. In this case, senators rushed to be first to beg for the marriage to be solemnized as soon as possible. Silanus, whom Tacitus says was innocent of the charge against him, timed his suicide for the day of the ceremony – the supposed perpetrator of incest casting his shadow over the nuptials of two blatant practitioners.

For Tacitus, there was a much greater irony: 'From now on the state was transformed, and the whole system became obedient to a woman – but not one, like Messalina, who had toyed wantonly with public affairs. Agrippina's domination was almost masculine in the tightness of its grip. In public she was austere, often arrogant; in private, she was chaste, unless it might be expedient for power.'[6] Can we take this astonishing statement at face value? Did Claudius really marry a woman who promptly took over the Empire from him? Tacitus was writing during the lifetime of at least some people who had spent their youth under Agrippina's sway; he could easily make credible accusations about her supposed sexual predations, but he would have found it difficult to sustain an obvious untruth about a vital public issue of state control. It is quite safe to assume that she did at some stage exercise a considerable degree of authority in important areas of the administration.

But it cannot be true that she immediately took charge of the Empire, with Claudius 'under her thumb', as Tacitus sneers. During the five-and-a-half years of their marriage the Emperor is shown taking various decisions to which she was opposed. Even in what might be thought an utterly trivial matter, he refused her request for a particular Gaul to be granted Roman citizenship. It did not seem trivial to Claudius, because he was intensely legalistic and a stickler for precedent. He loved to preside over civil cases, such as disputes between neighbours, which should properly have been heard by lower courts than the Emperor's, because of his lively interest in the mundane details of his subjects' lives. The business of state he seems to have left largely to others, except where considerations of his personal safety were concerned. That left her plenty of scope for hands-on management of affairs, while he indulged his passion for antiquarianism, delving into ancient documents and writing historical works, none of which have survived. He also enjoyed monitoring progress on his civil engineering schemes, such as a new harbour at Ostia and innumerable water works.

Great survivors like Agrippina tend not to act impulsively. Although living close to imperial power for much of her life, she had never before exercised it. She was on a learning curve, but we may suppose that she learned fast. With Pallas and his aides to brief her on events and policy, and guide her through administrative and diplomatic minefields, she was able not only to enjoy the *de facto* exercise of power but to build up a party of loyal supporters for Nero. The details of such work did not bore her, as they were to bore her son. She studied lists of officers in the Praetorian Guard, down to the level of centurions, and manipulated their career structure by promoting to higher rank in distant frontier legions those whom she could not trust. She replaced them with men who, in a crisis in Rome itself, would be prepared to do her bidding. Not until after she had re-arranged the minor posts to her satisfaction, did she move to have her staunch ally Sextus Afranius Burrus appointed sole Praetorian Prefect. That way, the junior officers knew they owed their appointments to her, not to their commander.

There is nothing in the written record to suggest that Agrippina followed a consistent line in specific policy areas. Her personal interest was not identical with that of the state. Her aim was the accumulation of power, and everything else was subordinated to it. She knew that at some indeterminate date in the future she would have to fight to retain that power by replacing her husband with her son. When that time came, she might need all the help she could get, both at home and abroad. Agrippina therefore tried to place her supporters wherever they would be most useful, and played on her position as the only surviving child of Germanicus to keep the army faithful to his memory and his grandson. The military settlement on the Rhine where she lived as an infant became Colonia Agrippinensis – which we know today as Cologne.

Dio Cassius gives a chilling example of her attention to detail in the case of Lollia Paulina, whom she had accused of consulting astrologers to see how long Claudius' new marriage would last. Agrippina was not content merely to send a trusted officer to kill her soon after her sentence of banishment took effect; she told him to bring back the severed head. In life, Lollia had livened up the conversation at many a dinner party by producing bills of sale to show how much her fabulous jewellery had cost. Now, Agrippina could not even be sure she recognized the grisly object that was presented to her. With her own hands she drew back the clammy lips and prised open the jaw. Only after subjecting Lollia's uneven teeth to careful scrutiny was she convinced that her old adversary was dead.[7]

Is it any wonder that Nero, just eleven years of age when Agrippina became Empress, went in awe of his mother? There is no suggestion in any of the sources that the boy ever stepped seriously out of line during his difficult apprenticeship to power. This was no 'spoilt brat' of the type so familiar in modern wealthy society in the West; he was an energetic, but watchful and sensitive child, who had known from infancy that some people wanted to kill him – and that one false move on his part might result in disaster both for him and his mother. He depended on her for protection and reassurance as well as for maternal affection, and he seems to have rewarded her with obedience. She, with her acute eye for other people's weaknesses, would have made sure he stayed that way for as long as possible. Mothers like Agrippina do not achieve dominance without knowing how to ration out love.

Agrippina's marriage meant that Nero now moved to the inner core of the royal family, in daily contact with Prince Britannicus, then aged about eight, and the two princesses – Antonia, aged about twenty-one, and Octavia, only about nine. Antonia was the Emperor's oldest surviving daughter by his second wife Aelia Paetina; for years she had evidently had to put up with a secondary role at court while Messalina lived to promote the interests of her own two children. It would scarcely be suprising if Nero appeared to her as another unwelcome interloper, but in any case it is hard to imagine a close friendship blooming between an elegant young lady and a boisterous schoolboy ten years her junior.

Claudius liked to dine at home *en famille*, so on most evenings Nero would have sat at the imperial table beside Britannicus and Octavia, within earshot of the adult conversation among the other guests, who would frequently have included the leading senators and occasional visiting generals. It must have been daunting for the boy at first, required to mind his manners, make conversation of a sort with his new brother and sisters, and reply to the Emperor himself if the great man should deign to ask him a question. It was a form of training in correct social behaviour at the highest level, and it is questionable to what extent the boy could actually have enjoyed his food – especially given the fact that each dish had to be tasted, before he received it, by a slave who nightly risked poisoning as a career.

Roman dinners could last for many hours, and Claudius, a noted gourmet, took his time over his favourite occupation and its associated pleasure of getting peacefully drunk. Obviously, the children would have left the dining room long before the party broke up, an event often definitively signalled by Claudius being carried, tipsy and comatose, to his bed. Equally obviously, there would have been evenings that dragged on endlessly for Nero, for he could not leave the imperial table without specific permission, and his mother would have told him what a bad impression it might create if he actually asked to go. His later preference for dining with congenial companions of any class rather than with senators who talked of nothing but state affairs was no doubt founded on all those tedious dinners he was forced to sit through as a new boy, conscious of his junior status and with his mother's basilisk eye eternally upon him.

Gradually, however, Nero must have grown in confidence. He was physically attractive, with blue eyes and a slim, athletic figure. He already knew he was popular with the common people. Now he had apparently become popular with the Emperor, who, after an interval, adopted him as his son and as a member of the Claudian family. It was at this stage that he dropped the name Lucius Domitius Ahenobarbus and became instead Nero Claudius Drusus Germanicus Caesar. At the request of the Senate – thoughtfully arranged by Agrippina – the Emperor betrothed him to his daughter Octavia. From Nero's perspective, Claudius had changed rapidly from uncle to stepfather to adoptive father and now also to potential father-in-law. To every politician in Rome and around the Empire, Nero's transformation was even more dramatic. From a once-despised poor relation, whom it was dangerous to befriend, he was now in the direct line of succession to the imperial purple.

Such a young man of great expectations needed a guide, philosopher and friend. The ideal man stood ready to hand – Seneca, still regarded as the greatest orator and literary figure of his day, in spite of nearly eight years of exile in Corsica. At Agrippina's request, Claudius recalled him to Rome and arranged for him to serve as praetor for the year 50. He came to the palace to meet the twelve-year-old Nero. It marked the start of a relationship that was to have momentous consequences for the Roman world. Seneca was well aware of the precedent set by Aristotle in tutoring the future Alexander the Great. Now he was to have charge of the education of a prince for whom an even greater inheritance and possible destiny beckoned.

Seneca, now aged about fifty, was supremely well qualified, by the standards of the day, for this challenging task. His father (of the same name) had an international reputation as a teacher of rhetoric. Seneca himself had studied the great writers of Greece and Rome, and continued for the rest of his life to emulate them. He had practised as an advocate in the law courts and held high public office. With his provincial background he was able to view the Empire from a wider perspective than the essentially narrow interests of city-centred aristocrats. As a young man he had spent some years in Egypt, where his uncle had been Tiberius' prefect. He had composed treatises on natural history, science and geography, as well as on the benefits of Stoic philosophy, for which he was especially noted. He had written – or had yet to write – a total of nine tragedies in Latin verse. To friends, he wrote voluminous letters, which still circulate to this day, on subjects such as providence, leisure, avoidance of anger, constancy, happiness and the brevity of life. These were not mere academic exercises to display his learning. Seneca was a man who had survived major illness, shipwreck, exile and the death of his only son.

Nero, for whom Seneca was to become an admired father-figure, was at an age where the stimulus of intellectual excitement takes over from the rote learning of words and facts. He had already acquired some fluency in Greek. Now Seneca taught him how to express himself in both his languages to secure the greatest effect on his listeners. In addition to these rhetorical exercises, he encouraged and deepened the boy's interest in literature. Together, they read aloud or recited from memory the acknowledged masterpieces of Greek and Latin poetry from Homer to Virgil. A streak of creativity surfaced early. Seneca must have constituted the first 'audience' on whom Nero tried out his juvenile efforts at composing original verses and songs, and performing them in his yet unbroken voice.

As a schoolboy, Nero naturally showed less interest in theory than in practice. He loved to draw and paint, play games, exercise his growing body and dream of one day drving a four-horse team in a chariot around the Circus Maximus in front of a cheering crowd. Suetonius gives us an attractive picture of him at about this age, but mixed with a degree of cynicism about Seneca's role: 'As a boy he tried his hand at almost all the liberal arts (*liberalis disciplinas*), but his mother warned him off philosophy as inappropriate for a future ruler. Seneca kept him from studying earlier orators so he would admire his own teacher for longer. Nero therefore turned to poetry, eagerly writing verses (*carmina*) with facility and without laborious effort.'[8]

Nero, of course, had had other tutors before Seneca, but none so distinguished. They appear to have been mostly Greeks, and they would probably have taught him in a class with other aristocratic youngsters. We know of Beryllus, who came from Palestine, and Anicetus, a former slave, whose later career in the imperial service included stints as Admiral of the Fleet, assassin and perjuror. At some stage – perhaps at Seneca's invitation – Nero was also taught by Chaeremon, a Stoic philosopher from Egypt, and by Alexander of Aegae, a 'peripatetic' (Aristotelian) philosopher; these may simply have been visiting lecturers, not of philosophy but of rhetoric.

Agrippina seems to have shared the common Roman prejudice that studying philosophy was a waste of time for the rulers of the world, and probably dangerous for unformed young minds. Philosophy has meant different things at different times; for the Romans, it was specifically associated with Greek ideas and manners. These were felt by many traditionalists to be subversive of the *mores majorum* – literally 'the moral attitudes and practices of the majority', representing the collective wisdom not only of living Romans but of all the dead ones as well.[9]

Up until Seneca's arrival, and probably for long afterwards, Nero would have been taught what this 'moral majority' considered good or bad behaviour, and would have been expected to conform without argument. In the home of every *Pater Familias* was a room set aside solely for the use of his ancestors. It contained their death masks and other relics, often dating back centuries. They 'participated' in family prayers and had outings on special occasions. When the *Pater Familias* died they would be paraded through the streets to accompany the corpse to its funeral. The eldest son would give the oration to a congregation partly consisting of retainers wearing the death masks of his ancestors, who in some vestigial sense were considered to be actually present and listening to the words, hopefully with approval. After the ceremony, the deceased's own death mask would join those of his parents and grandparents and the rest of the ancestral circle in the quiet little room back at home.

It took a very determined individual to break out of one of those haunted houses. Psychologically, to a highly strung child like Nero, it was comparable to having the undead sleeping by day in your cellar, and creeping out at night to drain off some of your blood if you didn't behave yourself and show them sufficient respect in your prayers. They were the supernatural confirmation of parental admonitions to do your duty and never disgrace the family name. Respect for seniority was virtually total. Adults respected the illustrious dead. Children respected their parents, or were beaten until they did. Pupils respected their tutors, and everybody respected the state.

And yet Nero did break out, after he was let off the leash. How did he manage it – and why? We can only make guesses, but we can be quite certain that it had little or nothing to do with Seneca's Stoic beliefs. Stoicism was a minimalist philosophy deriving from Zeno of Cyprus, who set out his doctrines in the *stoa* (porch) at Athens shortly before 300 BC, and attracted a wide following. He taught that everything that happened on earth was in line with the will of the gods and could not be changed. All a man could do was train himself to acquire wisdom and virtue, of which he could never be deprived by outside events. Seneca, in his voluminous writings, gives the example of a philosopher whose home town is burned down by an invader, all his worldly goods looted and his daughters raped. The chief raider jeers at him that his Stoic philosophy has not done him any good, because he has now lost everything and must be deeply depressed. On the contrary, the philosopher replies, he has lost only what was transient, like physical possessions and family, and therefore he is not depressed. His essential virtue remains, and with it his equanimity.

Whether Seneca fully believed in such extreme fatalism is questionable. Certainly he was notorious for not practising everything he preached. Stoicism seems designed to discourage people from protesting against their lot in life, much less trying to do anything to change it. The famous Epictetus, who was born into slavery in Rome at about the time Seneca started giving Nero lessons, became a revered Stoic sage, able to console himself for the inevitable problems of existence by reflecting on his virtue, which was its own reward. His career, however, does illustrate the point that Stoicism's outstanding moral advance on Roman traditionalism is its teaching that a slave can be as good as his master, and possibly much better. Given that Nero, in later life, demonstrated over and over again his general preference for the company of slaves and ex-slaves to that of most senators, it would seem that the doctrine of the underlying brotherhood of man struck an early responsive chord within him.

It may well be that, as an impressionable schoolboy, Nero accepted without question the instruction of the eloquent Seneca, whose job required him to advise the potential future Emperor on how to behave in public; but at some stage he evidently rebelled against it. Yet he was never to be just an uncomplicated hedonist. As Emperor, he was to be criticized for inviting philosophers to dinner and talking with them long into the night. In a later chapter we will look at the possibility that Nero embraced a form of Epicurianism, whose doctrine of the freedom of the human will would have been just as important to him as its better-known belief that pleasure is the ultimate good. Stoicism, of course, denies free will. Without some such belief in the possibility of what we would nowadays describe as 'existential choice', it is difficult to imagine that he could have persisted, to the bitter end of his reign, in a career so calculated in its refusal to follow the broad and simple path mapped out for him in advance by the moral majority of Rome.

For the moment, however, as he entered his teenage years, Nero was still deeply under the influence of his mother, who by now had succeeded in promoting herself to the status of Augusta, the first wife of a living emperor to bear that exalted name. Contemporaries noted with disapproval that when foreign ambassadors were received at court, she was often to be seen next to Claudius, though seated on a separate tribunal. When the British chieftain Caratacus was brought in chains to Rome, after his heroic resistance against the legions, he made obeisance first to Claudius and then to Agrippina, in front of the massed ranks of soldiers parading their standards, in a ceremony which effectively demonstrated to the world the partnership of a woman in the Roman *imperium*.

Honours came thick and fast to Nero, too. It was normal at the age of fourteen for a boy to receive the *toga virilis*, symbolizing manhood, but Nero was awarded his only a few months after his thirteenth birthday. At about the same time he was given the title of *Princeps Iuventutis*, 'Prince of Youth', elevating him still further above the Emperor's own son Britannicus. More significantly still, he was granted proconsular powers outside the city limits. These were real powers, not just a fancy title; Agrippina evidently intended that he should use them to secure the succession if Claudius suddenly died. When Britannicus, in his jealousy, called Nero by his former name of Domitius, Agrippina reacted as if the younger boy had done something treasonable. The outcome was that Claudius further humiliated his son by a severe reprimand, executed at least one of his tutors and replaced the remainder with his wife's nominees.

In an attempt to bolster his regime, the Emperor announced festivities to celebrate ten years in power and his sixtieth birthday, on 1 August 51. Nero was not quite fourteen. On public display in magnificent purple robes, embroidered with gold, the athletic Prince of Youth would very likely have outshone – and not for the first time – both his adoptive father, whose celebration it was meant to be, and his younger stepbrother, obscure in his child's regulation dress. But after the pageantry, there was famine in parts of the Empire because of bad harvests, and Rome was especially badly hit. The mob rioted in the streets, and on one occasion the slow-footed Emperor was lucky to make it back to the palace without suffering worse harm than a pelting with stale crusts. Special shipments of grain from elsewhere in the Mediterranean eventually ended the crisis in the capital, but the administration was coming under increasing fire for lack of competence.

Everyone had a favourite story about the successive fiascos at the Fucine Lake, north of Rome, where 30,000 slaves toiled for nearly 11 years to drain it for land reclamation and irrigation. On the first occasion, the city notables gathered around the lake to watch a 'sea battle' between rival fleets manned by gladiators and condemned criminals, who initially refused to fight. After they had been 'persuaded' by the usual threats, and had killed each other in satisfactory numbers, the plugs were removed from tunnels dug beneath the lake, and the vast crowd watched and waited for the promised rush of waters. Only a wretched trickle emerged. A year or so later, a second performance was given, and the festivities included a lavish banquet. The imperial table, seating the most distinguished guests, had an excellent view of the tunnel exits. This time the engineers had done their work too well. Emperor, guests and banquet were swept away by a wall of water, from which the half-drowned Claudius was rescued with difficulty.[10]

The Senate expelled all astrologers from Italy in 52, no doubt because they had been doing a roaring trade trying to predict what might happen next. It may not be a coincidence that Claudius himself was reported that same year to be gravely ill, and it appears that his illness may have dragged on well into 53. Nero impressed the Senate by entering their debating chamber and delivering a speech (presumably written for him by Seneca) calling for the Emperor's recovery. Later that year he gave several more set-piece speeches to the Senate on behalf of various communities around the Empire, including Troy (Ilium) and the island of Rhodes. He took the opportunity of referring to the supposed Trojan ancestry of the Julian clan, which claimed descent from Aeneas – legendary hero of Virgil's epic poem, the *Aeneid* – who sailed to Italy to found a settlement after the fall of Troy. There was, of course, no serious evidence for such a claim, but Julius Caesar had found it useful, a century earlier, in boosting his career. Nero was happy to follow his example, with the added compliment of delivering his speech in Greek.

After Claudius recovered from his illness he gave permission for Nero, now fifteen, to marry the thirteen-year-old Octavia, his daughter by Messalina. The wedding bound Nero even more closely to the Claudian family and to the line of succession, but it was never to be a happy union. Both bride and groom were far too young for a genuine marital relationship, and neither of them had any possibility of refusing. They were effectively trapped by the tradition of arranged marriages and by the evolving dynastic system. Was this sham marriage the catalyst that ultimately led to Nero's decision to dispense with tradition wherever it conflicted with his personal freedom? Certainly it showed him that, in spite of his apparent power in the state, he had no more true freedom than a slave when it came to taking a wife.

In that first year of his marriage, Nero moved further towards Agrippina's long-planned goal for him. During a three-day absence from Rome for a religious festival, Claudius put Nero in temporary charge of the city, advising the Senate that the youth was fit to rule. His duties during that brief period included presiding over a court room and making judgments in particular cases. It appears that he did his duty well, although no details are recorded; presumably he did not lack on-the-spot advice from senior magistrates, but it must have been a testing time for a boy of fifteen. To most outside observers his position must have appeared spectacular and enviable, and his future potentially glorious.

Nero's predicament, which he may not yet have fully understood, was that for him there was no way out. Having been elevated to the effective position of heir and presumed successor, he either fulfilled his mother's ambition and became emperor – or he would be killed. Anyone who now managed to outmanoeuvre Agrippina in the struggle for supreme power would almost certainly be forced to liquidate Nero, as an act of prudent public policy, to avoid perennial instability and the spectre of civil war. Was his manipulative mother honest enough to tell him so? Time was growing short for Nero to work out for himself that he had become a prisoner of his manifest destiny.

An event that must have concentrated Nero's mind was an accusation brought by Agrippina against Messalina's mother, Lepida, the aunt who had taken Nero into her household as a small boy. The charges were that she was practising magic against the Empress and allowing her slaves to get out of hand on her large Calabrian estates. On the face of it, the case seems absurd, and Tacitus seeks to explain it as a matter of rivalry between two jealous women, squabbling for influence over Nero: 'For Lepida was captivating his youthful spirit with her charm and generosity, whereas Agrippina, by contrast, was grim and menacing.'[11] Circumstantial evidence seems to indicate that it was part of a vicious power struggle within the palace, focused on the succession. Whether or not Agrippina believed in magic, she plainly thought that Lepida was plotting to remove her, as a preliminary measure to advancing the cause of Britannicus, who, of course, was Lepida's grandson as well as being Claudius' only natural and legitimate son.

The shadowy figure of Narcissus now moves briefly to the centre of the stage again. In spite of having hounded Messalina to her death, the influential freedman took up the cudgels on her mother's behalf, hoping to rid himself of a dangerous rival; Agrippina had accused him of malpractice and mismanagement of the Fucine Lake scheme, weakening his authority but failing to dislodge him from the Emperor's side. Evidently Narcissus hoped to turn the tables by securing Lepida's acquittal. Agrippina's counterstroke was to force Nero to give evidence against his aunt.

We do not know the strength or nature of Nero's testimony, but it can scarcely have related to the Calabrian part of the charge sheet. Presumably it concerned something that Lepida had said or done in his presence, touching on the accusation of practising magic against the Empress – a crime which carried the death penalty. For the first time in his life, Nero had to decide how to act in a situation that he knew could lead to a death in the family, for which he would have to accept a personal share of the responsibility. His evidence must have been crucial to Agrippina's case or she would surely not have tested his loyalty so severely. She was, in effect, inviting him to play the leading part in the judicial murder of his former mother-substitute.

It does not require much imagination to realize the anguish of the choice facing the fifteen-year-old prince. Knowing what we do of his future career, and its blacker moments, how can we not believe that this experience would ultimately make it less difficult for him to kill his natural mother, when her turn came? Agrippina herself was showing him the way, forcing him to suppress his feelings in order to achieve an objective in the endless struggle for power and survival. He did what she told him he had to do. The consequence was that his aunt, like her daughter Messalina before her, fell to the executioner's sword.[12]

Agrippina would have taken comfort from this further demonstration of her power over Claudius, who evidently acquiesced in the destruction of his former mother-in-law, although he still refused to dismiss his minister Narcissus. Once again, the loser was Britannicus, whose grandmother had been one of his few faithful allies. But as the months went by, and Britannicus celebrated his thirteenth birthday in February 54, the balance of power appeared to be shifting. By now Nero was 16, but the difference between a possible successor aged 16 and one aged 13 was far less gross than it had been when Nero had become Prince of Youth at the age of 13 while Britannicus was still only 10. Speculation around the court and in senatorial circles turned to the theory that perhaps Claudius had, from the beginning, intended to name his own son as his successor once Britannicus was old enough to fend for himself.

Rumour was fuelled by two new factors. First, Claudius was known to have altered his will, and to have locked it away under the seals of a number of senior magistrates. Secondly, he had taken to showing favour to Britannicus, embracing him in public and apparently acknowledging that he had neglected him in the past. According to Suetonius, he told the boy he would be giving him the *toga virilis* 'in order that the Roman people may at last have a true Caesar (. . . *ut tandem populus Romanus verum Caesar habeat*)'. But what may have alarmed Agrippina the most was a reported after-dinner remark to his cronies, all in their cups, that he seemed to be fated to suffer the misbehaviour of his wives – and then to punish them.[13]

Did Claudius suppose, during the long Roman summer of 54, that his wife would simply lie back in the shade and wait for events to brush her and her son off the turning page of history once they had served their purpose? He ought to have understood her better. At the very least, he and Narcissus should have inquired into the reason for the close relationship that now suddenly developed between Agrippina and the Emperor's personal doctor, Gaius Xenophon. As summer turned to autumn, they would have been even more interested to know that she was also consulting, in a professional capacity, a lady named Locusta, who later became infamous as one of the great poisoners of antiquity.

FOUR

THE TEENAGE EMPEROR

Claudius had a weakness for cooked mushrooms. A large, steaming dish of them was placed before him at table on the evening of 12 October 54. The Emperor had had a very busy and tiring day, much of it spent tramping around the temples on Capitol Hill for ceremonies commemorating the reign and deeds of the divine Augustus. He had managed to get a snack when he visited the priests of Jupiter, but now that he was back in the palace he was eager for his dinner. His food-taster, the eunuch Halotus, put his fingers in the dish and ate a mushroom with every sign of relish and no apparent ill effects. The Empress Agrippina followed suit while Claudius salivated. An especially large and succulent mushroom was among those left in front of his nose. He resisted no longer. The extra-large mushroom vanished down his throat, swiftly followed by most of the rest as he and Agrippina cleared the platter.

Some time later, Claudius began to complain querulously of feeling sick. By then he had drunk a lot of wine, and nobody was surprised when he was helped off to bed, staggering tipsily, for an early night. It was, of course, the big mushroom that had been poisoned, while all the rest were safe. Locusta had provided a potion to very specific requirements: it was not to be so deadly that it would kill its victim immediately, nor so slow-acting that he would have time to realize and reflect on what was happening to him, and take counter-measures. It was Halotus who had slipped the fatal mushroom into the dish when he fished out a good one.

Now Agrippina politely said good-night to the dinner guests and sent Nero and the other children off to bed, while she settled down next to the imperial bedchamber to wait to be told of her husband's death. We can safely assume that Xenophon, the palace doctor, was under standing orders, in the hypothetical event of Claudius' impending death, to bring the news to her alone. Hours went by, and the Emperor remained obstinately alive, if uncomfortable and restless. Flitting in and out of the dimly lit bedchamber, wringing her hands and wondering what to do, Agrippina learned from Xenophon that his patient had vomited after leaving the dinner table, and now seemed to be over the worst.

Agrippina realized the poison had probably not remained in his stomach long enough to kill him. He was still fuddled with drink, so he might not yet have worked out what had happened to him. But once it had passed through his system, he would be bound to wonder, in the cold light of day, if someone had tried to poison him. After more than thirteen years as Princeps, Claudius had almost totally subverted the rule of law when it came to dealing with any supposed offence against him personally. He sat as judge and jury in his own cases, conducting the trials in a private room of the palace – the notorious system of *intra cubiculum principis* – and torturing witnesses if he felt like it. And it was no use appealing against his death sentences. Agrippina would have reckoned that, at the very least, Claudius would interrogate the cooks, the waiters and Halotus the food-taster. Could Halotus be trusted to keep his mouth shut under torture? The Empress may have decided she could not afford to take the chance. She went off to consult Locusta.

The professional poisoner had a professional solution. She dipped a feather in a poison even more deadly than that which the mushroom had contained. Agrippina took the feather surreptitiously past the handful of Praetorians whose job it was to guard the Emperor while he slept, and handed it to Xenophon. What she said to him is not recorded. Xenophon would, in any case, have been feeling very uneasy; a Greek doctor who 'lost' a Roman emperor would need all the help he could get. By co-operating with Agrippina, who had already been showing him favour, he could reasonably expect to ensure his own survival.

There was no time to lose, because Claudius was complaining drunkenly about the pain in his stomach and demanding that the doctor do something about it. Xenophon took the poisoned feather from the Empress and tickled the back of Claudius' throat with it, ostensibly to enable him to vomit. Minutes later the Emperor sank back lifeless on his cushions.

It is chiefly to Tacitus that we owe the details of the murder,[1] but many other ancient writers mention it, and they are unanimous in naming Agrippina as the suspect. Nero is generally held to be innocent of the crime. There seems no need to argue with either of these verdicts. The circumstantial evidence, allied to the urgency of motive, would make the notion of death by natural causes hard to accept even if we were not already taking into account Agrippina's record as a ruthless murderess. Suetonius adds the further suggestive detail that, at the time, she was being accused by informers of responsibility for 'many crimes'.[2] If her enemies were, indeed, closing in for the kill, she may have decided there was more danger in delay than in action.

Although Agrippina could not have committed the deed entirely on her own, it is clear that few others were involved. Apart from the three people she needed successively to provide the poison, administer it and swear that death was due to natural causes, she had to be sure, at the crucial moment, of being able to control both the staff of the palace and the armed guards currently on duty within its walls. Pallas, head of the Emperor's treasury, was the obvious candidate to deliver the loyalty of the court. His task was made easier by the absence of Claudius' closest ally, Narcissus, who had gone to take the waters at a spa south of Rome – at Agrippina's timely suggestion – in the hope of curing his gout. Her protégé Sextus Afranius Burrus, as Praetorian Prefect, would issue whatever orders were necessary to the guards.

There is no conclusive evidence that Burrus or Pallas joined an active conspiracy led by Agrippina, but she would not have needed to disclose to them any murderous intention in so many words. She would have been able to achieve a similar result by voicing legitimate fears to them about the Emperor's health, perhaps going so far as to hint at the obvious possibility of a sudden natural demise. They would surely have replied, if they had any common sense, with some form of assurance for her and Nero. Of course, this is pure speculation, but the degree of co-operation that Agrippina in fact received on the fatal night and the following day was so effective and efficient, in spite of the suspicious circumstances, that it is difficult to believe it was entirely fortuitous.

For Agrippina, confirmation by Xenophon of her husband's death marked the end of only the first phase of her audacious bid for power. Now she had to put into action her long-matured plans, based on Claudius' own seizure of the Empire after the assassination of Caligula. Burrus, as Praetorian Prefect, is likely to have been the first person whom Agrippina summoned to the deathbed, probably along with Pallas and Seneca. She told Burrus to prepare discreetly for his guards to acclaim Nero as the new Emperor later that day. Meanwhile, nobody must know the old Emperor was dead. And nobody must enter or leave the palace without her permission.

Nero, too, was woken before first light and shown the body. We can legitimately imagine Agrippina taking her son's hands in hers, staring into his eyes and telling him that now his adoptive father was dead he must take his place as Emperor of Rome. What a prospect for a sixteen-year-old boy! By the time dawn broke, a sufficiently large detachment of Praetorian Guards, officered by Agrippina's supporters, surrounded the palace complex. They were told that the Emperor was ill and must not be disturbed. This message was also circulated to senators and soon spread through the city. As the corpse stiffened in the locked room, public prayers were offered up for his speedy recovery.

The situation was as alarming as it was exciting. Failure would almost certainly mean death for mother and son. The Principate was not hereditary in constitutional law but had simply remained, so far, in the hands of one family group because of their *de facto* control of the army and their long-accumulated prestige. Legally, the new Princeps – the 'first man' of Rome – had to be elected by a traditional assembly of the Roman people, the *Comitia*. In practice, he had first to be nominated for this election by the Senate. Tiberius and Caligula, successively, had each been nominated by the Senate as a formality, because each had already been designated for the position by his predecessor. Claudius, as we have seen, became Princeps only by initially bypassing the Senate, who, given a free vote, would unquestionably have nominated someone else.

With the Praetorians behind him, Claudius had nevertheless claimed the Principate on grounds of merit and experience, and as a *Pater Familias* who had previously served as consul. No such claims could be made by Nero. He was too young to have held any of the traditional magistracies, although he had been designated for a future consulship for the year following his nineteenth birthday. His pretensions to power rested upon adoption by Claudius, marriage to Octavia, descent from Augustus and Germanicus, notional proconsular authority outside the city walls, and the support of the Praetorian Prefect and the modest number of senatorial votes in his mother's pocket. The rest was up to him. He would have to rely on his own talents when the time came to go out and face the world.

Agrippina could not go with him, much as she must have wanted to. Her presence would indicate that he was still attached to her apron strings. As for Seneca, although he could not actually deliver Nero's speeches for him, he could – and did – write them. Perhaps the great philosopher of unbending morality had prepared them in advance. If not, he would have needed to write them quickly, because time was precious and there was much to do. Nero was no doubt left with Seneca to memorize his lines while Agrippina went back to sit beside the corpse until noon.

She had decided that Nero must not go out before midday. Astrologers had advised her that it was the most auspicious hour of that particular day. So Britannicus and Octavia, after being admitted to the royal bedchamber and shown their father's body, found they had to stay for hours on end. Tacitus describes how Agrippina embraced them, shedding crocodile tears, giving them words of bogus comfort and pretending to join in their mourning. She faced the Senate and the crowd at her gates on the Palatine Hill, providing bulletins on Claudius' supposed medical progress. Under pressure, she even allowed a troupe of entertainers into the palace complex under the pretence that her husband wanted to be cheered up.

But at last the long farce ended. At noon the gates were flung open and Nero stepped out. The waiting Praetorians, taking their cue from Burrus, gave a cheer, although it seems to have been rather a ragged one. Some of the soldiers are reported to have asked, in a puzzled way, where Prince Britannicus was. Burrus and the other officers turned a deaf ear. So far as is known, that is the only occasion that day when Nero's accession was openly questioned. Agrippina continued to cling on to Britannicus while her own son was carried off down the hill in a litter to be taken to the Praetorian camp.[3]

There, on the barrack square, Nero promised the serried ranks of guardsmen a repeat of the same huge payment of several years' salary that Claudius had given them thirteen years earlier as the price of gaining power. Now they cheered him to the echo. Nero marched under their escort to the Senate House, where he delivered Seneca's speech with great aplomb, while the man who had written it nodded his approval and joined in the tumultuous applause as they voted for him to be given all necessary powers as *Imperator*. These were almost certainly just as absolute in their scope as those voted to Caligula.

The years of training in rhetoric had paid off for the teenage Emperor. He was a fluent performer, slim and erect, boyishly handsome and speaking words of wisdom with the *gravitas* of a professional actor and the appealing ardour of youth. The senators, whatever their reservations about his age and qualifications, seem in most cases to have been genuinely impressed, if not entirely won over, by his manner and his statements of promised future policy, which Seneca had carefully tailored to fit their opinions and prejudices. Chief among these were pledges to restore to the Senate a range of legal powers that Claudius had taken away from them, and to end the process of 'government by freedmen'. He also vowed to rule justly and with clemency – there were to be no more secret trials and judicial murders.

There is no reason to doubt Nero's sincerity in delivering this speech, and for most of his reign he tried to live up to it. But the immediate problem for his mother and her associates, now that the Senate had acclaimed Nero, was to ensure the support of the legionary armies, who were many days' ride away. It would take weeks for the news of Claudius' death to penetrate to the remoter frontiers and for the legions' response to be brought back to Rome. While Nero was revelling in the cheers of the crowds, Agrippina and Pallas, with a team of imperial officials, were writing dispatches to the provincial governors and legionary commanders.

One courier, at least, was entrusted with a secret death sentence. The victim was to be Marcus Junius Silanus, Governor of the senatorial province of Asia, a man so laid-back and apparently unambitious that Caligula had dubbed him 'the golden sheep'. His misfortune was to be the brother of the unlucky first fiancé of the new Empress Octavia – the man who had committed suicide on the day of Agrippina's and Claudius' wedding. Agrippina may have feared that, as a great-great-grandson of Augustus, currently exercising proconsular authority, Marcus might contest the succession with the backing of the Eastern frontier army in neighbouring provinces. Her agents poisoned him before he had time to consider how to act.[4]

Another early victim of the new regime was Narcissus. There is an improbable story that, on hearing of Claudius' death, the freedman quixotically burnt his confidential documents because they would have implicated Agrippina in various acts of wrong-doing. It seems more likely that he would have kept them as a bargaining counter. And would he really have taken trunk-loads of documents with him on a health-cure visit to a spa? He was flung in prison on arrival back in Rome. Death, when it came, was announced as suicide. Agrippina had long been his enemy; and Narcissus knew where all the bodies from Claudius' blood-soaked reign were buried. If anyone burned his papers it was probably Agrippina herself, after sorting through them at leisure. His death would have boosted Nero's popularity with the many senators who had resented having to defer to Narcissus during his years of wealth and influence. Tacitus affirms, however, that Nero was grieved at the old man's fate.

The young Emperor would have known nothing of Agrippina's moves to kill these two eminent figures. After the most exciting day of his life, Nero returned to the palace in triumph and gave the guards – now become *his* guards – their password for the day: '*Optima mater!*' ('The best mother'). He would, of course, have received the congratulations not only of Agrippina but also of his young wife, now the Empress Octavia, and his many courtiers. Others may have cleared the path for him, but Nero himself had pulled off the stupendous coup that took him in a mere hour or two from obedient schoolboy to ruler of the Roman world and its millions of subjects. He would scarcely have been human if the experience had not, in some measure, gone to his head. Not for him the Stoic's advice to treat triumph and disaster as if they were just the same. We can imagine that Nero celebrated long into the night within his palace walls, although perhaps not in the company of Britannicus.

Agrippina would have been careful to remind him that over-exuberance in public would be counter-productive. His adoptive father was dead and a period of official mourning must ensue, so he would have to take pains not to give offence before the lengthy constitutional process of ratifying him as Princeps had been completed. Claudius' funeral was set for 18 October, five days after his death, and Nero, as custom demanded, had to give the oration. This was his first great formal occasion as Emperor when he had to meet and speak to his people as a whole, rather than simply their political and military leaders.

Unlike the perfunctory obsequies over Caligula, the ceremony that sent Claudius off to join his ancestors was extravagant in pomp and splendour. Following the tradition of Augustus' funeral, a life-sized effigy of the dead man, clad in robes of purple and gold, rode upright in a triumphal chariot. His mortal remains rattled along behind it, over the Roman cobbles, in a coffin encased in the imperial catafalque of ivory and gold, which had carried Augustus to his last resting place forty years earlier. These carriages were followed by the motley procession of family retainers wearing the ancestral death masks and by a vast crowd of mourners.

The panegyric was duly delivered by Nero, to Seneca's script. But unfortunately the great rhetorician had failed, on this occasion, to judge the mood of the people. The packed crowd in the Forum listened with due respect to the catalogue of Claudius' triumphs and literary achievements, but when Nero went on to praise the absent-minded and eccentric old Emperor's foresight and wisdom, it proved too much for their sense of humour. Laughter broke out, although Nero himself would appear to have kept a straight face. Agrippina must have been furious. She may have poisoned Claudius' dinner but she was not prepared to have him made a figure of fun. His reputation was inextricably bound up with hers, and she wanted the five-and-a-half years of their imperial partnership to go down in the nation's annals as a period of serious achievement.

If Agrippina did give Seneca a stinging rebuke for his rhetorical gaffe, it would help partly to explain why the two of them fell out with each other quite so early in the new reign. It may also explain why he went on to write a satirical sketch about her recently cremated husband, for private performance at court, under a title that is strictly untranslatable but is usually rendered in English as 'The Pumpkinification of the Divine Claudius'.[5] It affects to deal with Claudius' reception in Heaven, where the other gods treat him as a buffoon, especially the Divine Augustus, who thoroughly humiliates him. Some classicists find the brief play hilarious; others consider the petty spite to be unworthy of its author. But the fact that Seneca wrote it so soon after Claudius' death, and seems to have revelled in its authorship, tends to indicate that he was not directly involved in the plot to kill him. Guilt prefers silence.

The day after the funeral the Senate, in Nero's presence, formally declared Claudius a god. From that moment the young Emperor could – and did – call himself son of god. Latin has no means of expressing either the definite or indefinite article – so does not distinguish between them – and its script in the first century AD was entirely composed of capital letters. DIVI FILIUS or FILIUS DEI can therefore be translated in many different ways, from the fairly low-key 'a son of a god' all the way up to the unique and universal 'The Son of God'. It will perhaps be best for us to place Nero somewhere between these two extremes, without trying to be too specific.

Suetonius provides some colourful assistance.

> The main omens of Claudius' death were that a long-haired star arose (*exortus crinitae stellae*), the tomb of his father Drusus was struck from Heaven (*tactum de caelo*), and many magistrates of all ranks died in the same year. And in fact there is some evidence that he himself foresaw the end of his earthly life and did not try to conceal it. In choosing consuls he did not nominate anyone beyond the month in which he died, and in his last speech to the Senate he called for harmony between his children, begging the senators as fathers to take care of both boys while they grew up. And the last time he presided in court he announced that he was coming to the end of his mortal existence, although everyone present prayed to avert this.[6]

Such omens as a comet appearing in the sky and a family tomb being struck by lightning were believed to have significance for whole nations as well as eminent individuals. We can be certain that Suetonius' catalogue of strange events before Claudius' death would have been used by astrologers and soothsayers to demonstrate that Nero's arrival on the world stage represented the will of the gods. Nero's comet, trailing fire through the firmament, is in the same predictive category as the star that hung over Bethlehem for the Nativity of Jesus. The lightning bolt which disturbed the bones of Drusus would have marked, for Romans, a celestial announcement that the Claudian line was about to be eclipsed by the Julian, as now represented by the son of Agrippina.

Seneca makes his own distinctive contribution. Comparing the young Emperor to the sun rising over Rome, he writes: 'So already Nero appears, his shining face flaming in a flash of splendour, while the hair flows down his graceful neck.' Seneca puts this flattery in the mouth of Phoebus Apollo, god of music and song, who is made to describe Nero as 'resembling me in face and glory, not less in voice or making music'.[7] The *hubris* is extreme. To do Nero credit, the young man signalled his rejection of this pretence of equalling the god of music by taking daily lessons on the cithara, and sticking at it for years.[8]

These music lessons, given by Terpnus, the most accomplished soloist of the day on this traditional Greek instrument – a development of the lyre, with more strings and greater range – proved to be a personal success but ultimately a political disaster. Nero learned to play the cithara to professional standards and was unable to resist the temptation to perform on the public stage during the second half of his reign, shocking traditionalists who considered it was an activity more suited to a slave than to the ruler of the Roman Empire.

During the early period of his reign, however, Nero was able to retain the loyalty or acquiescence of a substantial number of conservatives, in spite of their reservations about his youth and lack of experience. He made an excellent impression when he addressed the Senate on the day of the vote for the deification of Claudius. The theme he chose – obviously after consultation with Seneca – was that the torch had passed to a new generation, uncontaminated by the blood-letting of the recent past. 'I do not carry with me any hatreds, any resentments, any thirst for vengeance,' Nero declaimed.[9]

The Emperor pledged not to set himself up as 'the judge of all cases' behind closed doors, nor to allow a minority to get their way by bribery or currying favour; and he would keep separate the private business of the palace and the administration of the state. That constituted an effective repudiation of the man they were currently honouring as a god. To the further delight of his aristocratic listeners, Nero confirmed the Senate's rights of government in Italy and the 'senatorial provinces' (effectively, those parts of the Empire that were sufficiently peaceful and settled not to require the permanent presence of a standing army). He himself, he declared, would be commander-in-chief of all the legions.[10] The senators were not to know that he would never once lead any of his troops into battle.

Tacitus confirms that 'his pledges were not dishonoured, and many decisions were made by the Senate itself'.[11] What shocked the senators, however, was that Nero did not read out to them the contents of Claudius' will. Evidently, none of them dared to mount a challenge. If precedent had been followed, the will would have been published at the Senate's meeting on the day of Nero's accession. To remain silent about it after almost a week was sufficient indication to everybody that its provisions would probably never be made known, and that it might already have been destroyed. Nero himself may not have been given the chance to read it, although Agrippina would no doubt have told him an edited version of what it contained, along with her reasons for suppressing it.

For Nero, there was no problem. In the absence of a will, he simply inherited the whole of the previous Emperor's property as well as his power. This, in fact, was to become the rule for all future imperial changeovers, so Nero was setting another constitutional precedent. Yet again, the loser had to be Britannicus. Some writers have speculated that Claudius might have decided, after all, to favour the younger of the two princes as his successor – but that would surely have been a recipe for civil war. It seems much more likely that Claudius intended to leave Britannicus a big enough slice of his personal fortune to enable the boy to pursue a significant political career when he grew up. Agrippina would no doubt have calculated that the risk of permitting such an inheritance, carrying a potential long-term threat to Nero's sovereignty, outweighed the offence of destroying the will.

The first weeks of the new reign marked the high point of Agrippina's amazing career. She moved around the city in a litter surrounded by her personal military guard, with Nero often enough seen walking respectfully beside her while she gave him the benefit of her advice. In front of her, to clear a way through the crowded streets, two lictors bore the *fasces*, the traditional bundle of rods signifying the power of a Roman magistrate (which she was not). She even arranged for the Senate to meet at the palace for her convenience, so that she could listen to the debates of the all-male assembly from behind a curtain, making sure they knew she was there.

At this stage she clearly had the Emperor's ear, and may very well have been in effective control of the army. But this period of dominance lasted only for a matter of weeks, and was certainly over before January 55, when Nero became a consul. What had gone wrong for her? There seem to have been differences over policy and presentation, as well as clashes of temperament and egos. Seneca, plainly, was serious about the pledges he had inserted into Nero's two speeches to the Senate, whereas Agrippina, while recognizing the need for fair words to attain an immediate objective, would have resisted attempts to make her change her ways in order to follow the new line symbolized by the young Emperor's 'clean-slate' approach.

We need to remember that Seneca, now in his late fifties, had spent years preparing Nero for his great role. He was just as far-sighted and clever as the dowager Empress, if not quite so ruthless. His own career had been blighted by eight years of exile in Corsica when he was in his political prime, and as Agrippina's faithful lieutenant after his return to Rome he had been unable to build up any significant following of his own. He had served as quaestor and praetor, which qualified him to sit in the Senate, but among all the ex-consuls his rank there was only middling. His great reputation as orator, author, philosopher and lawyer only partly compensated for the disadvantage of his provincial origins.

In its way, Seneca's sudden elevation was hardly less surprising than Nero's. He had no official position in the state beyond being known as one of the *amici Principis* (friends of the Emperor). From the outside he appeared to be just Nero's ex-tutor, hanging on incongruously after his task had been completed, until such time as his former pupil found a suitable younger man to replace him – or until Agrippina decided to pension him off. Certainly, she would not have expected to find herself sitting opposite him in the Emperor's *Consilium*[12] on a level of apparent equality.

The *Consilium* was an advisory council that had no legal

standing within the constitution, but was in practice the highest forum in the empire. It was at the summit of the secretive decision-making process that had evolved within the palace to replace functions Augustus had wrested chiefly from the Senate. Membership was very restricted, and there was no question of the Princeps being bound by a majority view. Its advisory nature is implicit in a novel system of decision-making that Nero adopted, perhaps on Seneca's advice. When members of the *Consilium*, among others, were sitting with him as a court to hear evidence in particular cases, he required each of his advisers to write out their judgments separately. He would then study these opinions 'privately and quietly' on his own before giving a verdict, usually the next day. It is a short step to the assumption that he followed the same method to deal with unresolved controversy on non-judicial matters when his *Consilium* met to consider state affairs, when its discussions and procedures naturally remained secret.

It is plain that such a system would prevent a particularly powerful and domineering member, like Agrippina, from getting her own way by inhibiting any outspoken opposition from other advisers, who would be certain to fear her capacity to take reprisals against them. Instead, it would be bound to favour someone skilled at writing a clear, concise and persuasive memorandum, and who pursued a coherent policy rather than personal and family aggrandisement. This role would be tailor-made for Seneca, and may explain his rapid rise to predominance. For Nero, only too conscious of his lack of experience, it would help to protect him against self-interested assertions masquerading as appropriate policy. His own interest, having given a number of unequivocal pledges to the Senate, was plainly to stick by his word, in order to build up kudos and credibility.

The war for the Emperor's ear was fought largely behind closed doors. Each of our three main historical sources gives a different answer to the question of who was really in charge of events at any particular time. Suetonius and Dio are agreed that at the very start of the reign Nero handed all the decisions over to his mother, but after that they diverge. Tacitus is rather more cautious, and rightly so, because he, like the others – and like us – is forced to try to work out what is happening at the inner core of power from the occasional glimpses of underlying rivalry and hostility which reveal themselves in connection with particular outside events.

There was trouble with Parthia early in the reign, for example, and senators expressed off-the-record worries about the capacity of a teenage boy and his mother to cope with the defence of the Eastern frontier. They got their answer when ambassadors from Armenia appeared before Nero on his dais, where he was being supported by Seneca and Burrus.[13] Suddenly Agrippina was spotted making her way up the steps with the obvious intention of sitting beside her son to hear the Armenians' plea. Seneca whispered to Nero, who immediately got up, walked down to greet his mother, and promptly led her away. No clearer demonstration could have been given that the Emperor would not allow a mere woman to interfere in Rome's foreign policy. The senatorial traditionalists could breathe again.

Things got much worse for Agrippina very quickly. The new year of 55, in which Nero became consul for the first time, brought her a series of hammer blows: the dismissal of her chief ally Pallas, the evident defection of Burrus to Seneca's side, the death of Britannicus from a suspected dose of poison and a potentially lethal accusation levelled at her of plotting against the new Emperor. Within a few months she was stripped of her military guard, deprived of her lictors and ejected from the palace.

The one thing on which all the ancient authorities agree is that the main cause of her downfall had been her furious, almost demented, reaction to a change in the Emperor's personal life. For the first time in his life, Nero, the married man of seventeen, had fallen head over heels in love. Unfortunately for their future happiness, the person he had chosen was a Greek freedwoman who worked in the palace. Worse still, from Agrippina's viewpoint, he wanted to divorce Octavia in order to marry this former slave and make her Empress of Rome.

FIVE

THE LOVER AND THE SLAVE-GIRL

The young woman's name was Acté.[1] She was bought as a slave in the province of Asia and shipped to Rome. That is virtually all we know about her up to the time when she attracted Nero, but there is much more we can deduce. The earliest references indicate that she had already been granted her 'freedom', which implies strongly that she was older than the Emperor. It seems unlikely that she was not at least in her middle twenties, because manumission of younger people was comparatively rare. The choice of an older woman fits well with what we shall come to know later about Nero's tastes. For him, it would appear, ripeness was all – and over-ripeness perhaps a bonus.

Certainly, Nero could not love his child-wife Octavia, who did not bear him a baby in nearly ten years of marriage. His second wife, Poppaea, regarded as the most beautiful and voluptuous woman in Rome, had already been married twice before he met her; and after Poppaea's untimely death he proposed marriage to Octavia's widowed sister, Princess Antonia, who was about ten years his senior. In addition, Suetonius reports that at one time Nero had a mistress who looked just like his mother. That list displays a clear enough pattern. We do not need to credit the allegation that he committed incest with Agrippina – part of the campaign of *damnatio memoriae* – to recognize in the affair with Acté the familiar picture of a teenager casting off the shackles of a dominant mother by falling into the arms of a mother-substitute.

Whatever the psychological reality, Nero was not the first or the last adolescent male to fall for a mature and sensuous female, one who could give him love and sympathy in a haven well away from his duties and from the feuding and bickering of the court. Significantly, in spite of his supposed 'absolute power', he tried very hard to keep all knowledge of his romance from his mother. One of Seneca's protégés, Annaeus Serenus (to whom the philosopher dedicated a book on the benefits of a tranquil spirit), pretended to be Acté's lover so that Agrippina should not suspect it was really Nero who was giving her expensive presents, having set her up in a comfortable apartment. Plainly, he was still afraid of his mother and her tongue; and she herself was presumably in a position to have noticed the sudden change in Acté's fortunes. Her (later) sarcastic reference to 'my daughter-in-law the maid-servant' (*nurus ancilla*) indicates fairly clearly what Acté's role must have been at the palace.

Secrets of that sort cannot be kept for long in the hothouse atmosphere of a royal court. We know that Nero had confidants other than Seneca and Serenus, because Tacitus mentions two of them as fashionable young men-about-town – Marcus Salvius Otho (the future emperor) and Claudius Senecio.[2] These scattered names, associated with Nero's first few months of rule, show clearly the young Emperor's disregard for social rank when choosing his friends: Otho, from the *nouveau riche* minor aristocracy; Senecio, son of a freedman who had been an imperial slave; Serenus, an ambitious equestrian; and Acté herself, whose early life as a child slave placed her on the lowest rung of all. What strength of character she must have needed, as well as fantastic luck, to rise from such a degraded level to such a height.

It could have been anyone, therefore, from any walk of life, who betrayed Nero's love affair to his mother. Agrippina became enraged when she heard the news. She not only stormed at Nero himself but had some of his friends beaten up, to teach them, and him, a lesson. 'I made you Emperor!' she raved, as if she had the power to take the title back and give it to someone else.[3] Nero promptly called her bluff by threatening to abdicate (*quasi cessurus imperio*) and take Acté with him to go and live on the island of Rhodes, where Tiberius had spent several years in self-imposed exile before becoming emperor. But his most audacious stroke was to try to suborn some former consuls to testify that

Acté was of royal descent. There is something touchingly naive about the thought of the teenage Emperor doing the rounds of senior senators trying to find one prepared to perjure himself in the cause of true love.[4]

The ex-royal family he had in mind as Acté's ancestors were the Attalids, rulers of the great Hellenic kingdom that had become the Roman province of Asia. As we have seen, that was where Nero himself may have lived briefly as a small boy when his step-father Passienus Crispus was provincial governor. Perhaps that was what originally gave the two lovers something to talk about together, some vital common ground. The Attalid dynasty of Greek philosopher-kings were exactly the sort of people Nero would have wanted as in-laws. They had made their capital Pergamum into one of the most civilized and beautiful cities in the Mediterranean world, creating a library extensive enough almost to rival Alexandria's. The Roman aristocracy, too, approved of the Attalids, because they had been faithful allies in the East. King Attalus III left the kingdom in his will to Rome on his death in 133 BC. A popular uprising against the provisions of the will was crushed, and then, as the *Oxford Classical Dictionary* records: 'On this wealthy land the Roman Republican governors and capitalists descended like vultures.'[5]

Such was the royal heritage that Nero tried to fabricate for his make-believe bride – one who, as a little girl, had been sold like a farm animal in the land the Attalids once ruled.[6] It was the first of his great fantasies. As yet, he did not have the political capacity or the will to convert his dreams into action, to force acceptance of his desires upon an uncomprehending and resistant establishment. That day would come. For the moment it was probably fortunate for him that, although the levers of power were within his grasp, he did not know how to use them effectively. The Romans would, no doubt, have accepted a brisk divorce of Octavia, but they were not ready for an empress who had been a slave.

Agrippina's continued violent opposition alienated Nero's affections, making him more determined than ever to stick by Acté. The previously amenable boy 'threw off the maternal yoke and put his trust in Seneca'.[7] It was a pivotal moment in Nero's emotional life, and also in the wider struggle for control of the political process. From now on, for years ahead, Seneca's star would be in the ascendant, while Agrippina's waned. She had forced Nero to choose between her and his lover. For a seventeen-year-old youth, not yet certain of himself but filled with masculine pride and protective love, there could be only one outcome.

When Agrippina realized she had pushed Nero too far she tried to retrieve the situation. According to Tacitus, she 'counter-attacked him with blandishments', offering him access to her personal wealth and even the use of her own bedroom for him and Acté. But it was too late. His friends warned him to watch out for trickery from 'a woman who had always been terrible (*atrocis*) but was now being deceitful as well'.[8] Nero was not fooled. He may have guessed that someone who could murder her aristocratic opponents while in pursuit of power would scarcely hesitate to maintain her position by disposing of a lowly freedwoman.

Nevertheless, perhaps at Seneca's suggestion, he tried to maintain tolerable relations with his mother. From the wardrobe of previous empresses he selected a priceless jewelled gown and sent it to her, gift-wrapped. Instead of thanking him, she complained to her circle of intimates that he had given her only a tiny fraction of what he owed her, of what, by rights, really belonged to her. Tacitus would have us believe it was because of this relatively trivial matter of the dress that Nero now moved against Agrippina's chief supporter at court, the financial secretary, Pallas, who had become one of the richest men in Rome through manipulation of the Emperor's treasury. It may well be, of course, that the millionaire freedman had spoken out of turn on the way Agrippina had been treated by the Emperor, but Tacitus makes the claim in the very paragraph in which he states that Nero had just transferred his trust from his mother to Seneca. And it was in Seneca's interest, above all, that the secretary should go.

Pallas must have become virtually a law unto himself as the new reign began. Hitherto, he had reported directly to Claudius or Agrippina. Even if he now reported to Nero, the inexperienced young man would hardly have been in a position to understand the details of what he was doing, let alone check on his probity. And Pallas, with Agrippina to back him, would certainly not have reported all his multifarious activities to Seneca, who now saw his chance to replace him with someone who would. As Burrus, at about this stage, apparently backed Seneca, that left Agrippina isolated and vulnerable in the *Consilium*.

Into this fraught and unstable situation at the top of the imperial power structure, there suddenly intruded a terrible family tragedy. Britannicus died at dinner in the presence of Nero and Nero's wife and mother, as well as other members of the court, so it could hardly have been more public. It was shortly before the prince's fourteenth birthday, in February 55, when he was about to become eligible to put on the *toga virilis*, the symbol of Roman manhood. For nearly two millennia the predominant opinion, in line with ancient sources, has been that Nero poisoned him. However, there are a number of reasons to give us pause for thought, among them the fact that Tacitus felt it necessary to preface his account of the 'crime' with an unbelievable speech by Agrippina, clearly designed to provide Nero with a sufficient motive for fratricide, which might otherwise have been lacking.

Ancient historians typically invented speeches for their characters, not with any intention to deceive, but because it was a traditional part of the genre in an age where verbatim reporting, except of occasional brief aphorisms, was virtually unknown. It was a tradition started by the Greeks and which the Romans, as in so many other fields, simply followed as a matter of course. They used the skills derived from their training in rhetoric to express in their own style the gist of what an orator had tried to convey, without troubling about word-for-word accuracy. Tacitus, convinced of Nero's guilt and wanting to make his story more credible, saw nothing wrong in presenting his readers with a dramatic set-piece – involving Locusta and some animals on which she tried out her range of poisons – which must be more a tribute to his imagination than to his knowledge of this particular historical event.

Tacitus shows Agrippina, alarmed by the dismissal of Pallas, seemingly ranting to the empty air with a raised and threatening hand. We do not know where she is speaking, or to whom, but we are told that her words 'were not kept from the Emperor's ears'. She allegedly confesses that Britannicus is the true heir of Claudius, that Nero displaced him because of her machinations, which included poisoning his father, and that she is going to take Britannicus, who is now sufficiently grown up, to the Praetorian camp, implicitly to remedy the injustice. 'Let them listen to Germanicus' daughter on one side,' Tacitus makes her declaim, 'and, on the other, to Burrus the cripple, with his mangled hand, and to Seneca, the exile, with his professorial accent – men who imagine they rule the entire human race!' As a grand finale, she invokes the spirits of her most notable victims: Claudius himself and the two Silanus brothers, descendants of Augustus. Agrippina's speech as a whole is like a soliloquy in classical tragedy, where one of the protagonists takes the stage alone to share her thoughts with the audience, because it is the most convenient way – perhaps the only way – for the dramatist to convey information essential to the plot.[9]

Brooding over what his ears are supposed to have heard, Nero now decides to kill his adoptive brother. What follows is a mixture of *grand guignol* and farce. First, he springs the poisoner Locusta from jail, along with the Praetorian officer who is supposed to be guarding her. Then he recruits Britannicus' tutors to give the boy her celebrated poison on the quiet. But the mixture fails to work, and the boy recovers. Nero, indignant, has Locusta tortured, and even flogs her with his own hand, presumably to teach her to be more efficient.[10] She prepares a stronger brew, but when they try it out on a baby goat the disobliging creature takes 5 hours to die. For her next attempt, she gives the deadly potion to a pig, which instantly drops dead. All is now ready for the actual commission of the crime, which is carried out with fiendish cunning. The young prince's taster samples a harmless drink and passes the cup to his master. Britannicus sips it – but it's too hot for him. The poison is in some cold water, which is added to the original drink to cool it.

So much for the traditional story. Britannicus did indeed fall down at the dinner table, but it was not generally realized at first that he was dying, except perhaps by Agrippina, who is said to have stared in horror. Nero himself showed no especial concern, saying that it was only another of the boy's epileptic fits, of which he had suffered many. Octavia, his sister, was equally unmoved. Tacitus claims that this was because experience had taught her to hide her emotions, but the more likely explanation – indeed, the obvious one – is that she agreed with Nero's diagnosis; and nobody would have known Britannicus and his fits better than she did. However, it is a statement by Dio that seems to confirm the accusation of murder. He says that Britannicus' skin darkened because of the poison, and so it was smeared with gypsum to conceal the crime. But at the funeral, in pouring rain, the gypsum washed off, revealing the frightful truth. Anthony A. Barrett, assessing the possibility that Britannicus died of an epileptic fit, affirms that 'the darkening of the body points to death by tetanoid epilepsy. No known poison except strychnine, not used in the ancient world, will turn the face dark.'[11] Taken in conjunction with the many implausibilities littering the ancient accounts, the modern forensic perspective provided by Professor Barrett, however cautiously expressed, seems to show beyond reasonable doubt the innocence of Nero.

In any case, how can anyone seriously believe that Agrippina would have doomed herself by confessing in front of an audience, however small, to the poisoning of Claudius in the same breath as she proposed to topple Nero and replace him with Britannicus, who would immediately have had her executed for murdering his father? No jury would condemn a dog on the tall tale of Locusta, the tutors, the goat and the pig – not to mention the poison that failed to kill Britannicus when adminstered to him direct, but caused him to drop dead when it was heavily diluted in cold water and some other harmless liquid. Tacitus, Dio and Suetonius derived their accounts from earlier writers whose work is now lost; the similarities among them plainly indicate a common source or sources. But that should put us all the more on our guard against accepting their second-hand assertions at face value.

This 'murder' narrative has to be considered in the context of what we know of Nero's attitudes and day-to-day activities at this stage in his life. He is a seventeen-year-old day-dreamer who wants above all to spend time with his sympathetic Greek mistress, whom he adores. But he has been forcibly married to a princess who, although now his empress, is still only fifteen and who plainly does not sympathize with him and his dreams at all. He is trying, simultaneously, to placate a mother who is constantly pressing him to do his filial duty – by which she means to manipulate for her benefit the power she has won for him – and to fulfil his matrimonial obligations by fathering a legitimate heir to ensure the succession stays in the family.

Meanwhile, Nero has inescapable duties concerned with the running of a vast empire. No doubt, as the sources allege, a lot of the work-load was placed on the willing shoulders of others. How could he have coped otherwise? Quite apart from his ultimate responsibility for so many senior appointments, civil and military, there were time-consuming legal matters to be considered, such as those famous 'appeals to Caesar' which we read about in the New Testament. A Roman Emperor was also High Priest (*Pontifex Maximus*) of the state religion, which involved presiding over ceremonies and rituals, including those in which the entrails of some animal or bird were inspected on the altar for clues to the future course of events.

Nero, at this period, was also taking daily lessons on the cithara, writing songs, learning and declaiming poetry, painting pictures and sculpting, among various artistic activities. He was an enthusiastic sportsman and athlete, who dreamed of competing in the Olympic Games – and who was later to encounter heavy criticism from the Roman establishment for making senators and their wives take to the sports field to run and to dance.[12] He was muscular enough to enjoy wrestling and to control a team of horses, which he would one day drive to victory. Much against his will, the Emperor was obliged to watch gladiators fight to the death in the arena, although he courted unpopularity with the mob by trying to reduce the vicious slaughter which passed for public entertainment there. Tied to this punishing schedule of public duties, private passions and domestic squabbling, it is difficult to see where Nero managed to find the time and space for the likes of Locusta and her experimental menagerie, especially when he spent almost every waking hour surrounded by guards and hangers-on, including his mother's team of spies, built up during the Claudian years.

Nevertheless, Nero did manage to have a social life of a sort and to enjoy himself. It did not take him long, once the apron strings were cut, to find like-minded friends near his own age – young people of dash and style, who would obviously have been flattered to have their Emperor for company on jaunts around the bars and night spots of the great city. They would not have nagged him about duty or despised his love of sport and the arts. If they had not shared – or, perhaps in some cases, pretended to share – his interests, he would no doubt have dropped them and found others who did. One of the hallmarks of Nero's reign is his constant attempt to attract to himself personal supporters from outside the usual ranks of the great and the good; and he was never too proud to pay for such support, if it became necessary, with patronage and hard cash.

Agrippina disapproved of her son's new friends and their nocturnal adventures. Judging him by her own standards, she obviously believed he had murdered Britannicus, and that belief must have led her to a radical reassessment of his desire for power. She had evidently assumed, when disposing of Claudius, that Nero would be her junior partner in government for many years, until such time as she was ready to lay down the reins and let him take over in his full maturity. Now she had not only been outmanoeuvred by Seneca but had to face the prospect, as she saw it, of having to adapt her behaviour to a son who had demonstrated his readiness to murder a close relative, whom he perceived to be a rival and who had quarrelled with him in the past. Nero was evidently aware of her mistaken belief that he had poisoned his adoptive brother, and that would have added to the bitterness between them.

Agrippina must have been confirmed in her new reading of the situation by Nero's decision to make her leave the palace. He phrased it diplomatically: it would be much more convenient for her, in view of her large number of 'clients' who visited her daily, to hold court at her late grandmother Antonia's house.[13] This building was in the same general area of Rome as the palace but far enough away to keep her out of intimate daily contact with the court. The Emperor was equally tactful, on the surface, when depriving her of her guards; he presented their withdrawal as part of a general redeployment of troops around the city. However, when Nero paid her an occasional visit, he came surrounded by his own armed guard and did not stay long. Other people took their cue from the Emperor. Perceiving her obvious fall from favour, many of her former supporters kept their distance, too.

The climax came later in the year when Agrippina's old enemy Domitia, Nero's surviving aunt, whose husband Passienus Crispus had divorced her in order to marry Agrippina, joined forces with another rejected wife, Junia Silana, whose husband Gaius Silius had divorced her in order to court Messalina. Acting through four men under their orders, they arranged for Agrippina to be accused of planning to marry Rubellius Plautus,[14] a young aristocrat not many years older than Nero, with a view to making him Emperor. The tale was carried one night to Nero by Domitia's freedman, Paris, who had become a well-known actor and dancer, and was a popular figure at court. He seems to have given the performance of his life in convincing the Emperor, who was a little the worse for drink, that he was in such grave danger that Nero, allegedly, considered having his mother killed immediately without trial.

This gives us a glimpse of Nero's tendency to panic in an imagined crisis and blurt out the first thing that came into his head. He had probably been expecting some sort of conspiracy, funded by Agrippina in retaliation for the humiliation she had suffered. Fortunately, when Burrus was sent for, the old soldier told the Emperor it could wait until morning. Burrus was famed for his abrupt, laconic way of speaking, but until quite recently he had been an active partisan of Agrippina. Even though Nero showed some suspicion of Burrus' motives, he was capable of recognizing good advice when it was so trenchantly given. Burrus, of course, had not made the mistake of directly opposing his Emperor's will, and he offered to go himself to Agrippina's house next day to question her and establish the truth.

Nero took the precaution of sending a number of his trusted freedmen to observe the interrogation, and it is no doubt because of their presence that Burrus felt it necessary to adopt a threatening manner towards Agrippina. Outraged by this treatment, she launched a devastating attack on her accusers, coupled with an emotional appeal to her undeniable record of maternal devotion. She triumphantly carried the day.[15] Nero met her and embraced her. Mother and son kissed and made up in public. Junia Silana was banished, one of her henchmen executed and two others given lesser punishments; but Domitia and Paris were spared, presumably because they were seen merely as bearers of the tale and not its originators. Nero further demonstrated his *clementia* by taking no action against Rubellius Plautus, who, as a great-grandson of Tiberius, was a plausible rival. He was lucky – for the moment. Claudius or Caligula, in similar circumstances, would surely have executed the young man without a moment's hesitation.

For Agrippina, it was an astounding reversal of fortune. For months she had been in disgrace and under suspicion, and only the previous evening she had appeared, at one time, to be as good as dead. A day later she was back in favour as the Emperor's devoted and long-suffering mother. All of Rome must have wondered what had taken place, but the likely explanation is that Nero had been distressed, too, by this separation, and probably felt guilty about the way he had treated her. The impulsive reconciliation was all of a piece with the earlier impulsive threat. Perhaps as a sign of good faith, he went on to appoint several of his mother's supporters to important positions, notably Faenius Rufus (who later conspired against him) to take charge of the corn supply to Rome.[16]

Another failed accusation, this time against Burrus and Pallas, briefly disturbed the newly established tranquillity. Paetus, a minor clerk at the Emperor's Treasury, which Pallas had controlled for so long, claimed they were plotting to make Faustus Cornelius Sulla emperor.[17] Faustus, despite his suggestive name, was a nonentity from a famous old family, who had been allowed to marry Princess Antonia, Claudius' elder daughter, perhaps because it was assumed he could never be a threat. Nero was so convinced it was a trumped-up charge that he permitted Burrus to sit among the magistrates hearing the case against him. He and Pallas were acquitted, which, in Pallas' case, seems to be further evidence of Agrippina's rehabilitation. Paetus was exiled while Faustus walked free.

After this first eventful year of Nero's reign, the historical record goes quiet. Between late 55 and early 59 virtually nothing is heard of Agrippina, and little more of Seneca and Burrus beyond the fact that the two men are widely credited with running the Empire in exemplary fashion and keeping the Senate happy. It may be that this period of apparent calm is what the later Emperor Trajan was referring to when he said, confusingly, that five years of Nero's reign had been worth more than five years of any other Emperor's. It is perplexing because some specific matters Trajan discussed, concerning building activity and foreign affairs, occurred late in the reign, at a time when the written record against Nero is almost unremittingly hostile. Nevertheless, it is a valuable corrective to the traditional caricature of the sadistic and incompetent monster, trashing his inheritance with blood-soaked paws.[18]

We do not know for certain which governmental measures during these early years of Nero's reign can be attributed directly to the Emperor himself. It seems not unreasonable to assume that, at first, few or none originated in his own head, but that as he grew more experienced he gained the necessary confidence to embark on policy initiatives. In 56 the Senate meekly acquiesced in the appointment of imperial prefects instead of the traditional quaestors to run the *Aerarium*, or senatorial treasury, thus giving Nero more effective control of state revenues, in addition to those that already flowed to his own fiscal office at the palace. To allay the suspicion that he might be trying to renege on his pledge to keep palace and state affairs separate, 40 million sesterces were soon transferred from his own funds to the *Aerarium* amid a blaze of publicity.

These financial changes would seem to be the work of Seneca, but a subsequent decision to give each citizen in Rome 400 sesterces, as a straight gift, sounds more like Nero's idea.[19] It is impossible to be precise about the relative values of money then and now, but there are grounds for supposing that, during the Neronic period, a sum of 400 sesterces would have kept an average family in wheat (the staple diet) for perhaps a year. As grain was issued free to all citizens, it follows that they could spend the money on other things, thereby sharing in the general prosperity derived from exploiting the Empire. This measure was so popular that Nero repeated it later in his reign.

Nero's administration also kept a tighter control over the activities of tax-collectors in the provinces, and some senatorial governors were put on trial before the Senate itself for extortion or related offences. But the proposal traditionally associated with the young Emperor personally was a move to replace some indirect taxes by direct ones. It is not clear what his motives were, beyond a desire to end abuses which caused frequent complaints from provincials against the officials who collected the taxes. The importance of his scheme lies in the possible opportunities it might have opened up for expanding trade thoughout the Empire. For many years customs dues had been levied on products for no better reason than that they had to pass through particular territories to reach their ultimate markets. The problem was not entirely dissimilar to that which would inhibit trade in Europe in the eighteenth and early nineteenth centuries; so many tax bites by rapacious local collectors on the same goods meant it was unprofitable to export very far from the original place of production.

The primitive capitalist activities of the Roman world were never successful in the way that modern capitalism is in our own era on the back of free markets. It is arguable that they would have had a better chance of doing so – or, at least, of expanding gross imperial product significantly – if Nero's plan had been put into effect, even taking into account the natural paucity of enterprise in an economy largely or partly dependent on slave labour. As it was, the interest groups involved in tax-gathering combined with Roman conservatism to block reform. The general view appeared to be that it would be reckless to forego an existing and fairly reliable source of income for a doubtful substitute. Not only was the possible opportunity for improved economic growth lost for another 1,800 years, but the chroniclers of the period clearly regarded Nero's idea as the utopian vision of a well-intentioned boy who needed wiser heads to keep him from bankrupting the state.[20]

The Emperor plainly did need wiser counsel than he sometimes got. By the time our sources resume their narrative of Agrippina's career, it seems evident that she had regained an uncomfortable proportion of the power of which he had earlier attempted to deprive her. The precise extent of her influence on events and on the Seneca/Burrus administration is not recorded in any detail, but it must have been enough to make Nero afraid of her again. When next we meet mother and son in each other's arms, after nearly five years of the reign, the 21-year-old Emperor is about to commit the least forgivable crime of his exceptionally chequered career.

SIX

ENTER POPPAEA

Judged by the criterion of the greatest happiness of the greatest number, the reign of Nero opened on a high note and continued at an exemplary level for nearly ten years. His 100 million subjects[1] were, for the most part, allowed to get on with their lives without undue interference and secure from armed invasion, so long as they professed loyalty and paid their taxes. This state of affairs was not due simply to a fortunate concurrence of events, although luck no doubt played a part. The chief reason was the peace policy of Nero's administration, based on lawful treatment of the provinces and on the conviction that Rome had little or nothing to gain – but much to lose – by military adventurism beyond the exisiting borders of the Empire.

The policy was plainly inspired by Seneca but could not have been maintained for so long without the young Emperor's active approval. It was intellectually underpinned by a philosophical essay, *De Clementia* ('On Mercy'), which Nero was given by his former tutor shortly after his eighteenth birthday. The essay offers plenty of advice on both the moral and practical advantages of showing clemency to (carefully selected) wrong-doers, but what strikes the reader most forcefully is the dramatic presentation of the ideal ruler as absolute monarch – a position totally at odds not only with republican tradition and sentiment but also with Augustus' formal concept of the Principate.

'I am the arbiter of life and death,' Nero states, as a character in the essay, using words provided for him by Seneca. 'Each man's lot is in my hand – and each man's status, too. Fortune tells through my lips what gift she means each one to have.' Not only individuals but whole nations must obey him – or suffer the consequences. 'At my nod, those many thousand swords held back by my peace will be drawn. Mine is the right to decree which nations shall be utterly destroyed, which transported, which given liberty or deprived of it, which kings shall be made slaves, whose heads shall wear kingly crowns, which cities shall be razed, which rise.'[2]

It is perhaps the most extreme statement of secular absolutism to have flowed from the pen of a philosopher and statesman. What Nero himself thought of it is not recorded, although he plainly did not repudiate it. Initially he declined the Senate's offer to award him the title *Pater Patriae* ('Father of our Country'), which does at least suggest some saving degree of modesty. The powers ascribed to him by Seneca are those more usually attributed to an omnipotent deity than to a youth of eighteen who has been reigning for little more than a year. Nevertheless, Seneca's text embodies a form of social contract between the Emperor, on one hand, and all his subjects on the other. Breaching the contract invites disaster.

'A great spirit befits an exalted station,' the philosopher continues, now in his own voice. An emperor's greatness, he writes, is firmly based only when everyone knows him to be as much a friend as a ruler. For the Emperor is the bond that unites the state, the breath of life (*spiritus vitalis*) for so many thousands, who, left to themselves, would be nothing but a burden and prey (*onus et praeda*) if Nero's imperial mind should be withdrawn. In their own mind's eye the people see the vision of a state enjoying the fullest liberty – except the liberty to destroy itself – and they will escape ruin for as long as they know how to tolerate the bridle and reins.

In the final analysis, Seneca tells Nero, an emperor ought to act towards his citizens as he would like the gods to be towards him (*ut se talem esse civibus quales sibi deos velit*). It is important to record the original Latin because this remark is so pregnant in its ambivalence. On the one hand, it implies that Nero is in some sense in the position of a god in relation to his people. On the other, if we turn it into the imperative, it comes close to saying: 'Do unto others as you would the gods would do unto you.'[3] No wonder St Jerome, from the perspective of the fourth century, supposed Seneca to have been an early Christian in correspondence with St Paul.

Miriam Griffin, the biographer of both Seneca and Nero, writes: 'Perhaps *De Clementia* is a pretence to convince the public that Seneca was training their ruler to be a philosopher king?'[4] But why should it have been a pretence? There is, admittedly, much room for disagreement over the extent to which Seneca succeeded in such an aim, but the intention itself is implicit in the work. The precedent of Aristotle tutoring Alexander the Great must have been in his mind. At those famous 'philosophy dinners' hosted by Nero at the palace – and so despised by the conservative nobility – Seneca must often have been present, to hear his star pupil expounding or criticizing the arguments of eminent thinkers, while he himself was no doubt obliged to defend, from time to time, his own favourite doctrines against the assaults of non-Stoic guests. Nobody would have dared to interrupt the Emperor, while only the Emperor would have dared to interrupt Seneca. We may safely assume they both enjoyed themselves immensely.[5]

Judging by his future actions, what Nero derived from *De Clementia* was the message that an intelligent ruler rarely needed to use his powers to the limit, but would achieve more – and be safer from the threat of assassination – if he could win the love of his subjects by being magnanimous and lenient whenever that was practicable. As a general principle of policy, it was an improvement on the attitudes and activities of his immediate predecessors, whether from a humanitarian viewpoint or in terms of the exigencies of statecraft. So far as one can judge from the inevitably limited nature of the historical record, with its gaps and distortions, Nero seems to have tried to apply this policy, with few exceptions, throughout the Empire.

It was the way Nero went about it, rather than any defect in the underlying priciple, that was ultimately to bring him down. He had the great good fortune, for more than half his reign, to have at his side both Seneca and Burrus to help him follow what appears to have been a surprisingly steady course. Except for two serious but geographically limited frontier problems, involving Armenia and Parthia at one end of the Empire and Britain at the other, he presided over a genuine and fruitful *Pax Romana* in most other areas during those early years. And even after he had dispensed with Seneca and Burrus in 62, replacing them with lesser men, he continued to maintain a general peace wherever diplomacy could reasonably avert serious conflict.

This outstanding record, not unworthy of comparison with the later, fabled peace of the Antonine emperors,[6] must be set against those very rare occasions in Nero's fourteen-year reign when, through fear, he displayed and used the proverbial mailed fist normally kept well hidden inside the velvet glove. The fact that his peace policy survived the departure of his two early mentors indicates clearly his personal responsibility for its continuity. It never found favour with the 'war party', which had always existed in the Senate and the army, but which typically concealed its aggressive intentions behind the mask of 'republican' rectitude – that pretence of never going to war except in self-defence which earned the later gibe that the city state of Rome had acquired its empire by accident in a fit of absent-mindedness. The idea sometimes debated that the main senatorial opposition to Nero was led by a party of high-minded Stoics seems uncomfortably like wishful thinking.[7]

The Emperor's peace policy was not grounded on ideological pacifism. It was peace through visible armed strength and, wherever thought necessary, through varying degrees of deterrence and intimidation up to and including punitive measures. Nothing less would have worked against neighbours who, along huge stretches of the frontiers, lived in tribal societies based on warrior cultures and were often subject themselves to external pressures from encroaching nomads and other land-hungry wanderers. The success of the policy depended crucially on maintaining the morale of the legionary troops through adequate pay and conditions, and by satisfactory settlement terms for discharged veterans.[8]

Seneca and Burrus, with their provincial origins, can be seen as natural supporters of a generally peaceful foreign policy.

Burrus had served only briefly in the regular army, having been invalided out because of a serious hand wound. He was appointed head of the Praetorian Guard after a civilian career in the service of various leading members of the imperial family. The Praetorians, based in Rome itself, would expect to fight in battle only if there was civil war, as the frontiers were so far away and so well guarded. War against a foreign enemy would do nothing for Burrus, any more than it would for Seneca, whose talents relied on peaceful civilization for their proper exercise. The men who chiefly wanted war were the senior aristocrats who had been trained up to it from childhood, who considered it the noblest of professions and who resented being deprived of the chance of making their names and their fortunes over the bodies of Rome's 'enemies'.

Claudius had given hope and gainful employment to the militarists through his conquest of Britain, which he undertook chiefly to bolster his personal reputation. By contrast, Nero never troubled to visit a single legionary outpost anywhere near the frontier during the entire course of his reign. He did talk of leading a great army to the East, beyond the Black Sea – and actually recruited a legion of 6-ft tall Italians for the purpose, naming it the Phalanx of Alexander the Great – but that was intended to show the flag rather than to engage in fighting. He also dreamed of conducting a similar expedition via Egypt to Ethiopia.[9] Nothing came of these ideas, except that a couple of centurions spent a year or two looking fruitlessly for the source of the Nile. But the fact that Nero had such plans indicates an interest in the world much wider than the boundaries of his Empire.

At the administrative level, Nero's senior military appointments were evidently based on professional assessment by his advisers of a potential general's ability rather than his social status, the classic example being Vespasian (the future Emperor) towards the end of the reign. The first important one was of Gnaeus Domitius Corbulo as Eastern commander in the Armenian crisis, a decision that pleased the Senate. Corbulo proved to be Rome's most capable soldier of that era; methodical and prudent, he was never personally defeated in the field, although not all of the subordinate generals under his overall command were so fortunate. The military successes that followed his appointment conferred popular favour on Nero and his government.[10]

Suetonius is prepared to give Nero credit as well as blame for governmental decisions in these early years, but Tacitus inclines to the view that Seneca and Burrus were effectively in charge – managing him by letting him have most of his own way in private arrangements. Theirs was a 'harmonious partnership of power', in which they exercised equal influence on the young Emperor, each by a different method – Burrus with his 'soldierly attitudes and austere character' and Seneca with 'eloquently expressed precepts and urbane manner'.[11] The pleasures that they condoned for Nero were those which chiefly outraged his mother. There are grounds for supposing that Agrippina's opposition suited them well enough, based on the theory that while she continued to nag him so mercilessly he would look to them – and no further than them – as his most trusted and understanding advisers.

Seneca and Burrus, in fact, needed each other in order to stay at the top. Seneca might have the ear of the Emperor but he had no independent power base to support him; at any moment he might be blown away simply through falling out of favour. Burrus, who did have wide official powers as Praetorian Prefect, was of course only of equestrian rank and was over sixty years of age; if he failed to support either Nero or Seneca he would be vulnerable to replacement by a younger and more ambitious man. One senses that he was more than content with the eminence he had already achieved from relatively humble beginnings.

Neither Burrus nor Seneca tried to stop Nero when he took to going out after dark in disguise. There was nothing sinister about this. He wanted to let off steam as an anonymous youngster among a crowd of others. Who, apart from his mother, could blame him for wanting that? Tacitus, for one. 'The year 56 was peaceful abroad but disgraced at home by the licentiousness with which Nero made his way through the city's pubs and brothels, disguised in a slave's dress, with companions who stole things from shop displays and attacked and injured people who got in their way; their opponents were so far from knowing who he was that they gave him blows and he bore the marks on his face.'[12]

It sounds fun only if you happen to be one of nature's hooligans – or a masochist (see Appendix Two). The Emperor was still a teenager, and can have known virtually nothing of life on the street, as lived by the majority of urban Romans. As a youth 'dressed as a slave', he would scarcely have made a credible gang leader among a mixed bunch of aristocratic younger sons and street urchins living on their wits. In any case, part of the attraction for Nero would surely have been the escape from responsibility, from the pressure of always having to be leader. This was his chance to be just one of the boys. He may also have felt a psychological need to place himself in a carefully limited form of physical danger. Those facial bruises would not have been marks of shame to him.

The other members of the gang presumably knew perfectly well who was the newcomer to their ranks. Young men need very little excuse for showing off, swaggering about and getting drunk. Knowing that the Emperor was with them *incognito* would have put them on their mettle to behave even more outrageously than usual. They seem to have played boisterous practical jokes on well-dressed citizens, and indulged in the sort of horse-play that ended with banged heads and with innocent passers-by being tossed in the *Cloaca maxima*, the main sewer of Rome. The athletic Nero was plainly in the thick of the brawling, the drinking and the wenching.

One night the Emperor staggered back to the palace with two black eyes, having been punched by a stronger, older man, who was trying to protect his wife from insult. Nero, unidentifiable in his disguise, had recognized the man as a senator, but refused to take action against him on the grounds that his assailant had been perfectly justified. Unfortunately, someone told the senator whose were the eyes he had just blacked, prompting him to write a hasty letter of apology. That put the incident in the public domain, and Nero was no doubt advised by his mentors that he could not overlook such a serious offence against the person of the Emperor, which, to the legalistic Romans, effectively counted as treason. The unlucky senator committed suicide to save his family from the ruin that a public trial and conviction would have brought in its wake. Nero, sadder and wiser, continued for a while to go out at night, but only with a military bodyguard following him and his friends at a safe distance.

It is possible to identify three other factors that may have played a part in his eventual abandonment of these nocturnal revels. First, other 'Neros' sprang up – imposters who used the cover of night to cut a figure and perhaps turn a profit. Secondly, a gang of thugs allegedly led by Princess Antonia's husband, Faustus Cornelius Sulla, waylaid a group of the Emperor's usual companions, beat up some of them and put the rest to flight; Nero luckily had not been out with them that night, but he arranged for Faustus to be exiled to Massilia (Marseilles) as a precautionary measure – and as a warning to others.[13] The third factor may have been conclusive: at the age of twenty he came under the spell of a society beauty who proved determined to wean him away from his low-life comrades and raise him to her own level of glamour and sophistication.

Poppaea Sabina had brains and personality to go with her widely acknowledged physical charms, which included auburn hair similar to Nero's and white skin kept soft by bathing in milk, said to have been drawn from a herd of 500 asses kept specifically for this purpose. But there were blots on her family record. Her father, Titus Ollius, had been mixed up in the Sejanus conspiracy of 31 during the reign of Tiberius, and may have died before she was born; if so, she would have been about six years older than Nero, and therefore about twenty-six or twenty-seven when she first attracted his attention in 58. Because of her father's disgrace she derived her name from her maternal grandfather, Poppaeus Sabinus, who had been consul in 9, under Augustus, and a very long-serving provincial governor under Tiberius as well.

Her mother, also named Poppaea Sabina, had been forced to commit suicide in 47, at the instigation of Messalina, because of her alleged sexual involvement with Asiaticus, the rich senator who had helped to plot Caligula's death and was suspected of conspiring against Claudius. Ironically, the younger Poppaea was at that time the sixteen-year-old wife of Rufrius Crispinus, then joint Praetorian Prefect, who arrested Asiaticus and brought him in chains to the palace. Four years later, Agrippina, as Empress, used her new influence to remove Rufrius from his post in order to replace him with Burrus. There was thus a powerful reason for Poppaea to hate Nero's mother, for blighting the career of her husband, who, although only of equestrian rank, had been awarded an honorary praetorship by Claudius for his part in the Asiaticus affair and also voted 1½ million sesterces by the Senate.

There are differing accounts of how Poppaea and Nero came together. Plutarch says that Otho, the future emperor, courted her on Nero's behalf while she was still married to Rufrius, but after he had seduced her himself he was unwilling to share her with the Emperor. Suetonius and Dio say it was Nero who first seduced her, but then he passed her on to Otho to marry – presumably so he could keep their romance a secret from Agrippina and Octavia. Tacitus gives two different versions, of which the most plausible – and the one now generally accepted – is that Poppaea divorced her husband Rufrius and married Otho, who could not resist boasting about her beauty. The Emperor asked to see her for himself, and was enraptured at first sight.[14]

Poppaea evidently did not take long to sum up Nero as a prospective husband. She had been a married woman for half her life, since the age of thirteen, and her successful love affair with one of Rome's most eligible bachelors had given her the confidence to embark on a royal flirtation. We may imagine fluttering eyelashes and coy looks among the 'cajoling and artfulness' which Tacitus says she practised on the much younger man, pretending at first that she was too smitten with his handsome face and figure to be able to resist her own passionate emotions. Nero was in no mood for resistance, either, but when she had him in a suitably ardent condition she changed her tactics.

'When he fell violently in love with her,' Tacitus writes, 'she became haughty. If he kept her with him for more than two nights together she would repeatedly point out that she was a married woman. "I can't give up my marriage," she told him. "I am bound to Otho by a way of life which nobody else equals. He is magnificent in spirit and in manner. It is in him that I see for myself the height of nobility and good fortune. But you, with Acté for a mistress, have got used to being chained to a servile housemaid – and nothing can come from the servants' quarters except what's degrading and sordid.'"[15] Her criticism of Acté may have been grossly unfair, but Nero evidently accepted the main thrust of her argument – that his long and intimate liaison with a freedwoman was effectively preventing him from presiding over his court in the style appropriate to a great ruler. There was an unbridgeable gap between her idea of life as the Emperor's mistress and the one he had grown used to in the previous three-and-a-half years. She would have agreed with Seneca's view that a great spirit befits an exalted station, but with the difference that her idea of a 'great spirit' would not be of a Stoic philosopher but of a ruler who lived in unashamed magnificence – with her on a throne beside him. It may well be that Poppaea met him at precisely the right psychological moment, when he was already outgrowing his low-life friends of the darkened streets. Her ambition must have appeared as attractive to him as it was to herself, or it would scarcely have fired him to the pitch where he would dare to run the risks necessary for its achievement.

Otho, the first obstacle in her path, was easily removed. After freezing him out of the imperial circle, Nero appointed him Governor of Lusitania (Portugal), even though he was only twenty-six years old. At that time Lusitania was considered to be on the very edge of the known world, and Otho was to remain there for the rest of Nero's life. A real tyrant would have had him killed after a suitable interval. As it was, the new post seems to have been the making of Otho. Tacitus, while continuing to criticize his private life, concedes that he proved to be an excellent governor. As for Acté, she seems to have given in without a fight, probably very wisely. She continued to live in comfort at Nero's expense, but evidently ceased to be his lover while remaining his friend. This cleared the way for Poppaea to be the Emperor's sole and undisputed mistress, leaving only Octavia – supported by Agrippina – between her and the throne.

Tacitus wrote of Poppaea:

This woman had every attribute except decency . . . From her mother, the most beautiful woman of her day, she inherited beauty and ambition in equal measure. Her wealth matched her pedigree, and her conversation was witty and to the point. She made a show of modesty but behaved wantonly. She rarely appeared in public, and even then was partly veiled, either to avoid satisfying those who saw her or because the veil suited her. She never troubled about her reputation, not differentiating between married lovers and bachelors. Nor was she susceptible to her own passions or those of others; expediency showed her where to transfer her favours.[16]

If there is a familiar ring to that last sentence, it is because it is the same insult that Tacitus earlier levelled at Agrippina. The Oxford classicist J.P.V.D. Balsdon has drawn attention to the suspiciously close resemblance of this entire passage to the description by Sallust, writing just after the middle of the first century BC, of an earlier Roman lady of doubtful virtue, Sempronia, who figures in his book on the conspiracy of Catiline. Balsdon comments that Tacitus' portrayal of Poppaea is thus 'perhaps more startling than true . . . Ambition led her to discard Otho in favour of Nero, but that was all. Otho never lost his love for her; Nero never tired of her.'[17]

It is necessary to examine on several levels the text that has come down to us from Tacitus in order to attempt an assessment of the probable truth. So consummate and individual a stylist as Tacitus would not simply have lifted that passage from Sallust, while making a few alterations to disguise its origin. The explanation must be that it had been lodged for a long time in his mind, thanks perhaps to the Roman educational system of memory training. He was also, of course, limited by the primitive psychology of his age, which tended to classify people as types. Thus, for him, Sempronia, Agrippina and Poppaea were successive examples of the kind of woman who disgraced her sex by behaving in a non-traditional way – hence the formulaic element in discourse about them.

Seneca, too, expresses his outrage about non-traditional women (while not referring specifically to any of the three individuals listed above). 'They stay up all night like men and drink just as much,' he complains in one of his *Epistulae Morales* (Moral Letters). 'Oiled like wrestlers, they challenge men at drinking neat wine.' And the wine often makes them sick. Just like men, too, they have active sexual desires when nature intended them to be passive. 'So they think up perverse types of unchastity, adopting for themselves the man's role.'[18]

Catharine Edwards, in her ground-breaking study *The Politics of Immorality in Ancient Rome*, commenting on this anti-feminist tract, says that 'the behaviour of the women Seneca describes challenged cultural rather than natural categories. Seneca was not reacting to naturally anomalous behaviour. He was taking part in the reproduction of a cultural system.'[19] To put it rather more simply, Seneca and Tacitus shared the common belief of their times that it was wicked, unnatural and dangerous for women to be on top, whether socially, sexually or in politics.

It is essential to keep this cultural tenet in mind as we approach the climax of the long-drawn-out and emotionally charged power struggle between Nero and Agrippina. Short of being a Vestal Virgin, the only acceptable roles for an upper-class woman in first-century Rome were as dutiful daughter (or dependant), faithful wife or responsible mother. In all cases, duty meant conformity with the wishes of the *Pater Familias* or senior male relative. In the little that remained of the Julio–Claudian dynasty, Nero was the senior male. Even if he had not also been Emperor, this adult male-female relationship of seniority within the family would have taken precedence over Agrippina's earlier seniority to him as his mother. He owed her respect but she owed him obedience. It was her refusal to concede this duty of obedience to him, even after four-and-a-half years of his supposedly supreme power as Emperor, that ultimately led to her untimely death.

As Dowager Empress, Agrippina was not content to be just one of the most influential individuals in the Roman world, tapping the Emperor's power whenever he let her, diverting it for her own purposes wherever possible, but acknowledging and accepting that in the final analysis it was *his* power to use as he chose. She wanted more than that. Having for several years before his accession dictated every waking activity of Nero's life, his mother found it impossible to accept 'No' for an answer. Her response to 'No' was to nag him repeatedly to change his mind, and, if that failed, to try to get her own way by some indirect route, obviously utilizing her many highly placed 'clients' as a pressure group. Agrippina had every right, of course, to regard herself as having been the necessary conduit through which power had passed from Claudius to him rather than to someone else, and that therefore he owed her a debt of filial gratitude that could never be repaid. But underpinning this commitment of reciprocal obligation was a deeper, darker emotion – bound up with her earlier dominance of a son trained to abject compliance – which, if it could have found appropriate expression, might have cried out in justification: 'Nero – I created him!'

Before meeting Poppaea, the young Emperor had been unable to break this second umbilical cord, whose imperious tug could still evidently turn his bowels to water. Even after Agrippina's earlier fright, when, as we have seen, she fought off accusations of conspiracy against him, she had continued to act as if she were in some degree an alternative source of power, trying to block or inhibit his free exercise of it. Everyone close to the political centre had become aware of this, and popular opinion took his side. It was one thing for Nero to defer to his mother as a matter of courtesy, but quite another for him to be perceived as caving in to her protests – effectively doing what she wanted, in exchange for a quiet life to pursue his artistic interests in peace. That could not be allowed to continue, or power would slowly but inexorably seep away from him to her – with incalculable consequences for his own hold on the Empire. This process of seepage may already have been well under way when Poppaea felt sufficiently confident of her hold over him to begin mocking him as a mother's boy.

Early in the new year of 59, Tacitus tells us, Poppaea accused him of not even being master of himself, let alone of the empire – he was still effectively a ward (*pupillus*) of his mother. Why, otherwise, she asked, was he continually postponing their wedding? 'Are you afraid that, as your wife, I might reveal the wrongs done to the senators, the people's anger against your mother's pride and avarice? Because if Agrippina can only tolerate as her daughter-in-law someone hostile (*infesta*) to her son, then let me go back to being Otho's wife again. I shall go anywhere on earth where I may hear the Emperor insulted without having to watch – and get mixed up in your perils.'[20] These are rather strange words to be directly attributed to Poppaea, and it is more likely that they express the underlying reality of the situation, as Tacitus perceived it. The alleged 'wrongs done to the senators' indicate his view that Agrippina was subverting the state, and 'the people's anger' his contention that she had seriously lost popularity because of the power struggle with her son. The references to unspecified 'insults' against the Emperor and to his 'perils' – whatever these might have amounted to – tend to validate the contention that some degree of power may indeed have been draining away from him through her activities.

The mention of the young Empress Octavia (without actually naming her) is interesting for the use of the adjective *infesta* (hostile) – typically used by Latin authors to designate the weapons or insignia of an enemy army – to describe her relationship with Nero. Octavia is characteristically presented in the sources as being no more than a helpless and harmless victim of Nero's neglect.[21] As a woman scorned, however, it would be surprising if she were not at least as much an enemy as a victim of her unfaithful and neglectful husband.

Tacitus quotes Cluvius – a contemporary historian whose work is now lost – as evidence of the strength of Agrippina's determination to hold on to power or influence (*potentia*): '[sometimes] at mid-day, when Nero was beginning to warm up through wine and feasting, she presented herself to him inappropriately dressed and ready for incest (*incesto paratum*)'. Bystanders in the palace saw them exchange 'lascivious kisses and disgraceful caresses'. It is a matter for subjective judgment how much kissing and caressing is appropriate between mother and son, but if they had truly been engaging in an incestuous relationship they would surely have been more discreet about it. And it is no doubt significant that Tacitus does not state it as a fact, but merely quotes Cluvius and others as sources, effectively leaving it up to the reader to believe or disbelieve.[22]

Cluvius' testimony cannot be dismissed out of hand because he was a senior member of Nero's court, in daily contact with the Emperor, and he later wrote a history of his times. However, mother-son incest is by far the rarest of all forms of incest, and its rarity is guaranteed by exceptionally powerful taboos in all known societies. I am unaware of any recorded case in which the incestuous son had as many alternative sexual outlets readily available as did Nero. What the passage from Tacitus does demonstrate is that, by 59, Agrippina had the free run of the palace again even though she was not actually resident, and that she and Nero were constantly in danger of being observed by censorious eyes. Seneca was sufficiently disturbed by these rumours of incest to call on Acté (but apparently not Poppaea) for help. He told her to warn Nero that Agrippina was reported to be boasting of her conquest of him – and that the army would not tolerate such a situation, which they would regard as sacrilegious.

In the end, we cannot be certain why Nero decided to take the extreme step of killing his mother. The problem with accepting the story that he did it in order to marry Poppaea – apart from the inherent lack of plausible motive – is that there was a gap of about three years between the two events. Agrippina died in 59; the wedding was not until 62.[23] To be fair to Tacitus, he does not specifically attribute this reason to Nero. What he does is to juxtapose in swift succession three key scenes: first, as we have seen, he shows Poppaea protesting to Nero because she sees no hope of his divorcing Octavia while his mother lives; second, Agrippina is shown offering herself incestuously to her son; third, Nero resolves to kill her. This narrative sequence leaves the reader with the impression – no doubt intended – that scene three of the unfolding tragedy is the direct consequence of scenes one and two.

The most one can safely say of this series of events is that Poppaea's pleading may well have been a contributory factor. The charge of incest looks like a deduction made afterwards on the basis of insufficient but suggestive evidence. Paradoxically, perhaps, Tacitus may have been on slightly firmer ground when he attempted to generalize about contemporary informed opinion: 'Everyone was longing to break the mother's power, but nobody believed that the son's hatreds would harden him all the way to murder.'[24]

It was surely Nero himself who was longing to break that emasculating power – not necessarily because of hatred but perhaps because Poppaea had succeeded in convincing him of how much better and safer life could be if he freed himself from Agrippina's intense and imperious, but ultimately warped and suffocating, love. At some point the Emperor decided that the only way he could achieve this was by killing his mother.

SEVEN

WRECKAGE AND RENEWAL

The murder of Agrippina stands out as one of the great 'true stories' of antiquity. It is rich in characters and incidents, as if some master dramatist had laid out all the twists and turns in its convoluted plot. The ruthless cunning of the conspirators is more than matched by the resourcefulness and courage of the woman they are trying to kill. At the last, when the masks are off and all pretence is gone, she meets death 'after the high Roman fashion', with defiance and justified disdain, directing the assassins' swords to her womb.[1]

Nero did not act alone. He had gathered around himself a small group of trusted advisers in order to devise a plan that would make his mother's death look like an accident. Suetonius says, rather implausibly, that they made three unsuccessful attempts to poison her. It is more likely, as Tacitus indicates, that poison was ruled out from the start; even if they were to succeed in such an attempt – rather doubtful in view of Agrippina's elaborate precautions against one – popular opinion would have been bound to suspect her son, especially when the suspicious death of Britannicus at the Emperor's table had not faded from public memory. The Praetorian Guards under Burrus were known to be devoted to her, and nobody outside their ranks could apparently be found with the hardihood to attempt a direct assassination by blunt instrument or dagger.

One day, probably in late 58 or early 59, however, Nero and some of his henchmen were watching a theatrical performance at Rome on the lake used for naval games when they saw a specially constructed ship begin to come apart. Some animals fell out through the gaps, and then the ship closed up again and sailed on, leaving them struggling in the water. The conspirators, Dio tells us, immediately decided to construct a seaworthy ship along the same lines, with a view to inviting Agrippina on board as a one-way passenger. For this task, an expert was available – the former Greek slave Anicetus, who, as a freedman, had been one of Nero's early tutors. Agrippina had replaced him by Seneca, thereby arousing his enmity. Nero, liking and trusting him, had promoted his career since becoming Emperor, and Anicetus was now Admiral of the Roman Fleet, based at Misenum on the northern edge of the Bay of Naples.

Dio also asserts – controversially but probably accurately – that Seneca was among the conspirators. The fact of his participation is important because it implies a political as well as a psychological motive for Agrippina's assassination. Modern historians have tended to give Seneca the benefit of the doubt; they have found it difficult to envisage why he should have soiled his hands with an act that would be so 'out of character' and directly opposed to his philosophical stance. In the *De Clementia*, for instance, Seneca had fulsomely congratulated Nero as a ruler who, unlike his predecessors, never stooped to crime.

Seneca was notorious, however, for not practising what he preached – especially for acquiring vast wealth through his position at the Emperor's right hand, and lending it out at extortionate rates of interest. He has even been assigned a share of the blame for Boudicca's (Boadicea's) rebellion in Britain; Dio's account suggests that it was partly in pursuit of the money to pay off debts to Seneca that the Roman occupiers used ruthless methods against members of the Iceni tribe and their warlike Queen.[2] But leaving aside Seneca's reputation as a moralist and financier, the key question is: did he have a strong enough reason for political murder?

We have already seen how Seneca first marginalized Agrippina in the Emperor's *Consilium* and then took over the role of Nero's chief political mentor, which she had planned for herself. Given her bloodstained record of disposing of political opponents, Agrippina could be expected to take advantage of any diminution in his *potentia* to do the same for him. Plainly, she could not hope to restore anything approaching her original position of dominance while Seneca remained in office, and it is difficult to believe that she would not have tried, at some stage, to persuade her son to replace him with one of her own supporters, if not with herself.

Dio claims that, in 58, Seneca was accused of adultery with Agrippina.[3] Evidently the allegation was not substantiated, but even the rumour of such a sexual liaison would have imperilled his position, if Nero should suspect his mother of plotting against him with his former tutor. Four years is a long time in palace politics. It no doubt suited Seneca earlier to keep Agrippina in a subsidiary but not contemptible position after her fall from grace in 55. But his use of Acté, in 59, to intervene at some risk in the presumed 'incest' crisis, shows his concern that the Dowager Empress had learnt nothing and forgotten nothing – and had once again become a destabilizing influence.

Acté, whose survival at that point in her career depended on Nero's continued hold on power, would surely have told him it was Seneca who had prompted her to warn him. For the first time, perhaps, Nero would thus have become aware of the possibility of Seneca's willingness to compromise or even betray his former patroness. If Seneca still had any doubts about Agrippina's view of him, Nero would presumably have been happy to clear them up. It is not hard to envisage a role-reversal in which the ageing philosopher, now advised by his former pupil, came to accept that Agrippina's murder had become a necessity for both of them.

Given the nature of the assassination plot and the time it must have taken to prepare, it would have been difficult to prevent any whisper of it leaking out. There is certainly evidence that word somehow reached Agrippina herself, but she indignantly refused to believe her only child to be capable of matricide. And if Nero had tried to act without at least the acquiescence of Seneca or Burrus, perhaps both of them together, there would have been a risk that they might try to wreck his plan before realizing who was directing it. Tacitus says frankly that he does not know whether Burrus and Seneca were parties to the original plot, but it is surely significant that, when he introduces them into his narrative of the assassination attempt, at the point when the plot has misfired, it is Seneca who, after a pause for thought, suggests her immediate execution by the Praetorians – and Burrus who declines to give the necessary orders.

The recruitment of Anicetus to the conspirators' group, and the construction of the collapsible boat under his supervision, directs the focus away from the capital city and its million prying eyes to the tiny and beautiful Bay of Baiae, tucked into the northern extremity of the much larger Bay of Naples, only 2 or 3 miles from the naval base at Misenum. Nero often stayed in a seaside villa there in the spring, so it was no surprise to his mother when he told her he intended to spend the holiday festival of Minerva (19–23 March) there in 59. She, too, had a villa in the neighbourhood within easy sailing distance of her son's. What could be more natural, marking the apparent reconciliation between them, than that he should invite her to dinner?

Baiae remains a beauty spot to this day, but the encroachment of the sea over two millennia has altered the coastline, and scholars' wars have been fought over the respective locations of the two villas. The poet Shelley refers in a letter written in 1818 to the 'antique grandeur' of the Roman ruins beneath the waves in Baiae's Bay. He later immortalized this sight in the 'Ode to the West Wind', where he imagines the Mediterranean Sea itself sleepily admiring the submerged 'old palaces and towers quivering within the wave's intenser day', overgrown with flowers 'so sweet, the sense faints picturing them!'. Pliny, too, in his *Natural History*, had enthused about this part of Campania and its coast, with its vineyards and olive groves and fertile fields.[4] This haven, then, was to be the beguiling backdrop for Nero's first attempt at murder, timed for a moonless night that was intended to end with Agrippina's drowned body being washed up among the holiday-makers and vendors who, as usual, were enjoying the Emperor's localized bounty there, some sleeping out in tents around the shoreline.

On the fatal evening, Nero welcomed his mother with open arms to his dinner party and led her personally to the place of honour beside him. He talked to her animatedly throughout the evening, plying her with wine and good food, and apparently deferring to her opinions. Shortly after midnight, when she took her leave, he embraced her again, kissing her hands, her eyes, her breasts. Agrippina then climbed on board the imperial boat waiting to take her across the bay to her own villa. With her lady-in-waiting Acerronia Polla, she reclined on a bench under a roofed area while her bodyguard, Crepereius Gallus, stood nearby, beside the tiller. It would be 2 hours or more before the moon was due to rise, so the boat, manned by naval oarsmen from Misenum, set off by starlight over the calm sea.

Suddenly, when they were sufficiently far from shore, the roof, which had been weighted with lead, began to collapse. Gallus, who presumably darted forward from his place by the tiller to try to save his mistress, was crushed to death. The two women were saved by the sides of the bench, which were high enough and strong enough to take the first blow of the impact. They extricated themselves from the wreckage to find everything around them in turmoil. The vessel was still afloat, but one group of men on board were trying to sink it while other sailors, not party to the plot, were attempting to keep it afloat.

Amid all the noise and confusion, a woman's voice was heard shouting for help and claiming to be the Empress Agrippina. It was a fatal error. Some men rushed towards the woman across the darkened deck and beat her to death with staves and anything else they could lay their hands on. The victim was not Agrippina, but the killers plainly did not realize it. It is not clear whether Acerronia had acted in panic on her own initiative, pretending to be the Dowager Empress, in an attempt to save herself, or whether Agrippina had told her to use her name, perhaps suspecting what might be the outcome. Agrippina herself was wounded on the shoulder, but managed to duck out of the way in the dim light and slip unseen into the water.

In spite of her injured shoulder, and all the wine she had drunk at her son's table, she was able to swim as far as some fishing boats which were near the shore. One can imagine the fishermen's incredulity and consternation when they discovered who it was whom they had just hauled up on to their deck. They sailed with her to a beach near her villa. From there, she was carried home among a small crowd of excited people, who by now had heard of the 'shipwreck' but did not have the faintest idea about what was really going on. Agrippina did not tell them, because she had already decided that her only chance of survival would be to pretend that she had not realized that there had been a deliberate attempt on her life.

By this time, or not long afterwards, a message may have got back to Nero – from Anicetus or the sailors who had mistakenly killed Acerronia – that his mother was dead. Meanwhile, the lady herself was being dried and pampered by her retinue of maids, and the steadily growing crowd outside her villa was offering up thanks to the gods for her safe deliverance from what they supposed to have been an accident at sea. Warmly dressed once more, she summoned a trusted servant, Agerinus, and gave him very careful and precise instructions. He was to run to the Emperor's house, inform him of her lucky escape from accidental shipwreck, but emphasize that Nero was not to trouble to come to see her immediately because she needed to rest after her ordeal and would be going straight to sleep. In fact, once her messenger had gone, she called for Acerronia's will to be produced – to confirm, it is said, that she stood to inherit part of her friend's estate.

News of Agrippina's survival threw Nero into a panic. He had Burrus and Seneca roused from their beds to advise him. The fact that they were staying with him, so far from Rome and their usual duties, does not necessarily prove that they were already his fellow-conspirators, although it does seem rather strange that one or other of them had not been left behind in the capital to deal with any important business that might arise in the Emperor's extended absence. Now, in the dead of night, as Nero faced the possibility of being accused of murder and attempted matricide, the two older men facing him certainly became his accessories in the crime that was soon to follow.

Tacitus describes Nero as being 'half-dead with fright' at the prospect that his mother might arm her slaves and come for revenge, or inflame the soldiers against him. Would she be able, he asked, to go before the Senate or an Assembly of the People to arraign him for the shipwreck and the murder of her friends? Both Burrus and Seneca remained silent at first, neither of them perhaps feeling it safe to try to dissuade him from finishing her off in case he rejected their advice. On the other hand, Tacitus adds, they may equally have felt that things had gone too far – that he would have to strike again at Agrippina before she had a chance to strike back at him.[5]

Breaking the uneasy silence, Seneca asked Burrus if he ought not to order his guards to go out and kill her without further ado. The Praetorian chief retorted that his men were so devoted to the whole imperial family and especially to the memory of Germanicus that they would not agree to attack his daughter. He said it was up to Anicetus to see it through. Anicetus unhesitatingly agreed to finish the job in person. Nero exclaimed: 'Today you have given me my empire!' He told Anicetus it would be best if it were done quickly, and to take with him men who would obey orders to the letter. As for his mother's messenger, Agerinus, Nero had him admitted to his presence, dropped a sword at his feet and pretended that the man had been sent by Agrippina to assassinate him.

By the time Anicetus reached Agrippina's villa at the head of a menacing armed column, the crowd outside had swelled to huge proportions. Neighbours, fishermen, holiday-makers brandishing lighted torches were all celebrating the Dowager Empress' miraculous escape from the disaster that had claimed the lives of her two companions. The crowd parted and fell back as Anicetus and his men forced their way through to the gates, surrounded the entire building and then smashed down the front door. Once inside, they arrested anyone who got in their way. Agrippina heard them coming as she lay in her bedroom, attended by just one maid. 'Are you leaving me, too?' she called out, as the maid took to her heels.

Anicetus burst into her bedroom followed by a naval captain named Hercules and a ship's lieutenant, Obaritus. She had thought of what to say, in a final attempt to save her life by confusing them. As they had come to visit her, she said, they could report back to the Emperor that she was feeling better. When they closed in for the kill, she shouted that her son had never ordered his mother's death. For reply, Captain Hercules clubbed her on the head. It was as she sank down under the blow that she is said to have pointed to her womb and cried: 'Strike here!' Lieutenant Obaritus thrust his sword in, and she died under a hail of further blows.

For nearly 2,000 years people who have read the accounts of this terrible and savage execution have asked themselves how on earth the 21-year-old Emperor could have justified to *himself* his actions in bringing it about. There is no satisfactory answer. Even if his mother did have some residual power in the state, it was utterly dwarfed by his own. Could he not have kept her under some form of house arrest, in comfortable circumstances, while depriving her of the financial means and the opportunity of conspiring against him? But rationality is unlikely to provide the key. It is in the realm of abnormal psychology that an explanation may lie.

The eminent psychologist Anthony Storr cites a modern case history of a man with feelings both of inferiority and omnipotence. The man was intellectually gifted, academically successful and had been brave enough as a schoolboy to win all his playground fights; but although, at least as an adolescent, he felt omnipotent, he was 'paralysed by fear' as an adult at the thought of being in situations where someone else could have power over him. For example, before watching a film he had to ensure that an easy 'escape route' out of the cinema was available to him, because if scenes of violence were shown he could not help identifying himself imaginatively and distressingly with the victim on the screen. According to Dr Storr's diagnosis, the man 'did not believe himself to be lovable, only powerful'.[6]

I am not, of course, attempting to make some anachronistic claim about Nero's psychological state matching that of this anonymous twentieth-century patient, however suggestive Nero's combination of a taste for street fighting and dislike of gladiatorial death agonies may be. The importance of the modern case history for our purposes is precisely its demonstration that just because an individual appears outwardly powerful, and may even believe inwardly that he is omnipotent, he may nevertheless also feel deeply insecure and threatened, and – in a crisis – inferior and terrified. The fact that the case history is published in a study devoted solely to 'creative' people helps to reinforce this message.

The probability, from the discussion of Nero's actions in the ancient sources, is that the Emperor could not simply shrug off his mother's disapproval of his way of life, his love affairs and his ambitions as a performer in the creative fields of music, poetry and drama. The mere existence of that disapproval – whether or not she possessed the physical means to enforce her will – was enough to inhibit his actions.[7] In some important sense, no doubt inexplicable to outsiders, Agrippina had retained much of her old ability to make Nero feel inadequate: nothing that he did, short of abject surrender, could ever satisfy her. The resentment that must have built up inside him, coupled with the belief that she was holding him back from his destiny as the choice and master spirit of his age, crystallized finally in his resolution to eliminate her from his world.

As we shall see, Agrippina's death was in fact followed, after an uneasy interval, by a surge of creative activity which, communicated with manic energy to his subjects, stamped a new authority on his reign. It seems incredible to suppose that Nero killed his mother partly out of frustrated creative instinct – that she had to die, not simply be sidelined, in order that he could live as artist-emperor. Yet that is what the facts of his career before and after the event seem to suggest. Under the shadow of his mother he had incubated artistic longings but had lacked the essential capacity of the artist to dare to put these longings to the test of reality. When the shadow finally lifted – and it was to linger on for some months after her death as he struggled to come to terms with what he had done – it would appear that Nero had taken control of his life, that he set his own agenda for each day instead of having it set for him by one or other of his advisers.

It is a striking transformation, but before considering it in more detail it is necessary to take account of the immediate reaction to Agrippina's murder. There is a story that Nero went straight to the scene of the crime, stripped his mother's corpse and, after gazing at it for some time, remarked: 'I didn't know she was so beautiful!' Even Tacitus acknowledges the doubtful truth of this macabre scene of incestuous necrophilia while nevertheless reporting it for posterity's titillation. She was cremated that same night, stretched out on her couch, in a hasty ceremony during which one of her freedmen, Mnester, stabbed himself to death.[8]

If Nero had feared the reaction of the Praetorian Guard his worries were quickly set at rest. Burrus, no doubt anxious to reinstate himself in his master's confidence, led in a succession of officers who congratulated the Emperor on having survived the 'attempted assassination' by Agrippina's messenger, and reassured him with hearty hand-clasps of their loyalty and devotion. Deputations arrived from neighbouring towns and villages expressing similar messages of support. But the young man himself was gloomy and could not sleep properly. Observers reported that he started up at sudden noises, at times even leaping out of his bed in terror during nightmares. Suetonius says that Nero confessed to dreaming he was being chased by the Furies with whips and burning brands. Wailing sounds allegedly arose from Agrippina's grave on the headland above her villa, and the Emperor engaged Persian magicians to lay her ghost.[9] Back in Rome a baby was abandoned in the Forum, with a message attached: 'I won't bring you up in case you kill your mother!'[10]

Seneca composed a letter to the Senate for Nero to sign. It explained that Agrippina had killed herself as the price of her treason in sending Agerinus to assassinate the Emperor. The letter listed as many crimes as could plausibly be pinned on her, including her desire to be co-ruler of the Empire and her murderous activities dating back well into the reign of Claudius. In a none-too-subtle appeal to the mercenary self-interest of the citizens, it pointed out that she had opposed the gifts of money that Nero had paid out to both civilians and soldiers. After the letter had been read to the Senate in Nero's continued absence,

Publius Clodius Thrasea Paetus, the leading Stoic, walked out ostentatiously without a word.[11] The rest stayed on and voted to erect twin gold statues of Nero and Minerva in the Senate House in thanksgiving for the Emperor's safety.

Nero spent some months in Campania, chiefly in the Greek-founded city of Naples, apparently still worried about the possibility of a hostile reception in the capital. Presumably he sent for Poppaea to keep him company and boost his confidence.[12] When at last he returned to Rome, having sent a team of agents in advance to prepare a welcome, he was cheered by enormous crowds, all decked out in their best clothes and headed by the senators. The much-despised mob wanted his peaceful reign to continue, even if most of the senators may have been there only because they were afraid to be numbered as his opponents. Nero ascended to the Capitol and gave thanks in the Temple of Jupiter. By that time Agrippina's statues had been removed from all public places, her birthday declared a day of ill omen and various of her enemies allowed back from exile. These included Junia Calvina, whose brother had committed suicide on the day Agrippina married Claudius. It was too late for Junia Silana, who was already dead; but even the ashes of her earlier rival, Lollia Paulina, Caligula's Empress, finally found a resting place in Rome.

Now that he had been welcomed back to his capital, Nero 'gave himself up to all the lustful passions (*libidines*) which some measure of respect for his mother had delayed, if not quite repressed. He had long yearned to race in a four-horse chariot; no less vile was his desire to sing to the cithara in the manner of a stage professional . . . Now he couldn't be stopped.'[13] Tacitus' view, expressed so strongly here, that it was utterly reprehensible for a young ruler to want to take part in a chariot race or sing in a concert in a park, shows the importance of what was at stake in this struggle between traditionalists and the Hellenizing reformers – a battle in which Agrippina had just forfeited her life.

If culture consists of all the beliefs and practices that differentiate any given society from another, and constitutes moreover a dynamic process rather than a fixed sum of attributes,[14] then Agrippina and her son can be seen as inveterate opponents – cultural adversaries warring to the death for the soul of the Roman people. Like the Greeks in their former city states, the Romans resisted attempts to differentiate between morals and politics. They would have considered it strange for a citizen to take a different attitude to 'right and wrong' according to whether he was acting in public or in private; and their 'culture' depended crucially on example being set at the top. In the days of the Republic that example was generally set by the senior magistrates, and from the time of Augustus by the *Princeps*.

From one perspective, Agrippina symbolized in her person the self-seeking, power-hungry rottenness of the system founded by Augustus to replace the old Republic, and as such she drew down upon her head Tacitus' searing contempt. But at the same time he clearly acknowledged and approved of her traditional views on how an emperor should comport himself in public. Rome's great leaders had not won all those famous victories of the past by prancing around on a public stage but by directing their armies in battle; and they might not hold on to the Empire, some prominent citizens feared, if a maverick like Nero forfeited the imperial *dignitas* by performing in a manner considered appropriate only to a slave.[15]

It was not, therefore, a question merely of Tacitus' personal distaste for Nero's Hellenizing initiatives, especially the Greek-style artistic and sporting competitions in which even senators and their wives would soon be required to participate. It was a factor affecting the prospect of long-term national survival. It threatened not only the particular time in which the 'bad example' occurred but future eras as well, because the transmission of 'good example' from one generation to the next was regarded as an essential part of the process, almost as if it were a sort of genetic inheritance.

In the early autumn of 59, when Nero returned from Campania, free now from his mother's restraining influence, he found himself quite suddenly at new heights of power and influence, with nobody daring to oppose him directly. It was the Faustian reward for his demonstration of ruthlessness. A young man who could murder his mother and yet keep the favour of the mob was a new and dangerous phenomenon in Roman history. In his capital city the aristocracy kept their heads down – for the moment. On the frontiers, which Nero never visited and where news from Rome arrived slowly and in a generally expurgated form, those many millions of his subjects who had never seen him must have wondered what manner of man or god it was who had been set over them.

The more Hellenized among them would, no doubt, have reflected that even Zeus had become almighty only through murdering his father.[16] But in Britain, Boudicca would use the reports of the Emperor's stage performances to encourage her rebel army to regard the Romans as effete.[17] She was probably not the only enemy to assume that the great empire was going soft at the core, once Nero began to reorganize Roman high society to dance (literally) to his own tunes and play the games he chose for them. From now on, any young man who wanted to make his mark in the world might usefully aspire to win athletics or poetry prizes rather than slog with the legions as a junior officer. Tacitus bemoans the 'degradation' of ancient family names, whose bearers were strutting daily on the stage or competing with all comers on the running track.[18] For him it represented cultural pollution; for the youth of Rome it marked a break-out towards cultural diversity.

Tacitus says that Burrus and Seneca initially co-operated with Nero's plans for chariot-racing in the hope that this might prove to be enough to satisfy him. In any case, it was an activity that at least required some display of manly virtues, even though it was considered below the dignity of the Emperor to perform in a public arena. Their solution was to adapt and improve a private race track originally laid out by Caligula in the flat bottom of the Vatican valley, roughly where St Peter's stands today. As it was well away from the city centre, on the far side of the Tiber beyond the Field of Mars,[19] they presumably thought that Nero could safely amuse himself there to his heart's content, driving his chariot-and-four against non-professional opposition, with only his usual entourage of courtiers for an audience. But, of course, once word got around the city, ordinary Romans flocked to witness this unprecedented spectacle and stayed to cheer.

Stimulated by this evidence of his popularity, Nero instituted the *Juvenalia* ('Youth Games') to mark the first shaving of his red beard. This shave was an occasion of great symbolic significance in a Roman male's life, and of infinitely greater importance in the case of an emperor who was, unprecedentedly, young enough to qualify. After the painful iron razor had done its work (the Romans had not yet discovered soap), his straggly hairs were gathered up and placed in a golden box studded with pearls to be dedicated in the Temple of Jupiter. Admission to the games, which accompanied the dedication ceremony, was by invitation only. Even Nero evidently felt the time was not yet ripe for him to appear on a public stage instead of his own private one, if only because he could not be sure of a suitably enthusiastic reception from the uninitiated mob for his voice, his poetry and his skill at playing the cithara.

The description 'youth' attached to these games did not necessarily have to apply to the competitors. Tacitus agonizes over the fact that neither age nor rank prevented people from participating, as he contemplates what he considers to be instances of members of the male nobility performing on stage in an effeminate way, while respectable matrons learn improper roles. He does not specify precisely what his criticism is supposed to mean in practice, any more than he does when he refers to 'provocations to debauchery' (*irritamenta luxui*) being on sale there. His tirade becomes even more bizarre when he alleges that money was handed out – presumably as an incentive to participants in the games – and 'good people were forced to spend it', while those lacking self-restraint gloried in frittering it away. 'It's hard enough to remain pure even in decent circumstances,' Tacitus protests. 'How much less could chastity or modesty or any grain of integrity be preserved among this contest of the vices? Finally Nero himself walked on to the stage, taking great pains to test his cithara by twanging some practice notes for his trainers.'[20] It sounds as if the Emperor was a little nervous about this first performance, with his music teachers supporting him in the wings as he began to sing in his husky and tuneful, but perhaps not very powerful voice.[21] The songs, both words and music, are believed to have been of his own composition, on fashionable tragic subjects. The applause was sensational. Even grizzled old Burrus joined in the clapping, though he was said to be grieving inwardly.

But if the climax of all this supposed immorality was the young man's stage debut – not even in public but in front of a carefully invited audience composed largely of the social elite and their retainers – it raises serious doubts about the validity of Tacitus' moralizing testimony on this and related subjects, except on his own puritanical terms. What he describes as 'debauchery', on this reading, may well have been no more than non-traditional amusements, and exercises in short tunics rather than dignified togas. It is true that in Greek-style games the male participants traditionally ran their races naked, but Nero was not built physically for the running track, and there is no unequivocal evidence that he ever stripped completely in public, except perhaps in the public baths where everyone else did likewise.

As for people being forced to spend money that has just been given to them, it is scarcely surprising if Nero should have gained in popularity because of this. One of his methods was to throw wooden balls to the crowds watching his shows; whoever was lucky enough to catch one would read on it the description of a gift awaiting collection at the palace.[22] These presents were often very valuable, ranging from food and jewellery to horses and houses and slaves. He also formed a select group of Roman knights to act as his paid cheer-leaders. They were the forerunners of the 5,000-strong company of the *Augustiani*, young men who followed him around from concert to concert later in his career to organize rhythmical applause and call out praises of the Emperor's voice and musical ability.[23]

Meanwhile, the poets Lucan (Seneca's nephew) and Calpurnius Siculus, were beginning to emerge as the stars of Nero's salon, whose work, along with his own, he hoped would mark the literary renaissance he dreamed of. 'The Age of Gold is born anew,' Calpurnius gushes, in the first of a series of eclogues based on the celebrated examples of Virgil. The young Emperor's clemency has 'thwarted the crazy swords' (*insanos enses*) and he has ordered the trumpets to sound for holy things, not for war. Calpurnius, of course, is an ambitious young man. His poems may be derivative and often sycophantic, but the sentiment is fair enough – allowing for appropriate poetic licence – as a reflection of its hero's intentions, if not quite his actual achievements.[24]

For most of his subjects, Nero deserved such tributes. He had promised a reign of peace and justice, and by and large he had delivered on his promise. The early years of his reign were evidently a period of general prosperity, or we would surely have heard to the contrary. Within the Empire, free-born people were generally able to travel between provinces without undue hindrance or serious danger of armed attack – a situation that would have been rare indeed outside its carefully patrolled frontiers. In such a context, the murder of his mother may have seemed a forgivable aberration. Nero's capacity to rule, however, was about to be tested by a violent crisis in an unexpected quarter.

EIGHT

THE GREAT BATTLE OF BRITAIN

The news from Britain was as bad as could be imagined, and rapidly got worse. First, two supposedly co-operative and disarmed tribes in the 'peaceful' eastern area of the country (now East Anglia) rose in revolt. They destroyed the Roman capital of Camulodunum (Colchester), burning it to the ground and killing everyone inside, including the entire colony of retired legionary veterans and their families. Nero and his advisers would have been shocked but not, at first, dismayed. While they and the rest of Rome grieved at the slaughter, they knew that the four legions stationed in various parts of the province should be more than adequate to deal with an isolated regional conflict. The Governor of Britain, Suetonius Paulinus, had between 40,000 and 50,000 troops (including non-Roman auxiliaries) at his disposal, and he was an experienced and skilful general.[1]

But hot on the heels of news of Camulodunum's fall came a message from Nero's agent in Britain, Catus Decianus, that he had been forced to flee the island. One of the four legions had been routed, and a huge rebel army under the warrior Queen Boudicca was heading for London, where Catus had his tax-gathering office, and there were not enough soldiers available to protect the town. Nero would scarcely have had time to digest this apparent confession of cowardice in the face of the enemy – tempered by the reassurance that the collected taxes were now safe in Gaul – when confirmation came that London had indeed gone the way of Camulodunum. And the smoke was still rising from London's corpse-strewn ruins when the neighbouring town of Verulamium (St Albans) suffered an identical fate.[2]

Boudicca's revolt was threatening to build up into the most

serious frontier crisis of Nero's Principate. We can imagine him, along with Seneca and Burrus and his other advisers, receiving these reports via the post-horse service from northern Gaul with a mixture of outrage, bafflement and sinking hearts. What had become of Suetonius Paulinus and the other three legions? Was he allowing them to be picked off piecemeal? Or was he already dead, along with other senior officers? The imperial agent Catus would have reported to Rome that Governor Paulinus had turned up at London's gates before the British assault, only to strip the town of its garrison and march away, leaving the remaining inhabitants defenceless. The hope of the Emperor's *Consilium* must have been that Paulinus was gathering together a force big enough to defeat the rebels in the field. But Boudicca had cut him off from the Channel ports and therefore his quickest line of communication with Rome.[3]

The most pressing question before the *Consilium* was whether they should send immediate reinforcements to Britain from the German frontier. But that raised the logistical nightmare of how to transport them there, if Boudicca already controlled the southeast, and thus the short sea routes to and from Gaul. Underlying all of these problems – on everybody's mind if not yet on their lips – would have been the wider consideration of the viability of Britain itself as the newest province of the Empire. Even if they ultimately managed to defeat Boudicca's warriors, was the province worth keeping at such cost in terms of scarce resources and Roman blood? As an earlier British rebel, Caratacus, had said when taken to Rome in chains under Claudius and shown the great marble buildings around the Forum: 'What on earth do you want with our mud huts?'[4]

Nero's biographer Suetonius, writing more than half a century later, confirms for us – but without specifying the date – that the young Emperor did in all seriousness consider total withdrawal from Britain.[5] The country was too primitive to generate enough wealth to pay for the upkeep of the troops who held it down. There was tin, lead and even a little silver to be mined, and ores of iron and copper among the deeply forested heartlands; but the island's chief resource was its human inhabitants. Even the

Romans would have acknowledged that there were limits to the number who could be sold into slavery without alienating all the rest.

Nevertheless, Roman money had been invested quite heavily since the conquest of 43. Claudius himself had made substantial loans to various local chieftains, who may have supposed them to have been outright gifts. Seneca had outstanding British interests amounting to some 40 million sesterces, according to Dio; and the case for imposing some part of the blame for the uprising on the old philosopher rests on the supposition that he suddenly called in his vast loans at an especially sensitive time.[6]

Boudicca's husband, King Prasutagus of the Iceni, had recently died, leaving half his fortune to Nero and the other half to his two daughters. Seneca, at the centre of Roman government – perhaps even specifically responsible for British affairs, in which he had such a strong financial interest – was in a position to know that the Empire intended to absorb the whole of the tribal kingdom of the Iceni, effectively disinheriting the two girls and their mother. He would therefore have had a powerful incentive to try to get back the money he had loaned before the imperial agent Catus went to work with his team of officials, mostly freedmen and slaves, to seize any portable valuables the Iceni possessed.

The move against the Iceni in the name of the Emperor was only too typical of the way the Romans added to their territory and pushed forward their frontiers. King Prasutagus had made a treaty with Claudius under which he would continue to rule his extensive tribal lands as an honoured friend of the Roman people. But the treaty was to lapse on his death, and it was in the hope of protecting his tribe's autonomy and his family's status that he had named the Emperor himself as co-heir in his will. He had reason to put some confidence in his Queen's capacity to deal with the Romans: she was tall, with flashing eyes, a ferocious expression and waist-length tawny hair. She is also described as wearing a sort of tartan plaid, fixed with a golden brooch, as she stood upright in her war chariot before battle, commanding her troops with a raised spear.

Dating is impossible to establish with precision; Prasutagus probably died in 59 and the likely year of Boudicca's revolt is 60, but possibly 61. There does appear to have been a significant interval between the king's death and the arrival of Catus and his bailiffs, with their military escort. It is arguable, therefore, that this time-gap was to allow Seneca's representatives to collect the money owed to him while the Iceni still possessed any. Whatever the truth of that particular matter, Queen Boudicca resisted the depredations of Catus. As all the world knows, she was flogged for this impertinence to a Roman official, and both her daughters were violated.

If this account of imperial sharp practice – not to mention robbery with violence and rape – fails to square with popular belief about the rectitude of ancient Romans in their mission to civilize barbarians, that is because generations of classicists have taken it for granted that incorporation within the Empire was really in the barbarians' best interests. Few, until recently, would have quarrelled seriously with the Augustan poet Virgil's time-honoured justification: 'Remember, Roman, your virtuous art shall be to rule with power the peoples, to impose the lawful ways of peace, to spare those who submit and to crush the proud (who don't).'[7] In seeking to degrade the Iceni, whose weapons they had confiscated on the grounds that Roman soldiers were there to protect them from their tribal enemies, the imperial administrators were following a well-trodden path.

Tacitus, who respects the fighting spirit of the Celts while despising the ignoble and cowardly Catus and his minions, does not try to disguise what was being done in Rome's name. 'The kingdom was plundered by centurions, and the royal household by slaves, as if they were prizes of war . . . The leading men among the Iceni were deprived of their ancestral estates, and the king's close relatives were reduced to slavery.'[8] Indeed, failure to pay taxes and debts could result, under the law, in enslavement, either of the debtor or his children. No wonder the Iceni fought back, recruiting other tribes, most notably their southern neighbours the Trinobantes,[9] many of whom had already been evicted from their land to make way for Roman settlers in Camulodunum – once the capital of the great King Cunobelinus (Shakespeare's Cymbeline), father of Caratacus.

There is no evidence that Nero knew (or cared) anything about the administration of Britain until Boudicca's revolt woke him up to his responsibilities. His later decisions over imperial appointments in the province, however, suggest that if he had known more of the details, he might have intervened earlier. For the present, any reform would have to wait upon recovery. No emperor could tolerate the blow to his and Rome's prestige of an apparent defeat at the hands of painted 'savages' led by a woman. Rome's many enemies on other frontiers would seek to take advantage of any perceived weakness. The priority for the *Consilium* was inevitably to try to crush the revolt, before considering any other option.

If Nero had possessed even the smallest spark of military spirit he would surely have called for his armour and saddled a horse. The news that he was riding north with a Praetorian escort would have sent a thrill of martial energy through the soldiers on the frontier. He could have sent messengers ahead to detach at least two of the legions watching the Rhine, with orders to join him at the Channel, where a new fleet of transports could have been prepared. The beleaguered troops in Britain would have taken fresh heart from the knowledge that a relieving force under their emperor was on its way, while the Britons who had not yet joined Boudicca's growing army would have been justly fearful of reprisals if they did.

But beyond probably putting some of the Rhine troops on standby, Nero did none of these things. Instead, he decided to leave the situation, for the moment, in the hands of Suetonius Paulinus. And it is undeniably the case that leaving things to the man on the spot had had a long and generally successful history in the centuries during which Rome accumulated her empire. If Julius Caesar had waited for orders from the Senate he would certainly not have conquered Gaul, and therefore never have set foot in Britain, as he did during his two brief expeditions of 55 and 54 BC. But Suetonius Paulinus, Nero's man-on-the-spot, was no Julius Caesar. He had made the elementary mistake of

leaving south-east Britain virtually undefended while he went off
to harry the Welsh. But Paulinus' ability as a battlefield tactician
proved to be outstanding, and he inspired his men to fight like
tigers when they were finally at bay.

Paulinus received the news of Boudicca's revolt while he was
mopping up the last of the resistance on the Isle of Anglesey, in
the north-west corner of Wales. He had launched a daring
waterborne assault by infantry in flat-bottomed boats and by
cavalry swimming across the Menai Strait beside their horses.
Tacitus, whose father-in-law Agricola (a later Governor of Britain)
was a member of Paulinus' staff, has left us an unforgettable
description of the Druids and black-robed, long-haired women
among the Welsh warriors on the shore, waving their arms and
shrieking curses at the invaders.[10] There would have been few
survivors among those defenders of the last Druidic stronghold.
Too many captured Roman soldiers had been sacrificed in their
sacred grove, which Paulinus now destroyed. He would have been
unable to take prisoners now that his presence was so urgently
required on the far side of the country.

The grave news from East Anglia would almost certainly have
been brought to him by a messenger from Cerialis Caesius
Rufus, commander of the 9th Legion, whose headquarters were
at or near Lincoln but who had a fortified outpost near
Peterborough on the north-western edge of Iceni territory.
Paulinus had directly under his immediate command the entire
14th Legion and a large part of the 20th. He sent orders to the
2nd Legion, based in south-west Britain (probably at Exeter or
Gloucester), to join him at London. Then he set out for London
at the head of his cavalry, leaving the infantry to march after him
as fast as they could. He plainly intended to link up with Cerialis'
9th Legion *en route*.

It was a good plan but it went hopelessly wrong. The 9th
Legion – either the whole of it, or the section based near
Peterborough – took the field prematurely and were
overwhelmed on the march to Camulodunum by vastly superior
numbers. Cerialis managed to escape with some of his cavalry,
but the infantry died where they stood. As for the 2nd Legion

in the south-west, they were temporarily without a legate to command them, and the camp prefect Poenius Postumus, who had been left in charge, refused to take the risk of leaving his fortified position. Consequently, when Paulinus and his cavalry eventually arrived at London, he found only a handful of soldiers in the garrison there instead of two full legions with their auxiliaries.

If the 2nd Legion had obeyed orders and the 9th had not sacrificed itself in vain, Paulinus would no doubt have defended London while waiting for his infantry of the 14th and 20th to arrive. They were having to foot-slog roughly 250 miles from Anglesey, probably via their forts near the Welsh border at Chester and Wroxeter, where they would have been able to leave behind their wounded and pick up supplies. They were several days' march behind Paulinus when he took the ruthless but undoubtedly correct decision to abandon London to its fate while he retreated back along the way he had come, accompanied by a swarm of refugees. Boudicca should have moved to cut off his retreat, but her warriors could not resist sacking the defenceless city first – and impaling those taken prisoner. By the time they caught up with Paulinus, having also stopped to destroy Verulamium, he had not only rejoined the main body of his troops but had carefully selected a place to make his stand.

The decisive battle was fought somewhere in central England. It has no name because nobody knows where it took place.[11] We cannot even be sure of the year, whether 60 or 61. Yet of all the armed encounters on British soil it was arguably second in importance only to the Battle of Hastings a millennium later. As many as 10,000 Roman and auxiliary soldiers, packed into the mouth of a rocky and wooded defile, faced a British horde said to have numbered 230,000. If Paulinus had tried to fight in the open, his men would have been surrounded and forced to defend all sides simultaneously. Here they could form a line of battle in some depth without the immediate fear of overwhelming attack from flanks or rear. Boudicca's warriors were so sure of the outcome that they drew up their waggons to form a barrier behind them, from which their women followers could watch the slaughter in comfort and hinder any attempt at escape by the Roman cavalry.

For the Roman infantry there could be no possibility of escape except through outright victory, because their position in the defile would become a death-trap if their line was broken. Each foot-soldier was armed with two javelins and a short sword, designed for close-combat stabbing. They wore light, flexible body armour and helmets, and carried big wooden shields with a metal boss in the centre.[12] By standing in close order, with each man's shield almost touching those of his comrades on either side, the men in the front line presented a difficult target and a formidable threat. By contrast, the Britons generally fought bare-chested, covered with painted patterns intended to provide some assurance of supernatural protection. They, too, carried spears, but their aim needed to be much more accurate if they were to get past the tall rows of curved shields and protective armour. Their swords were longer than those of the Romans, but were made for slashing rather than stabbing.

Paulinus instructed his troops to stand firm and await the attack. When it came they threw their javelins at close range straight into unprotected British chests. Then they moved forward over the fallen bodies, still in close order, in a disciplined formation, which they had practised many times on the barrack square and which enabled those in the front line to be methodically relieved and replaced by the fresh soldiers behind them. They used their shield bosses to smash at the faces of the warriors immediately in front of them – who could not dodge away because of the enormous press of other warriors behind them – and thrust their short swords into their bellies. The British had little or no room to swing their swords and were slaughtered like cattle. At last they broke and ran, but the line of their own waggons and livestock impeded their escape.

'The soldiers gave no quarter – not even to the women – while the speared pack-horses added to the mounds of bodies. It was a glorious victory . . .'[13] Tacitus adds that, according to one report he had read, no fewer than 80,000 rebels were killed for the loss of 400 Roman dead and only a slightly larger number of Roman wounded. Even allowing for the exaggeration typical of ancient chroniclers of battles, it had clearly been an astonishing victory against apparently impossible odds. Boudicca took poison; Poenius Postumus, of the absent 2nd Legion, fell on his sword. Catus simply disappears from the pages of history.

Back in Rome, rejoicing was tempered by reflections on how near Paulinus had come to disaster. An estimated total of 70,000 Romans and 'loyal' Britons and their families had died in the various massacres. If the general had taken adequate precautions before going off to fight in Wales, and maintained better liaison with his subordinate commanders, the revolt could have been confined to a smaller area and many fewer people. The city of Camulodunum did not even have adequate barricades, behind which the veterans of the colony might have held off the rebels for long enough to stand some chance of relief.

The heroic last battle could not have been won against even moderately competent generalship. Boudicca had enormous advantages in numbers, mobility and supply. She needed only to hold back a substantial reserve, preferably out of sight, while she winkled the Romans out of their defensive position by probing attacks down the wooded sides of the defile, where parade-ground tactics would have been impossible. The chaotic frontal assault by her entire force was aimed precisely where the Romans were strongest. When it failed she had nothing in reserve. Back in Rome, there was no shortage of armchair strategists to explain to Nero how lucky Paulinus had been.

The Emperor owed a huge debt to the fighting qualities of his troops – those gallant few in this first great Battle of Britain. If Paulinus had lost, it is hard to see how Rome could or would have held on to its new province. All the tribes would have thrown off their allegiance, if only to avoid local reprisals, leaving Nero with the choice either of mounting a new, full-scale invasion against a determined and triumphant enemy, or, more likely, seeking a diplomatic withdrawal of the remaining troops pinned down in their forts. 'Roman Britain' would have been a 17-year phenomenon instead of a 360-year civilization, and the young Emperor's reputation – given his incapacity for military command – would have been trampled in the dust.

So Paulinus was not awarded the honours that a successful general might have expected. Instead, Nero moved cautiously to cut short his tour of duty. First, he appointed a Romanized provincial, whom he obviously trusted to share his views, to replace Catus as his procurator in Britain. Gaius Julius Alpinus Classicianus came from Trier, of a newly distinguished equestrian family, which only a few generations earlier had been tribal warriors not greatly dissimilar to those of the Iceni and Trinobantes. Classicianus reported back promptly that there would be no secure peace in Britain while Paulinus remained governor.

Paulinus, in fact, was having his revenge on the British. He organized his soldiers into wrecking bands to roam the countryside wherever rebellion had raised its head. They burnt crops and homesteads, driving the peasants off the land at a time when sowing and harvesting had already been neglected in favour of war. The result was famine, and an untold number of new deaths, which inevitably must have been concentrated among the most vulnerable – the very young and the old and sick. Tacitus, an admirer of Paulinus, says that the unfavourable report by the new procurator, Classicianus, was motivated by personal animosity, and that he was acting against Roman interests by advising Britons to wait for the appointment of a new governor before surrendering and giving up their arms.

Nero, uneasy about arousing the wrath of the army and the Senate if he simply dismissed Paulinus out of hand, temporized by sending a senior palace administrator, Polyclitus, a freedman, to assess the situation independently. His official report from Britain glossed over some of the problems; that was perhaps understandable from the pen of a civil servant who found himself in a socially inferior position even to rank-and-file soldiers.[14] Presumably his verbal report to the Emperor was more frank, because after a brief interval Paulinus was replaced as governor, on the apparent pretext of having lost some ships and men.

His successor, Publius Petronius Turpilianus – well known to Nero because of his recent consulship – was a conciliator who worked with Classicianus to try to heal the wounds that Boudicca's revolt and its suppression had opened. Two years later, needing Turpilianus back in Rome, Nero replaced him with an equally conciliatory governor in Trebellius Maximus. Classicianus, who continued in office until his death – his tombstone is in the British Museum – has justly been hailed in modern times as a champion of the British people. The significance of the appointments of these three men is that they demonstrate the change of British policy that Nero initiated and which continued for the rest of his reign. It was not until after his death that Rome resumed its aggressive expansionary programme in Britain.[15]

Foreign affairs, however serious, did not distract the young Emperor for long from his self-appointed task of encouraging Romans to share his own – and his mistress Poppaea's – love of Hellenistic ways. The games of 59, which had celebrated the shaving of his first beard, were followed in 60 by an even more elaborate and prestigious festival, presided over by former consuls, whose names were drawn by lot as if they were being appointed to some important command in a senatorial province. Music and poetry were high on the agenda, along with athletics and chariot-racing.

This time, Nero did not take part personally in the contests, but the judges thoughtfully awarded him some of the best prizes anyway. The proceedings, over a number of days, were so successful that it was decided to hold them at five-year intervals – a deliberately marginal difference from the traditional Greek adoption of four-year intervals for their Olympics – under the name of the Neronian Games. Even Tacitus has to admit that they were popular with the majority of Romans, and that they passed off without notable debauchery.

Nero followed up this success by laying the foundations of an enormous public bath house and an associated gymnasium; they were completed at his own expense over the next two years. The poet Martial, in a splendidly back-handed compliment, wrote later: 'Who was worse than Nero? Whose baths were better than Nero's!'[16] Not only was admission free to both buildings but the

Emperor also provided complimentary body oil to encourage potential gymnasts among senators and knights to work out before taking the plunge. Unfortunately, the gymnasium – the first of its kind to be built in Rome – was struck by lightning in 63 and burnt to the ground, in such intense heat that a bronze statue of the Emperor melted out of shape. He reconstructed the building as soon as possible, perhaps not simply to demonstrate his continuing enthusiasm for gymnastics but also to counter what must otherwise have seemed a bad omen about his future.

The situation had not been helped by the appearance in the night sky a year or so earlier of a comet, popularly supposed to herald a change of emperor. It may have come at a time that coincided, for Nero, with a bout of serious illness, because it caused so much speculation about the identity of his possible successor that he felt obliged to advise Rubellius Plautus (descended from the Julian clan on his mother's side) to leave Rome quietly so that he would no longer be the innocent focus of seditious gossip.[17] Young Plautus departed for his large estates in the province of Asia, taking his wife and much of his entourage with him. He would never see Rome again.

Nero's baths became a hugely popular recreational centre, even in a city that prided itself on the number and quality of its many bath houses. They were used by both men and women, slaves as well as free citizens. Most Romans lived in cramped apartments in rickety blocks without running water; for many of them, Nero's public generosity improved their daily lives and greatly expanded their social circle. Moralists among the elite – who, of course, enjoyed more exclusive bathing facilities – tended to criticize the public baths as immoral places, where pleasure was preferred to virtue.[18] Warm water, in particular, was believed to have a softening effect on moral fibre. It certainly does appear to be true that communal nudity was favoured, even for mixed bathing, which may lend some credence to the moralists' strictures – or speak volumes for Roman self-control.

The Emperor himself was devoted to the pursuit of physical fitness. He found it only too easy to put on weight, thanks no doubt to over-indulgence at the banqueting table. He used to diet severely at intervals, partly to keep fit for his favourite sport of chariot-racing and, more interestingly, to improve his musical performances. Suetonius describes how he used to lie on his back with lead weights on his chest to strengthen his breathing capacity; at the same time he abstained, curiously, from eating apples, which were believed to be harmful to the voice.

When playing the cithara before judges, Nero stuck scrupulously to the arcane rules for competitors, which included a veto on using a cloth to wipe the sweat from one's brow during a performance, deploying his bare arm instead – a tricky manoeuvre if he was holding the heavy instrument in one hand while picking out the notes with the other. This all creates a convincing picture of the effort, enthusiasm and high seriousness which, among all his other responsibilities, he continued to expend on his chosen art. The Emperor's evident embarrassment when he dropped a prop during a stage performance and thought he was going to lose points, is further testimony to his quest for artistic professionalism.[19]

In his daily encounters with his subjects, Nero took pains to be pleasant and affable. According to Suetonius, he rarely forgot a face and made a point of addressing people of all classes by name. He increased his popularity by putting on a wide variety of public entertainments in addition to his Greek-style games, including a gladiatorial show in a specially built wooden amphitheatre. These were gladiatorial fights with a difference. None of the losers were to be killed, not even criminals, and the combatants included many senators and knights, some of whom fought wild beasts – presumably with the odds well stacked in the humans' favour. Nero's reputation for singular behaviour was enhanced by his ultra-realistic production of an old comedy (now lost) by Afranius, called the *Incendium*, in which a house burns down. The actors, who were required by the exigencies of the plot to rescue the furniture from the actual blaze, were allowed to keep it all afterwards.[20]

When in Rome Nero reputedly never missed watching the professional chariot-racing at the Circus Maximus,[21] where he supported the 'Greens', one of the four major racing groups on which the public laid bets and in whose support they occasionally rioted. Like many of his subjects, Nero had been obsessed with the sport from an early age, when he had played with toy chariots. As a schoolboy, reprimanded by one of his tutors for chattering with fellow pupils about the races, he pretended, plausibly enough, to have been discussing the exploits of Hector, as described by Homer in the *Iliad*.[22] As Emperor, he raced at least once with a team of four camels instead of horses.

But although revelling in his freedom from maternal restraint, Nero was far from shedding all his inhibitions. In particular, he did not feel confident enough to divorce Octavia, who retained a devoted following among the masses, as well as the sympathy of the aristocracy. His mistress Poppaea continued to press him to name a date for their wedding, but she herself was deeply unpopular with the people, for reasons that remain obscure. It may be that she was seen as an adventuress, intent on stealing the legitimate Empress' husband. Burrus put his finger on Nero's weakest spot when he was asked for his advice on whether divorcing Octavia would be acceptable. 'Give her back her dowry,' he replied bluntly. Her 'dowry', of course, was the Roman Empire.[23]

It is, perhaps, significant that Poppaea did not get her way until both Burrus and Seneca ceased to be the Emperor's chief advisers. Burrus died quite suddenly, still in office, after developing a tumour in his throat. Tacitus repeats a highly implausible claim that Nero murdered the old man by having his throat painted with poison in pretence of soothing the pain, but acknowledges that he does not know if that was true. Burrus was about seventy; even if he had recovered, he would surely have had to be replaced as Praetorian Prefect sooner rather than later. His was arguably the most important and politically sensitive executive job in the whole of the Empire, next to that of the Emperor himself, and physical fitness was essential.

The death of Burrus is commonly seen as heralding a major turning point. Within a short while Seneca offered his resignation, which was accepted, albeit with a show of reluctance.[24] The abrupt departure of the two men who had guided Nero – and, through him, Rome and its vast empire – for more than seven years, did not so much alter specific policies of the regime as its tone. Seneca and Burrus had always tried to respect established rights and liberties, so far as practicable, to achieve their ends, believing it to be especially important to carry the Senate with them if at all possible. The man who was effectively to replace both of them in Nero's counsels, Gaius Ofonius Tigellinus, the ne'er-do-well son of a poor Sicilian family, was despised by the senatorial elite, whom he was to repay by building up an apparatus of state terror aimed at forcing their submission. For him, the law was something to be manipulated by those in power. Among his early victims was the Empress Octavia.

NINE

MURDERER MOST FOUL

The rise of Tigellinus from humble beginnings to commanding heights sheds much light on Neronian society and on the character of the Emperor himself. But it is important to be clear about the nature of their relationship. It has proved only too easy to caricature Tigellinus as a serviceable villain, game for any sort of depravity, and delighting to whisper evil counsel in his master's ear. The truth is more interesting. He was a clear-sighted opportunist of undoubted executive ability, who had the brains to analyse correctly the power structures of imperial Rome, and was able to manipulate them for his own benefit through his understanding of the Emperor's character.

Nero evidently assumed that Tigellinus sympathized with his aims and ambitions. He was to keep him in his post to the bitter end because Tigellinus was willing and able to operate the levers of power in his favour, without fuss, without moralizing – perhaps, above all, without making Nero feel he was just a tiresome young man who ought to know his duty better and ought to stop trying to get his own way against the grain of Roman tradition. But Tigellinus had his own reasons for hating the traditionalist Roman aristocracy, and was an eager collaborator in cutting them down to size.

Unfortunately, we know virtually nothing of Tigellinus' origins except that he came of a poor family from the Greek-founded city of Agrigentum in Sicily. We may safely deduce that he was born free and that his father was a Roman citizen, or the universally hostile sources would have emphasized the contrary. Sicily was multi-cultural: Greeks and Phoenicians had colonized it long before the Romans arrived. It was also a social backwater.

The conquerors had turfed the peasants off the best land and replaced them with slaves owned by largely absentee landlords.[1] An ambitious young Sicilian who wanted to make his way in the world would naturally have to try his luck in Rome.

Tigellinus somehow found his way into circles close to the royal family, perhaps while still a child whose father was serving them in some capacity. He must have been personable and attractive, as well as useful to his aristocratic patrons, because as a young man he became overly friendly with both Agrippina and her sister Julia Livilla. His reward was to be sentenced to penniless exile by the Emperor Caligula, who is reported to have accused him of going to bed with both the royal sisters.[2] The historical evidence for these alleged sexual misdemeanours is not strong; it is hard to believe that Caligula would have permitted him to live if he had really been guilty of such high-level adultery.[3] But the exile was real enough. He spent it in Achaea (Greece) where he kept destitution at bay by selling fish, and where he had plenty of time to brood over his treatment. If he had originally been ambitious to serve Rome, he no doubt came to see himself as someone who had been punished for having the effrontery to try to rise above his station.

As a quick-witted outsider serving the aristocracy, Tigellinus had been in a position, while still in Rome, to observe the manners and customs of those privileged insiders, and to profit from the experience. He would soon have understood that one did not need to be a coercive bully to be a successful Roman – but it helped. Enforcing other people's respect was much more important than seeking love. A 'good' family man expected unquestioning obedience from his children and servants, and not very much in the way of argument from his wife. The whip would be in routine use in his household on the backs of unsatisfactory slaves, of whatever age or sex, and one was not supposed to be moved by their cries – or, at least, not to the extent of showing pity or allowing such weakness to interfere with discipline.

If birth put a young man in line for leadership of one of the noble families, he would be trained to adopt a haughty manner towards rivals and his social inferiors, who would naturally comprise almost all the rest of the human race. Such a man would be expected to repay infringement of his *dignitas* with appropriately severe retaliation, and any serious insult to his clan with implacable hatred, not stopping short of homicide. If, in addition, such a man hoped to live up to the reputation of his ancestors, he would want to demonstrate on the field of battle those qualities of courage, endurance and capacity for slaughter that had made Rome master of the world.

Tigellinus evidently grasped that Nero did not want any of that, while he himself could never hope to qualify for it. When he finally returned to Italy from exile, thanks to Agrippina's influence, and set up in business as a horse trader, he seems to have made an instantly favourable impression on the teenage Emperor, who was obsessed with driving horses in his racing chariot. Their mutual interest in the sport was obviously an advantage. Tigellinus had not seen Nero since he had been a baby. Now he evidently looked beneath the young man's good-natured exterior, identified before long the vanity and the weaknesses within and saw his way to exploit those characteristics. If the story of Nero's reign of more than thirteen years is, in some measure, the story of his various strategies of escape from the traditional burdens of office, Tigellinus is the dedicated accomplice who provided the necessary means – and who may have relieved him of much, if not all, of the associated guilt.

Tigellinus knew that the touchy young Emperor could not abide disapproval. Nero had been prepared to accept it, however reluctantly, from his previous advisers, no doubt because he had relied from his youth upwards on the honesty of Burrus and the political shrewdness of Seneca. But disapproval of her son had ultimately cost his mother her life. Tigellinus had known Agrippina intimately and no doubt learnt much from her. He may even have had the benefit of listening to her own assessment of her son's character. Certainly he must have shared some of her other secrets, because, as his patroness, she would surely have expected to rely on his services in return for what she had done

The adolescent Nero receiving a leafy crown from his mother Agrippina – a symbolic public acknowledgement that it was she who put him in power. He wears a breastplate and military tunic, but has taken off his war helmet (bottom left) to show his peaceful intentions. Agrippina, in a matronly robe with fruits of the earth at her shoulder, is probably meant to represent Demeter, the Greek corn-goddess, who brings bounty when propitiated but famine when crossed. These outstandingly beautiful sculptures were unearthed in a temple complex devoted to emperor worship in the Roman province of Asia (now part of modern Turkey), at Aphrodisias, about 75 miles inland from Ephesus. (Aphrodisias Excavations, Institute of Fine Arts, New York University)

Nero was a precocious student of rhetoric, as this charming statue of him as a schoolboy orator suggests.
(Photo RMN – Chuzeville)

The Stoic philosopher Seneca, Nero's tutor, became effectively his chief minister but later plotted against him. (Florence, Galleria degli Uffizi. Photo: AKG London)

Coins were not simply money but a lasting form of public relations. Nero is shown (right) as Apollo playing the lyre and (left) as mature ruler.

(Museo Archeologico Nazionale, Naples, Italy/Bridgeman Art Library)

(© British Museum)

After she married Claudius to become Empress, 'the state was transformed, and the whole system became obedient to a woman . . . Agrippina's domination was almost masculine in the tightness of its grip' – Tacitus' assessment of Nero's power-driven mother, whose bust is seen here. (Photo RMN – Arnaudet)

Potential violence simmered just below the surface of imperial Roman society, and was often lethal when it broke out, as in this riot between rival groups of spectators at the amphitheatre at Pompeii, near Naples, in 59. Nero was in the Naples area for six months of that year, when he organized the murder of his mother. Twenty years later Pompeii was buried by the eruption of Mount Vesuvius. (Museo Archeologico Nazionale, Naples, Italy/Bridgeman Art Library)

The violence demonstrated by Jesus in driving out traders from the Temple at Jerusalem with a whip (imaginatively pictured above in this nineteenth-century engraving by Gustave Doré) is believed by many modern scholars to have been the underlying reason for his crucifixion by Pontius Pilate. Nero's uncle and step-father, the Emperor Claudius (left), loved watching people die in horrible ways. (Pat Hodgson Library)

Nero built his great palace, the 'Golden House', on a large area of central Rome that had been mostly destroyed in the fire of 64. Its internal walls and ceilings were decorated with paintings, of which only a few, faded examples remain (opposite, above). Their quality and beauty can be better gauged by visiting the Vatican, where Renaissance artists painted a papal corridor from copies made when they were lowered on ropes into what they believed to be under-floor grottoes but was in fact the buried ground floor of Nero's palace.

Rooms of the Golden House open to the public today include (above) this high chamber containing a statue of Terpsichore, Muse of Dancing, who is associated with the lyre and lyric poetry, and (right) the octagonal hall believed to have been covered originally by a revolving dome. (EPA/PA Photos)

This detached fragment of a mural from the Golden House, now in the Ashmolean Museum, shows the birth of Adonis. (Ashmolean Museum, Oxford, UK/Bridgeman Art Library)

Praetorian Guards, seen in this second-century relief, had a special duty to guard the Emperor's person. Their sudden, unexpected betrayal of Nero triggered his downfall. (Louvre, Paris, France/Bridgeman Art Library)

The legend that Nero 'fiddled while Rome burned' – imagined, here, in an oil painting by Hubert Robert (1733–1808) – will probably never die. In reality, he led the fire-fighting operations night and day for more than a week, and at great personal risk, until it was finally extinguished. Afterwards, he imposed strict new building regulations to inhibit future outbreaks. (Musée des Beaux-Arts André Malraux, Le Havre, France / Giraudon / Bridgeman Art Library)

for him. It is even alleged that he made his first substantial amount of money, with her support, by successfully claiming an inheritance under a forged will.[4]

Tigellinus' first important official appointment was as Prefect of the Watch, in charge of the city's firemen, who also doubled as night-time police officers patrolling the darkened streets, on the look-out for fire and crime. It was no doubt in this capacity that Tigellinus kept an eye on Nero's nocturnal revels. He would also have met regularly with Burrus, who, as Praetorian Prefect, had overall responsibility for public order in the city. Tigellinus would have been able to see at first hand how the old soldier behaved towards Nero – and how Nero responded. Burrus was noted for being a man of few words. A well-known anecdote relates how he declined to repeat himself after Nero asked him twice for his opinion on a particular subject, answering brusquely that once was enough.[5] That would never have been the style of such a glib courtier as Tigellinus.

After Burrus died, Nero decided to revert to an earlier practice of appointing two praetorian prefects, which was an attempt to prevent too much power being concentrated in one man's hands. Tigellinus' colleague in the new joint post was a better qualified man, Faenius Rufus, one of Agrippina's protégés, who had achieved a reputation for efficiency and honesty by organizing the grain supply without conspicuously enriching himself in the process. It quickly became clear, however, that Tigellinus had much the greater influence of the two with Nero, who had raised the Sicilian's son-in-law, Cossutianus Capito, to the rank of senator (a promotion that would have been impossible for Tigellinus himself, as only an equestrian could command the Praetorian Guard).

Early in 62, Capito stood up in the Senate to demand the prosecution under the old law of *maiestas* (treason) of the Praetor Antistius for libelling the Emperor. It was the first time this law had been invoked in Nero's reign, and it carried an especially gruesome form of the death penalty. Capito was, of course, acting on Tigellinus' instructions. Tacitus indicates that Nero did not intend to have Antistius executed, but to exercise his veto in order to demonstrate his clemency while at the same time giving a warning that he would not tolerate mockery. It appears that jokes were circulating freely among the aristocracy about Nero's artistic performances, although the exact terms of Antistius' 'libels' are unknown. He had written a lampoon in verse, which he recklessly declaimed before a large audience at a banquet.

At the trial in the Senate, members voted one after another for the death penalty, until it was the turn of Thrasea Paetus, the leading Stoic. He astutely lavished praise on Nero while arguing for Antistius to be spared the cruelty of the ancient punishment. The great majority of senators then changed their votes to a sentence of exile and confiscation. Nero was annoyed at being deprived of the opportunity to add to his reputation for mercy, but he accepted the Senate's decision.[6]

It is not clear whether the trial of Antistius took place shortly before or after Tigellinus' appointment as joint Praetorian Prefect, but his growing influence with Nero, combined with the death of Burrus, prompted Seneca that same year to consider his own position at court. Deprived of the support of the Praetorians, and detecting a sudden lack of warmth in his relations with the Emperor, Seneca did not wait to be outmanoeuvred and dismissed, but voluntarily offered his resignation. It is hard to work out from the excessively polite exchanges (reported by Tacitus) between Nero and his former tutor, whether Seneca genuinely wanted to retire to private life to resume his philosophical studies and literary output, or even whether Nero, on reflection, wanted him to go or stay. But go he did.

It may be significant that during their conversation Seneca apparently invited the Emperor to help himself to the wealth he had amassed during more than seven years as his chief adviser. That may show his vulnerability to criticism over past financial activities, perhaps even a fear that Nero might be seeking to justify his dismissal on grounds of corruption. At any rate, he indicated that he would no longer need more than a sufficiency to maintain himself. He may, indeed, have been speaking the simple truth when he referred to his desire for a quiet life amid intellectual pursuits. He was in his middle sixties and had perhaps endured more than enough of politics in the service of an increasingly unpredictable master.[7]

With both Seneca and Burrus gone, there was no longer any outspoken opposition within the *Consilium* to Nero's long-contemplated divorce. Poppaea's discovery that she was pregnant added urgency to her cause. If Nero would agree to marry her, she would be able to present him with a legitimate heir. If he held back for fear of public opinion – or a senatorial coup – the child would be born out of wedlock and therefore lack the status necessary for ultimate succession. So far as is known, this unborn infant was the first whom Nero had ever fathered. Octavia, his wife of ten years, appeared to be barren, which was sufficient grounds for divorce under Roman law, even for an empress. The main problem, of course, as Burrus had pointed out, was that the Empire was, in a sense, her dowry; Claudius' dynastic plan must undoubtedly have been that even if his own son could not succeed to the throne, a grandson, via Nero and Octavia, could hope to do so. The secondary difficulty was that she was loved by the people, while Poppaea was despised.

Tigellinus advised Nero that it would be prudent, before divorcing Octavia, to dispose of the two men who might, in an emergency, be considered to have the best claim to the Principate: Faustus Cornelius Sulla Felix, his brother-in-law, and Rubellius Plautus. Nero had already exiled them as a precautionary measure, Sulla to Massilia (Marseilles) and Plautus to the province of Asia. They appear to have done nothing during their banishment to justify execution, although at one point a rumour emerged that Plautus was conspiring with Corbulo, the general controlling the eastern frontier; but as Corbulo was to stay in office for a further five years, Nero can scarcely have believed it – and may even have started the story himself. Sulla, married to Princess Antonia and only a few days' journey from Rome, was probably considered the more immediate threat.

It is a measure of the regime's rapid descent into tyranny, under the malign influence of Tigellinus, that Nero, having already resurrected the law of *maiestas*, now used his executive power to order the assassination of both Sulla and Plautus without bothering to put them on trial. Soldiers were sent to cut off their heads and bring them back to Rome as evidence. Nero told the Senate that the two men were agitators, but omitted to add that they were now dead agitators. The senators thus went through the charade of voting to expel them from their ranks, while announcing a public thanksgiving for the Emperor's deliverance. In the face of such supine grovelling – where, as Tacitus observes, Nero's crimes were now praised by the Senate as virtues[8] – he divorced Octavia without further ado and married Poppaea twelve days later.

A straightforward divorce of Octavia for barrenness, however, was not enough to satisfy the new Empress, who immediately set out to destroy her rival. This gave Tigellinus another outstanding opportunity to show his mettle. He and Poppaea put their heads together and came up with a plan that found favour with Nero, who presumably chose not to disbelieve their allegation that Octavia had committed adultery with an Egyptian slave, a flute-player named Eucaerus. Octavia's maids were then tortured one by one to make them 'confess' that she had had sex with him. It is a tribute to the young Empress that this vicious enterprise proved a failure. Most of the maids defied the torturer, and one of them spat in Tigellinus' face, crying out: 'My mistress' private parts are cleaner than your mouth!'[9]

The mob rose twice in Octavia's defence. The first time, Nero tried to pacify the protestors by talking of recalling her from Campania, where he had sent her under an armed guard. But this only encouraged them to further demonstrations. A great crowd invaded the Capitol area, overturned Poppaea's statues and set up Octavia's, covered with flowers, in the Forum. This caused genuine alarm at the palace. No doubt the strange new triumvirate of Nero, Poppaea and Tigellinus took counsel together, in search of a solution. All three, in their different ways, were outsiders: Nero psychologically, Tigellinus by birth and Poppaea because she wasn't Octavia. All three had totally miscalculated popular reaction to their activities. In their hour of need they drafted in a man who was more of an outsider than any of them – Anicetus, the tutor turned admiral, who had expressed his devotion to the regime three years earlier by murdering Agrippina.

Nero himself seems to have handled the details, presumably to make sure that everything went according to plan. He personally interviewed Anicetus, who was still Admiral of the Fleet, and made him a proposition: he must either confess to adultery with Octavia or be killed. Anicetus chose to live. He not only 'confessed' before a special meeting of the *Consilium*, stacked with friendly faces, but did it so convincingly that Nero was able to announce that Octavia had tried to suborn his admiral in the hope of getting the navy to switch its allegience to her. The inconvenient fact that she was also accused of procuring an abortion for herself, when she had just been divorced for sterility, seems not to have affected the outcome of the case.

While Anicetus sailed off with a big financial reward to comfortable exile in Sardinia – he died a natural death there later – Octavia was transported to the prison island of Pandataria and murdered there a few days after arrival. She was still only twenty-two. The centurion who trussed her up in cords and cut open her veins was too impatient to wait more than a few minutes, while she remained obstinately alive, so he dumped her in a steaming-hot bath to finish her off. The Senate voted for more thanksgivings after her severed head was sent to Poppaea as a trophy.[10]

The only good to come out of the entire episode was a play, *Octavia*, which deals imaginatively with the main characters and incidents. Until quite recently it was generally believed to have been written by Seneca, who plays an anachronistic role in it as if he were still Nero's chief adviser; but internal evidence suggests strongly that the unknown author was aware of events that took place after the philosopher's death. In the play, Seneca is so depressed about the sheer awfulness of the times that he questions whether the present human race will survive; perhaps, he speculates, a day of chaos will wipe them out as the sky falls in, to be replaced by better creatures. He looks back longingly to the fabled Golden Age of remote antiquity when there was no conflict and all goods were held in common (*communis usus omnium rerum fuit*). His speech develops into a tirade against contemporary wickdness and lust, until Nero strides on, bellowing: 'Bring me the heads of Sulla and Plautus.'

This stage-Nero is a remorseless villain, but the author provides him with some useful lines of argument to explain, if not fully justify, his actions. When Seneca protests at the injustice to Sulla and Plautus, the Emperor retorts: 'It's easy for someone to be just whose breast is empty of fear.' Urged to be more like Augustus, Nero points out that his 'divine' predecessor slaughtered so many people in his proscriptions that the Forum was polluted with tainted blood, dripping from the rotting faces (*putres vultus*) of those whose severed heads he had left there as a warning to others.[11] He adds sarcastically that, just as Augustus' virtues evidently merited heaven because he ruled by fear, so there will be a place for himself (Nero) in heaven,[12] too, so long as he continues to wield a savage sword against his enemies, and founds a dynasty with worthy offspring. Octavia must die, he asserts; at first he had been deceived about her feelings towards him, but now he knows that her unresponsiveness is due not to modesty but to hatred.[13]

Octavia herself never directly encounters Nero in the play, but tells her old nurse about a nightmare in which the Emperor kills both her and her brother Britannicus. The nurse urges her several times to try to win back her husband by being compliant – advice which implies that, to some extent, it was her refusal to be a conventionally obedient wife that ultimately led to her divorce. But Octavia compares him to a savage tiger, adding: 'He hates those of noble birth, and scorns men and gods alike.'[14] Poppaea appears only briefly, pale and in tears after a dream in which she fell into an infernal abyss. The potential show-stopper is the ghost of Agrippina, who comes hot from Hell, brandishing flaming torches and prophesying Nero's downfall in suitably blood-curdling language.[15]

The whole play is less than a thousand lines long, and may not have been intended for public performance. But it is written with verve and often with eloquence, and is unique in surviving Latin literature as the only Roman 'history play'. It cannot, of course, be taken as 'real' history, except insofar as it represents evidence of an intelligent and roughly contemporary view of the imperial court during a particular crisis. The effective acknowledgement that Augustus persecuted and killed far more people than Nero ever did – and that his supposed divinity was a cynical sham – could scarcely be more cogently expressed. Above all, a close reading of the work feeds the imagination in a way that no official report could ever match, and leaves an indelible picture of the spurned young Empress and her sufferings.

But the play does not deal adequately with the important question: what had happened to the originally benevolent young prince who had set out to rule with such good intentions? The corruption of absolute power was no doubt taking its seemingly inevitable course in a personality unsustained by firm beliefs in traditional virtues, inadequate though some of those specifically Roman virtues might often be in practice. Another factor, of course, was the growing influence of Tigellinus and Poppaea following the abrupt departure of both Burrus and Seneca. But we must keep a sense of proportion. Nero now employed murder as a weapon, but he used it very sparingly and only if he felt personally threatened; he did not take pleasure in it, as both Caligula and Claudius had done.

That may not sound like a reasonable excuse, but it needs to be judged in the context of a governmental system that conferred on Nero the effective power of life and death over any of his millions of subjects, some of whom undoubtedly wanted to assassinate him or control him, motivated by personal ambition and not because of concerns for the welfare of mankind. It is surely legitimate to wonder, given what we all know to be the frailty of human nature facing the temptations of power, that he was quite as restrained as in fact he proved to be. The arithmetic is compelling. In those first eight years of his reign the total number of his murder victims was four: two women and two men: his mother, his wife, his brother-in-law and a cousin. In each case he tried other solutions than murder, over a period of years, before deciding there was no effective alternative. The accusations that during this period he also poisoned Burrus, Britannicus and his terminally ill Aunt Domitia (supposedly for her money!) are highly implausible and almost certainly false.

This tally of four confirmed killings in eight years, all confined to the same extended family grouping, is not the mark of the homicidal monster of popular imagination, but the long-delayed reaction of a cautious ruler who knows that if he is going to be stabbed in the back, it will be one of his relatives or 'friends' who will most likely be wielding the knife. Nevertheless, it is scarcely the mark of the philosopher-king he had intended to become. Seneca was undoubtedly disappointed and disillusioned at the way his former pupil had turned out, but Nero himself had reason to complain that some of his worst enemies were Stoics in the Senecan mould. The Emperor continued to study philosophy and to debate with philosophers because he still needed to answer, to his own satisfaction, the puzzling question of his true identity.

This was not an issue that ought to have troubled a good Roman, but it reared up before him with much greater force than it would have done for ordinary mortals, precisely because he was worshipped as a god. It is no use objecting that the question 'Who am I?' is one that would never have occurred to anyone before the advent of modern psychology, because it had evidently already confronted Jesus of Nazareth – for not totally dissimilar reasons. Nor is it valid to object that it was not Nero himself who was worshipped, but his 'spirit' or his 'genius', in the established Roman formula, because Roman traditionalists formed only a minority of Nero's worshippers. Throughout the Hellenistic world the concept of a god-king was universally known and avidly discussed, in an age of superstition and of competing mystery religions, including Christianity.

Nero was aware that he was the most powerful ruler in the known world, and therefore more entitled to divine status than any of the many lesser monarchs who were also daily worshipped as gods, not to mention the various 'wonder-workers' who arose from time to time in that era, chiefly in the Near East. As for the true identity of Jesus, various authority figures asked him who he was, or claimed to be, and they usually received evasive answers.

The gospels tell us that Jesus himself put the question more than once to his own disciples: 'Who do you say I am?' The claim is widely made that Jesus already knew the answer to this question and asked it in order to test his followers, but that would be much more plausible if it were not for the earlier evasions.

Jesus certainly believed that he had a divinely sanctioned mission in life and that he had a special relationship to God the Father, such that God, for example, would save him from bodily harm even if he should jump off the top of the Temple in Jerusalem. Long after his crucifixion by Roman soldiers, Christian theologians, believing that he had been resurrected bodily from the dead, succeeded in identifying him as the second person of the triune God who had created the universe; thus the person known on earth as Jesus had 'always' existed outside time, partaking of God's essential attributes of infinity, almightiness and omniscience. Jesus, of course, made no such claims during his lifetime; his belief in his special relationship with God was evidently based not on a theological definition but on direct personal experience, presumably of a revelatory or intuitive kind. His experience of other men and women – in contrast to his experience of God – was that only a small minority of them accepted his inner belief in this special relationship.

By contrast, Nero's personal experience of other human beings was that untold millions of them worshipped him – or, at least, went through the motions of doing so. He therefore had plenty of justification for assuming that he might have a special relationship with whatever power or powers had created the universe and placed him on earth to be a ruler. 'Who do you say I am?' would have been a far more complex question for one of Nero's 'disciples' among the 'Arval Brothers' than it would have been for St Peter and the rest of the Apostles in replying to Jesus. A wrong answer might have very serious consequences in this world rather than in the next. No doubt as a young man, Nero would initially have treated the question fairly lightly. But that would not have been the case later in his reign, when Nero's mature aim as a ruler was to create a specific impression of himself as in some sense God-like.

Some among his courtiers, hoping by flattery to achieve power and profit, would surely have been tempted to reply to him along the lines of St Peter to his master: 'Thou art the anointed one, the son of the living God.'[16] And where there is great temptation there is usually, sooner or later, direct action. We can be quite sure that during nearly fourteen years of supreme secular power, some of Nero's courtiers would have treated him – or, at least, affected to treat him – as if he were really divine. Nero, while perhaps retaining much of his earlier personal scepticism, would have been unlikely to have discouraged too strongly such openly avowed worship. After several years of it, he would perhaps have treated it as quite normal, as something not to be discouraged at all.

There is always a risk that such an artificially constructed persona, or mask, will ultimately take over the mind that created and cultivated it. Perhaps, at times, it did. There need be nothing surprising about that. It is a phenomenon related to a believer's personal faith in God in our modern, largely secular world. Believers characteristically feel the need to have other believers around them to ward off scepticism. Sometimes their faith is weak, sometimes strong to the point of moral certainty; at other times it may vanish altogether, leaving the 'believer' in despair at a lack of faith in the value of anything at all. Just as suddenly, it may return in full force. The existence of millions of Nero's subjects consistently and regularly expressing belief – year in, year out – in his divinity would have had a powerful effect on his mind. So far as the reactions of *other people* were concerned, therefore, Nero would have had much more reason than Jesus to suppose himself to be in some way special, chosen or divine. Moreover, the activities of Nero, however 'morally bad' at times, were for the most part rewarded with mass adulation, while those of Jesus, however morally good, aroused threats of communal stoning for alleged blasphemy – and ultimately to the cries of 'Crucify him!' from the inflamed mob.

There is no evidence that Nero ever seriously considered the teachings of Christianity, although it is just possible that he met St Paul face to face in order to judge his case. Certainly Nero never became a Stoic. But if we may judge from his actions, he probably favoured aspects of Epicureanism, the great rival system to Stoicism.[17] Epicurean teaching on physical reality, arrived at by rational deduction from limited natural observation, is uncannily close to modern scientific hypotheses. The universe is infinite, consisting of matter and space – and nothing else. Our cosmos is not ruled by Fate or Providence, but came into being by the random collision of material objects. All matter is ultimately reducible to microscopic material particles which cannot be further divided but are capable of reassembling and separating again and again in an endless process of change, during which our earth and all who live on it will be recycled an infinite number of times.

These indivisible particles are called 'atoms', but we must be careful not to confuse the terminology of the atomic theory of Epicurus (derived and adapted from the teaching of Democritus) with that of modern atomic science, where atoms can be split into even smaller particles. The Greek root of our word 'atom' effectively means 'that which is indivisible', and expresses the logical impossibility, for Democritus, of dividing a finite material object into an infinite number of parts. The modern splitting of the atom, therefore, does not invalidate the logical basis of Democritus' fundamental deduction. Epicurus' great contribution to Greek atomism was to introduce randomness into the movement of particles – what he called the 'swerve' of atoms deviating from a supposedly predictable line.

The importance of Epicurus' 'swerve' for the philosophical debaters of Nero's court was that if it were true it would indicate that events on earth are not entirely predictable, even to the gods, and that the notion of an all-seeing Providence is therefore a mistake. Cicero, writing a century before Nero, had derided this Epicurean view for effectively claiming that there could be effects without causes – a proposition so utterly against reason that no self-respecting thinker could possibly entertain it. Philosophical opinion generally supported Cicero until the twentieth century, when the random behaviour of sub-atomic particles was confirmed by scientific experiment.

Epicurus' teaching that there is no such thing as Providence or an after-life effectively freed his followers from the fear of divine punishment for their actions or failures. Conveniently for Nero, Epicurus also taught that the gods nevertheless exist, but that in order to maintain their state of heavenly bliss they do not interfere in the affairs of humans, because any such intervention would be bound to involve pain, or, at least, a preponderance of pain over pleasure; the one thing for which Epicureanism has remained notorious down the centuries is its insistence that pleasure is the ultimate good, and that any sensible person will choose it in preference to pain.

Nero, for whom eclecticism seems to have been second nature, was thus in a position to believe both that he could do exactly as he liked without fearing a heavenly thunderbolt, and at the same time hope to be numbered among the gods after death. It is true that Epicurus was such a thorough-going materialist that he held that even human souls disintegrate into their component 'atoms' at death, effectively wiping out each individual person for ever, but that part of his philosophy has never been very popular, and was daily denied by Nero's many worshippers. At the very least, the prospect of an honoured seat in Heaven among the rest of the gods, after his death on Earth, would have been an open question. It would have made perfect sense to him that immortality, like earthly power, was only for the select few in each generation.

Marriage to Poppaea transformed Nero's court and brought him closer to their favoured model of Hellenistic monarchy, where the supposed divinity of rulers was not a matter for argument. She had already enjoyed ample opportunity, as the Emperor's chief mistress, to carve for herself a dazzling role as an individual leader of fashion. Now, as Empress, she set the tone for all those who moved in court circles or hoped to do so. Whereas neither Octavia nor Acté had cost the regime more than a modest allowance, Poppaea helped to inaugurate an era of spectacularly high spending designed to make the court the most magnificent the world had ever seen, with herself as its most fabulous jewel. Nero needed little encouragement to scour the Empire for works of art to beautify the palace[18] he was now building for the two of them and for the little Princess Claudia, who was born to them in January 63.

Lavish celebrations throughout the empire greeted the birth of the Princess. Senators flocked to the imperial villa at Antium for the privilege of being admitted to the baby's presence. She and her mother were each awarded the title of Augusta. The Senate issued a formal commendation for the efficacy of Poppaea's womb and voted to build a Temple of Fecundity. Nero's loving and joyful response to his daughter was 'more than human' (*ultra mortale*), Tacitus remarks mordantly, and his grief was equally extravagant when she died less than four months later.[19] It was both a personal tragedy and a dynastic setback. Little Claudia was officially deified, but Nero and Poppaea were never to have another child. Perhaps to ward off his depression, the Emperor now finally took the decisive steps to a professional stage career, in defiance of all precedent.

TEN

ORDEAL BY FIRE

By striking out on his own, and by the new emphasis on his exalted status, Nero greatly increased the number of his opponents. Senators who had been prepared to tolerate his perceived eccentricities when they assumed that Seneca and Burrus were exercising effective control, were much less disposed to support him now that he had chosen to ally himself with Tigellinus and Poppaea. The murder of Agrippina, while unnatural and horrible, could at least be justified by reasons of state. The divorce and murder of Octavia not only looked like self-indulgent spite but eradicated one of the fundamental tenets of the regime – the dynastic mingling of the Julio–Claudian bloodline.

Although it was true that Augustus himself had scandalously stolen another man's pregnant wife – Livia, the mother of Tiberius – he had taken great pains to present her publicly as a traditional Roman matron, even to the extent of insisting that she weave his and her own clothes on the family hand-loom. The contrast with Nero and Poppaea could hardly be more striking, especially now that Nero, doubtless under his new Empress' influence, made a point of never wearing the same clothes twice.[1]

Roman aristocrats, whose ancestors had literally taken turns at ruling the civilized world, had been forced to cede the realities of power to successive members of a particular family grouping, but now they baulked at giving up the trappings too. Few of them were content to knuckle under to an apparently vainglorious young couple whose way of life struck them as immoral and hubristic, inviting the anger of the gods. Among Nero's regular tasks was the examination of the entrails and vital organs of sacrificed animals at Rome's many temples, precisely in order to try to discover the will of those self-same gods, so as to ensure that his activities and those of the state marched in harmony with divine wishes. Nero himself may not have taken his function as *Pontifex Maximus* too seriously, but most of his subjects did. Their superstition was soon to be put to the test.

On the surface all seemed calm, but the Emperor's agents must have informed him of the underlying discontent, at least in the capital, because although he had at last come to the firm decision to pursue a career as a professional singer and instrumentalist, he lacked the nerve to stage a full-scale performance for the general public in Rome itself. Since his debut at the Youth Games, where the audience had been carefully restricted, he had sung only to guests at the palace or to privileged groups of friends in their private houses or gardens. For his first professional appearance, he chose the former Greek colony of Naples, intending it as a springboard for his long-projected tour of Greece, where he dreamed of establishing his reputation as a bard by winning competitive victories over his artiste peers.

Excitement was intense in Naples and the surrounding district when the news got out. The Neapolitans must scarcely have believed it at first. Nor, one must imagine, must the people of Rome, who may be forgiven for perceiving it as a snub. Their Emperor had been fond of saying that only those of Greek culture could truly appreciate his music-making. Now he was matching his action with his words. Long before he and his entourage reached Naples it had become obvious that he would have to give not merely one performance but a whole series if he was to satisfy all those who wanted to hear him. No conventional Neapolitan theatre was big enough to cope with the demand for tickets, so he decided to use a large, open-air arena which had tier after tier of seats on all sides. The acoustics must have been excellent, or it would have been hard for his unamplified voice – variously described as 'celestial' or 'husky but not very strong' – to reach the upper levels.

Nero duly performed before a capacity crowd for several days in succession, and enjoyed himself so much that he could not bring himself to leave even during the intervals when he had to rest his voice. Instead of walking off after playing and singing, in order to relax with Poppaea in the privacy of a dressing room, he would happily eat a snack in the orchestra area while the audience milled around him. He told them in Greek that after he had drunk a glass or two he would soon be singing again. He was particularly pleased at the enthusiasm of a group of Alexandrian sailors, who happened to have arrived in port at Naples. Although Alexandria was in Egypt, it was basically a Greek city, which had been founded by Alexander the Great. Nero responded to their tumultuous applause by sending a messenger to Egypt to invite more of them to sail across.[2]

An untimely earthquake brought his concerts to an end.[3] He sang on, regardless, through the first tremor, until he finished his programme, which shows courage, or foolhardiness, of a sort. The audience stayed on with him, perhaps because they had no choice. He had no doubt rehearsed long and conscientiously, in line with his usual seriousness of approach to artistic endeavours, and once he had his cithara in his hand he was not easily stopped. But shortly after that day's show ended and the audience had left, the theatre collapsed in ruins. Some said this was a warning from Heaven. Nero, however, took it as an auspicious omen and composed a poem of gratitude to the gods for the happy outcome, in which not a single person was injured.

The Emperor then set out for the Adriatic coast to take ship to Greece, but stopped on the way at the former Samnite hill town of Beneventum, where a man of humble origins, Vatinius – described as deformed in body, scurrilous in wit and pre-eminent among the wicked – was giving a gladiatorial show. The introduction of Vatinius into Tacitus' narrative (he does nothing to justify it) makes sense only in the context of the prevalent Roman belief that physical deformity was a form of punishment inflicted by the gods on those who deserved to suffer.[4] Tacitus' mention of Nero's friendship with such an unsuitable person – 'bred in a cobbler's workshop' – can be taken as a further example of the Emperor's supposedly ungodly behaviour: the head of state ought not to be consorting with menial cripples.

News reached Nero, while he was still at Beneventum, that Decimus Junius Silanus Torquatus, last of Augustus' great-great-grandsons (except, of course, for the Emperor himself), had just committed suicide. His servants had been arrested on imperial orders and held in chains for interrogation. Torquatus, whose two brothers had both fallen victim successively to Agrippina and her son, had drawn the obvious conclusion. Nero, with an air of injured innocence, protested that although Torquatus had obviously been guilty of wanting to supplant him – he had given certain of his freedmen job titles equivalent to those of the imperial freedmen in the palace – he would nevertheless have been spared if only he had stayed alive to trust in the Emperor's clemency.[5]

As a consequence, abruptly, Nero decided to postpone his intended visit to Greece. He gave orders for his huge travelling court to turn around and head back to Rome. This was no quick and easy logistical exercise. Suetonius tells us that Nero seldom travelled with fewer than a thousand carriages in tow; even allowing for a certain amount of exaggeration about such a big round number, it is obvious that an Emperor of Rome would not have contemplated making his first official visit abroad without a large train – and adequate military protection. It was colossally expensive, too. Even his mules, it is said, were shod in silver, and his drivers wore clothes made of the best woollen cloth from the sheep-raising Italian region of Apulia. In addition to his Praetorian detachments and his personal bodyguards, Nero was accompanied by fearsome Moorish cavalry from the North African province of Mauretania – horsemen jingling with exotic jewellery as well as weapons, who were eager enough to show off their mounted skills to the Roman peasant infantry.[6]

Tacitus says that Nero took this costly and difficult step of turning back at Beneventum for no known particular reason. He must already have made arrangements for a fleet to convey him and his enormous entourage from the port of Brundisium, and for his reception in Greece. The fact that his decision coincided with the news of Torquatus' suicide is surely the key. Torquatus had been consul in 53, the year before Nero came to power;

assuming that he was at least thirty-five years old (the normal qualifying age) at that date, he would have been at least forty-six when he died. On grounds of ancestry, maturity and experience, therefore, Torquatus had been the obvious successor as Emperor if Nero had died without an heir. Structuring his domestic household along similar lines to that of the palace, thereby implying that he was ready to take over the imperial role at a moment's notice, would have alarmed any emperor, let alone one as suspicious as Nero had now become.

We know that Nero had general cause for suspicion, because the next year, 65, was to see the thwarting of the biggest conspiracy of his reign, involving dozens of highly placed men, with evidence of their secret meetings going back well into the past. It is legitimate to suppose that Torquatus may have been the original nominee of the plotters, and that his downfall caused them to postpone their plans for the time being. Tigellinus would certainly have tortured those members of Torquatus' household whom he was keeping chained up; although no accomplices were named, the Praetorian Prefect perhaps gained enough in the way of forced confessions to convince both him and Nero of the probable existence of such a web of treason, requiring the Emperor's return to his capital as a measure of simple prudence.

Whatever the truth behind the sudden volte-face at Beneventum, Tacitus says that on his way back to Rome Nero was 'secretly turning over in his imagination the idea of journeying to his Eastern provinces, especially Egypt'.[7] As a descendant of Mark Antony, he had a particular interest in the land of the Nile, which his own grandfather, Germanicus, had visited – to the disapproval of Tiberius. Meanwhile, speculation must have been rife in Rome about what their unpredictable young Emperor was going to do next. On arrival there, he issued an edict to his baffled people, swearing that this projected new foreign trip would not keep him away from the city for long, and that while he was abroad all public business would continue to run smoothly.

Nero then went in solemn state up to the Capitol, the steep hill overlooking the Forum, to venerate the gods whose spiritual presences were believed to dwell there, especially those of Jupiter, the king of the gods, and of Apollo, the divine musician, to whom the Emperor was especially devoted. He sought by the customary sacrifices to discover whether the time was propitious for his proposed journey to the East. All apparently went well until he descended to the Temple of Vesta, on the edge of the Forum. Here he suddenly began to 'tremble in every limb' and appeared to go temporarily blind. Tacitus speculates over whether his trembling was due to terror of the gods or to a supposedly guilty conscience because of his crimes.[8]

The astonishing outcome was that Nero, again without adequate explanation, abandoned his plans to visit Egypt and the East as suddenly as he had conceived them. The Senate scarcely knew whether to be glad or sorry. Perhaps it was at this stage that some of the more venerable members began to think back to the days of Caligula, and to wonder whether Nero was becoming as mad as his homicidal uncle. His public excuse was that, having seen the sad faces of his subjects and listened to their whispered fears, he could not bear the idea of leaving them, where they would no longer have the daily comfort of being able to look upon his face. Their real comfort, of course, was that his presence among them would make it more likely that they would continue to receive uninterrupted supplies of free grain. To demonstrate his sincerity in claiming to love Rome more than anywhere else on earth, he now embarked on a series of lavish street parties, 'treating the whole city as if it were his own house'.[9]

The climax was an orgy organized by Tigellinus. It sounds like a very special and unusual event, but Tacitus insists it was only one of many, and that he is describing it in detail in order to avoid having to recount any of the others.

A banquet was laid out on a raft which had been constructed for the purpose on the Pond of Agrippa and was towed around by boats ornamented with gold and ivory, and manned by depraved rowers who were graded according to their age and sexual skills. He [presumably Tigellinus] had collected various birds and animals from around the world, as well as sea-creatures from the ocean. On the banks of the pond stood brothels [*lupanaria*] full of high-class ladies; opposite them, some naked prostitutes could be seen outside. At first there were obscene gestures and movements; after dark, the nearby groves and the neighbouring houses rang with singing and blazed with lights. Nero polluted himself by his actions, whether legal or illegal . . .[10]

Dio adds some suggestive details to his account of what seems evidently to be the same orgy that Tacitus describes. Nero and Tigellinus feasted with a select group of revellers on board the raft, lounging on cushions and colourful rugs while watching the riotous activities on the illuminated shores surrounding them. Men were crowding into the brothels, having supposedly been told they could have sex with any woman they found there, even from the most aristocratic families, whether married or virgin; none of the women or girls, Dio says, were allowed to refuse.

Not surprisingly, there was a lot of shouting and elbowing going on among the crowd on shore, which turned into free fights; a few women were said to have been killed as well as men. Some of the more muscular and enterprising clients carried women off on their shoulders. Dio's account, however, seems to be entering the realms of rhetorical fantasy when he claims that, in one place, a slave would be seen having sex with his mistress in front of his master, while, in another part of the orgy, a gladiator would be violating an aristocratic girl in front of her father.[11]

When considering any of these reports of orgies, it is important to test them against what we know of the physical and emotional limitations of human beings. Social life in first-century Rome was, indeed, very different from that of our own in the twenty-first century, but not so different as several generations of Hollywood directors have tended to make out. Films depicting ancient orgies have typically shown large numbers of scantily clad young women posturing among a group of slavering, pop-eyed men, who embrace them ardently and simultaneously while the music builds towards a furious climax – which is never shown. Life is like that in imagination, rarely in practice. This sort of theoretical orgy could scarcely have maintained its manic pace for much longer than 5 minutes, with perhaps a few heroes managing to hold out for 10. Nero's orgies went on for half the day and part of the night as well, and were notable for feats of eating and drinking that, in some cases, could be sustained only by visits to the vomitarium.

Nero and Poppaea loved to dress up and display their finery at these parties. It would be truly amazing if either of them took their clothes off to entertain their guests. If they had done so, we can be sure that the ancient writers, freed from the need to rely on innuendo, would have stated it bluntly and in detail. What probably happened was that dancers or mimes, individually or in groups, would give performances of an erotic nature, which may or may not have culminated in intercourse. There may have been a limited degree of audience participation, but the event as a whole would have been carefully stage-managed by some such figure as Petronius, who was not known as the 'arbiter of elegance' for nothing.[12]

Vulgar brawling, of the sort that evidently took place on shore while Nero's pleasure raft floated on its placid lake, would never have been allowed to spoil his and Poppaea's party, in which matters of style and aesthetic pleasure would have been as important as eroticism. Nor would the entertainment have been allowed to degenerate into random promiscuity. No doubt there was some bodily contact and much sexual banter, while the wine flowed freely. But Nero was obviously a voyeur – and obsessive voyeurism is more often a substitute for sex with another person than a stimulus towards it. Sex in the head is always a mark of decadence.

Suetonius' account of these events skates lightly over the surface, but he encapsulates the young Emperor's philosophy of sex in an admirably plain statement, that rings only too true: 'I have learned from some people that Nero felt strongly that nobody is chaste (*pudicus*) and that no part of one's body is pure, but that most people pretend otherwise and are skilful at hiding their vices. That is why, if people admitted frankly to having obscene feelings, Nero was prepared to forgive them their other faults as well.'[13]

Nothing could have been further removed from the ethical teachings of his discarded former tutor. 'Virtue is something high, exalted and regal – unconquerable, inexhaustible!' writes Seneca in one of his moral essays. 'Pleasure is something low, servile, weak, fallen, whose home and fitting haunts are brothels and eating-houses.' Pressing the argument to the limit, Seneca expands his catalogue to demonstrate that virtue is pious, public-spirited and hard-working, whereas pleasure is soft, enervating, reeks of liquor, lurks in the bath, and is 'either pallid-faced or plastered with make-up like a corpse'.[14]

Seneca and Tacitus clearly thought of sexual immorality as a canker gnawing away at the body politic. But, as always, their indignation was highly selective. They would have been outraged at Dio's story of a slave embracing his mistress in public in front of his master (if it ever happened!) but they would have shown much less concern – if, indeed, they would have shown any concern at all – at hearing of the master copulating with an unwilling slave in private, even if that slave happened to be an under-age girl or boy. That, after all, was one of the things slaves were bought for. Sex with slaves was normal and traditional. It was routine. It was simply not worth recording, except where it provided material for insult. Cicero, for instance, in a speech, compared his political enemy Mark Antony to 'a boy bought for sex' (*puer emptus libidinis*);[15] Antony later had him killed, in revenge.

Paedophilia was punishable only if the victims were free-born. The practice was certainly not considered virtuous, but, equally, it was not perceived as a threat to the state if it was kept private. Effectively, without fear of the law, a Roman *Pater Familias* could go to the slave market and buy half-a-dozen assorted children from anywhere in the world for his personal gratification. It would not harm his career or his reputation, even if he were a senator or a priest – nor even if he were the Emperor himself – so long as a decent reticence was observed in public, and he did not make the mistake of boasting about it. Hypocrisy has rarely been considered a crime. The Romans liked to believe it was the Greeks, not they, who enjoyed sex with boys, in spite of such varied literary evidence as the poems of Tibullus and Martial, the plays of Plautus and the novelistic *Satyricon* of Petronius.

It was Petronius, of course, who helped to set the tone of Nero's court as his 'arbiter of elegance', advising him and Poppaea on fashions in such matters as dress and personal appearance, literature and interior decoration – and showing by his own example how a perfect courtier should behave. But his famous *Satyricon* – a picaresque narrative in prose interspersed with passages of poetry – demonstrates how *not* to behave. Its narrator, Encolpius, is a bisexual drifter of no perceptible morals who is in love with a sixteen-year-old runaway slave-boy, Giton. They make their way through the dregs of Neronian urban society in a story which seems to be incoherent only partly due to the fragmentation of the surviving pieces of manuscript.

Satyricon is vivid and often horrifying; until quite recent times, English translations tended to be abridged or bowdlerized because many of the episodes were considered pornographic. The longest continuous passage concerns a dinner party given by a *nouveau-riche* freedman, Trimalchio, whose desire to display his wealth leads him to ludicrous excess in the size and style of the dishes he serves. Presumably, this is meant to provide a contrast to Nero's feasts, which, although they were said to have lasted often from noon to midnight, with breaks for guests to take a dip in the pool or visit the vomitarium, were highly sophisticated and well organized.

The running joke thoughout the narrative is that Encolpius is obsessed by sex but is never able to achieve consummation. Some of the flavour can be gauged from an early episode in which Quartilla, a female votary of Priapus, the phallic deity, arranges for young Giton to deflower 'a pretty enough girl who was no more than seven years of age'. Encolpius, who has pretended that Giton is his brother, tries to stop it, saying that the boy is too modest and the girl too young. Quartilla retorts scornfully that she herself was at least as young as seven, and probably younger, when she lost her virginity. After a mock marriage ceremony featuring a chorus of drunken women, the two children retire while Quartilla and Encolpius watch avidly through a crack in their bedroom door. The reader is evidently meant to laugh at this appalling scene, especially at Encolpius' discomfiture; his motive in objecting to the act is not basically because of scruples over the girl but because, as a jealous though largely impotent lover, he wants to keep Giton sexually and emotionally dependent upon himself.[16]

There is no evidence that Nero had any specific inclination towards paedophilia. It is true, of course, that after Poppaea's death he is said to have castrated and made love to a youth, Sporus; but his overriding interest in Sporus was because he looked so much like Poppaea, not because he was a boy.[17] We do not know how old Sporus was at the time. In any case, paedophilia does not fit with Nero's known predilection for older women. An allegation that he raped a Vestal Virgin seems very unlikely to be true. The penalty for both parties in such a case would have been death; for the woman it would have meant being buried alive. Moral scruples would evidently not have deterred Nero, but he was generally careful to avoid sacrilege and he had a finely developed sense of self-preservation.

Suetonius levels an even more bizarre accusation against him, but it is one which is less easy to disbelieve. He reports that Nero thought up a game in which he pretended to be a rampant wild animal. Dressed in skins, he would be 'released' from a cage in front of a row of men and women tied to stakes. '*Inguina invaderet*', Suetonius writes, and this is translated in the most widely read modern English versions as 'he attacked [their] private parts'. This almost certainly gives a false impression of what was happening. If, as Suetonius asserts, Nero was doing it '*quasi genus lusus*' ('as a sort of game'), it seems improbable, given his squeamish reaction to combats in the arena, that the object was to hurt the people who were trussed up.[18]

What Suetonius is describing is easily recognizable in today's terms as a sexual bondage romp, rather than a sadistic attack. The root meaning of *invadere* is 'to go in, to enter'; the secondary meaning, 'to attack', arises simply because, in military discourse, an invasion is necessarily also an attack. Nero, however, is not playing at soldiers. It is surely easy enough to imagine him bounding out of his cage on all fours while the 'victims' reply to his tigerish roars with their own simulated squeals of terror. All of them were acting pre-arranged parts. No doubt he performed some sort of invasive, but not physically harmful, sexual assault on them before, as Suetonius adds, 'he was finished off' (*conficeretur*) by his obliging freedman, Doryphorus.

From a Roman point of view, however, the most serious sexual accusation against their Emperor was that he dressed up as a bride and went through a wedding ceremony with one of his freedmen, who then subjected him to anal intercourse in front of witnesses. There are good reasons for disbelieving this story, quite apart from a discrepancy in the surviving accounts, whereby Tacitus says the freedman concerned was Pythagoras, while Suetonius again names Doryphorus. Ancient Roman attitudes to homosexuality were radically different from those of later times. The dominant, penetrative partner would not have been thought of as specifically 'homosexual', in the sense of that term as a descriptive label of sexual orientation. The passive recipient, however, would have been considered utterly debased – no better than a slave.[19]

Even such a high-minded moralist as Cicero kept a slave-boy, Tiro, for this purpose. As Professor Eva Cantarella states: 'Cicero, in his moralistic invectives, does not condemn homosexuality as such; he condemns only one particular form: pederasty, in the Greek sense of the term – making love to freeborn boys.'[20] Romans were brought up to be dominant, and they saw nothing abnormal about expressing this at the sexual expense of other males. Penetration, whether of a man or woman, did not of itself involve any loss of manly virtue or *pudicitia* (chastity) on the part of the dominant male; but a passive male recipient would be deemed to have irretrievably forfeited both.

There would be no way back from such loss of status, as Nero would have been well aware. A slave had no choice but to submit; even a freedman might be expected to do so at the insistence of his former master. But a free-born Roman who deliberately chose passive sex in the way alleged by Tacitus and Suetonius, would have been regarded with universal contempt, which, in the case of an emperor, would have exacted a terrible political price in terms of public outrage and revulsion. It is much more likely that Nero, whose taste for dressing up to play women's parts on the stage is well attested,[21] had simply invented another exciting game, like that of the tigerish beast. The little cries he is said to have uttered, in imitation of a bride in the throes of passionate love, give an undeniably theatrical flavour to the proceedings.

Most of the curious incidents discussed in this chapter are treated briefly and impressionistically by Tacitus, one after another, in a rhetorical crescendo that reaches a climax with the Great Fire of Rome. He does not state directly that these incidents, which cumulatively represent for him a world turned upside down, were the cause of the fire as a punishment from Heaven, but that is obviously his intended effect. In the ancient world virtually everyone except the Epicureans believed that God or 'the gods' intervened in human affairs to punish transgressors, expecially those rulers who had committed outrages against morality or had demonstrated overweening hubris. What could have been more deserving of fire from Heaven, according to the moral majority of Rome, than the sins and the ignored warnings enumerated by Tacitus?

It is a cautionary and instructive catalogue. The Emperor had performed on a public stage and wilfully misinterpreted the portent of the collapsing arena; he had hob-nobbed with the deformed Vatinius while the noble Torquatus was forced to suicide; his wild schemes for a concert tour of Greece or a visit to Egypt (in emulation of his immoral ancestor Mark Antony) had been followed by a further warning from the Roman gods, causing him to tremble blindly in the very precincts of the Vestal flame; his sexual orgies had staffed the brothels with high-born ladies instead of slaves, and his 'marriage' as a homosexual bride had finally put him for ever beyond the pale of decent society. It is perhaps due to Tacitus' determination to present Nero as an evil ruler who brings disaster on his own people that he is the only ancient writer about the fire who does not accuse the Emperor of starting it himself.[22]

On the evening that the fire broke out,[23] Nero was in fact enjoying a seaside holiday at his favourite resort of Antium, 35 miles from Rome. It was a brilliant moonlit July night in the great city, after the heat of a summer day, and a small fire evidently got out of hand somewhere among the rows of cheap cafés and cook-shops near the Circus Maximus race-track. The huge stadium, capable of holding about a quarter of a million people, occupied the valley floor at the base of the Palatine hill, on which Nero's new palace, the *Domus Transitoria*, overlooked the track as well as much of the rest of the city. The valley district was one that Nero knew well from his incognito wanderings when he first became Emperor. The cook-shops represented a constant fire hazard. Wood and charcoal were their standard fuels for heating food, and they also stored large amounts of cooking oil on the premises. They specialized in hot take-away meals for the race crowds and for the poorer sort of people who lived in the overcrowded neighbourhood tenements.[24]

On the fatal night a brisk south-eastern wind was blowing. It carried the flames into the stadium and spread rapidly along the wooden upper levels. Roaring out of control, it moved north to engulf the wooded hillside and smart houses of the Palatine.[25] The next obstacle in its path was the palace itself, on which Nero had already spent a fortune. Its elaborately decorated corridors and high-ceilinged rooms, filled with art treasures collected from around the empire, were now filled with unstoppable flames. At some stage a messenger was dispatched post-haste to Antium, using the organized relay system of horses, to break the news to the Emperor.

The message arrived in the middle of the night. Nero leapt into the saddle and rode through what remained of the hours of darkness to his stricken capital. Dawn brought no relief. The air was hideous with smoke and flames – and the shrieks of trapped humans and animals among the narrow streets of the poor, as men abandoned the attempt to check the fire and tried, often vainly, to lead their women and children to safety. But as the fire pursued its relentless course, spreading death and destruction ever wider, the smoke-blackened and dazed survivors found they

had to run for their lives a second or even a third time as more
and more of the city was consumed.

When Nero finally galloped up to the city gates, he set to work
to organize the fire-fighting and to arrange for help, shelter and
food for the crowds of homeless refugees. He threw open the
public buildings and temples on the Field of Mars, the former
army exercise area beside the sharpest bend of the River Tiber, to
give them somewhere to sleep and eat and bind up their burns.
Meanwhile, the flames roared on to new residential districts in
spite of the efforts of demolition teams to clear spaces too wide
for the sparks to jump.

The Romans had great experience of fire-fighting, but this
mammoth conflagration defeated their best efforts for days on
end. The city had been able to call on the services of a
professional fire brigade since 21 BC when the aedile Marcus
Egnatius Rufus had formed one with his own slaves. When Rufus'
term of office ended, Augustus was so impressed with the value of
their work that he instituted a bigger brigade, composed of 600
public slaves. Even these, however, proved unable to cope in the
mushrooming imperial capital, with its thousands of often jerry-
built tenement blocks, some rising to six or seven storeys, where
people of many races and languages crammed into insanitary and
easily flammable rooms – where those who were slow to wake up
in an emergency might never reach street-level alive.

In AD 6, after a number of serious fires and much loss of life
and property, Augustus set up the extensive organization which,
in essence, still operated in Nero's day, whereby seven cohorts,
each of a thousand men, were given responsibility for preventing
and fighting fire in two each of the fourteen administrative
districts into which Rome was divided. By this time they were no
longer slaves but 7,000 freedmen, and Tiberius had ordered that
any who served for six years would qualify for Roman citizenship
– sufficient indication, in itself, of the dangers involved.

Nero now took over personal leadership of these already
exhausted men, whose prefect, until recently, had been
Tigellinus. The young Emperor was to be seen rushing about his
city, directing operations by day and night, unprotected by his

usual armed guards, whom he had presumably already pressed into temporary service as fire-fighters, along with any other able-bodied men he could find. After six days of intensive struggle, this tattered army of bucket-carrying, axe-wielding heroes at length managed to bring the fire under control. Or so they thought. No doubt almost all of them, including Nero, thankfully went off to try to get some sleep wherever they could find an unburnt spot. But in their absence, the flames started up again, this time in the area of a property owned by Tigellinus.

For three more days and nights the chaotic destruction continued. By the end of this period, only four of the fourteen districts had escaped unscathed, including the Trans-Tiber area on the far side of the river. Three districts were almost completely destroyed: that of the Circus Maximus, along with most of the Palatine and the easterly area of Isis and Serapis. Damage was widespread elsewhere, but virtually the whole of the Forum survived, due to the big open space at its heart and the high quality of its predominantly stone and concrete buildings, the exceptions including the Temple of Vesta where Nero had suffered his trembling fit.

Under the pall of smoke and floating debris that hung over the ruins, Romans began to reckon up the cost in terms of material destruction:[26] the ancient Temple of Jupiter Stator, reputed to have been built by Romulus; the Temple of Diana, dating back to the pre-republican age of the kings; the *Atrium Vestae* where the Vestal Virgins lived; the Regia, ascribed to Romulus' successor, Numa Pompilius, which had for centuries been the official residence of the Pontifex Maximus; the original House of Augustus and its palatial successor, the *Domus Tiberiana*, where Caligula had held court; and almost all of Nero's own *Domus Transitoria*, which linked the palace complex on the Palatine with the Gardens of Maecenas on the neighbouring Esquiline Hill.

These were just the most notable of the architectural casualties. Of the human loss of life, nobody knows. Apart from the direct victims of the flames and smoke and collapsing buildings, many more must have succumbed in the days and weeks that followed. The Great Fire of Rome appears to have been the biggest in antiquity. Nero's capital held at least a million people, possibly twice that number. No medieval European city reached such a size. The Great Fire of London of 1666 burnt for only about half as long a time, and was confined to a smaller area with a lower population. It is hard to think of a more devastating inferno in European history than that of Nero's Rome until the fire-storms of the Second World War destroyed Hamburg and Dresden.

Modern historians are virtually unanimous in dismissing the ancient view that Nero started the fire deliberately. It is arguable that, but for the crippling cost of rebuilding the city, thereby imposing unacceptable burdens on the tax-payers, both great and small, he would not have forfeited that essential core of support at the centre of the imperial power structure that was necessary for his survival. Indeed, he worked harder to put out the fire than he had ever worked at anything in his life. He was accused of wanting to destroy the city in order to rebuild it to his own Greek-inspired standards of taste and glamour, but the area that he took over to build his new palace was far from the spot where the blaze actually began.

It was rumoured that gangs of men, claiming to be acting on official orders, had gone around the city feeding the flames and preventing the fire-fighters doing their duty. Further suspicion was added by the fact that the blaze had renewed itself on or near the property of Tigellinus, his right-hand man. Above all, it was alleged that, at the height of the destruction, the Emperor ascended the Tower of Maecenas, wearing a lyre-player's tunic, and sang to his own accompaniment on the cithara of the burning of Troy, with words of his own composition.[27]

This legend of Nero fiddling while Rome burned has taken on a life of its own over the centuries, acquiring proverbial status along the way. It would be vain to imagine that any amount of modern demythologizing will prove capable of debunking it. Historians will, however, continue to ask awkward questions – such as where Nero managed to find either the cithara or the tunic among all the chaos while the fire raged, as he plainly would not have packed them when he jumped on his horse at

Antium in the middle of the night, and the ones he kept in his palace in Rome would presumably already have gone up in smoke. It is certainly possible – even probable, given his histrionic attitudes – that at some stage of the fire-fighting he turned to his nearest companions and quoted a line or two from his Trojan epic. The rest is surely embroidery.

But the falsehoods about Nero and the fire were to have alarming consequences for the followers of his hitherto obscure rival for the loyalty of his subjects – Jesus of Nazareth, once apparently a mere wandering preacher in Palestine, but now the revealed Christ of Faith to a numerous and expanding flock. These men and women, mostly very poor in material circumstances but strong in spirit, were now to take their first steps on the stage of secular history as an identifiable religious group separate from the Judaism from which they had sprung.

ELEVEN

Saving Rome from the Christians

Nero shouldered the task of clearing and rebuilding his shattered city with the same energy that he had shown in fighting the fire. But the religious dimensions of the disaster plunged him immediately into fresh trouble. It was a religious problem as well as a social crisis because of the almost universal ancient belief that disaster on such a scale was due to the anger of the gods. Both the *Iliad* of Homer and the *Oedipus Tyrannus* of Sophocles start with a situation in which a deity is inflicting punishment on ordinary people because of the unacceptable actions of a ruler. Thus it was not simply a question of Nero having to prove that he did not deliberately start the fire himself or order his servants to do so. He also had to prove that the gods who normally protected Rome were not angry with him.

This was close to an impossibility. A straightforward assertion of innocence would not be enough. Oedipus had been innocent; he had been totally unaware that the man he had killed was his father or that the woman he had married was his mother. The gods who had put a blight on his kingdom of Thebes would not lift their curse until he made amends by giving up his crown. Nero was far from innocent, which made him fear the more for his own crown. He had murdered his mother and was suspected of having had an incestuous affair with her. He had ordered the killing of his first wife Octavia, and was widely believed to have murdered his step-brother Britannicus. He was even said, by the ultra-suspicious, to have murdered his young stepson, Rufrius

Crispinus, Poppaea's only child by her first marriage (in fact, the boy drowned while out swimming). He had even profited from the murder of his step-father Claudius by seizing the empire.

In order to hold on to power, therefore, Nero needed to be seen in public actively placating the gods of Rome. In the immediate aftermath of the great fire, the smoke of burnt offerings rose up from the city's remaining altars, to mingle with the clouds of floating ash. Untold numbers of animals were ritually sacrificed as 'sin-offerings' to purge the supposed human guilt. Experts consulted the Sibylline Books, those venerated oracular records of past communications with supernatural forces. They recommended prayers to Vulcan, god of fire, and also to the ancient fertility goddess Ceres and her daughter Proserpine, who spent part of each year in the sulphurous Underworld. 'Then the Roman matrons propitiated Juno, drawing water from the sea at its nearest point to Rome and sprinkling her temple and statue. And married women whose husbands were still alive held the special banquets sacred to the goddesses, and stayed up all night to keep vigils. But neither human works, nor the Emperor's largesse, nor measures to appease the gods could overcome the suspicion of infamy – that the fire had been deliberately started by order.'[1]

Meanwhile, thousands of men, women and children who had lost everything they possessed in the fire were scavenging around the city like walking scarecrows for what they could find. In some cases, even the clothes they had stood up in would have been burned off their backs. Nero had, of course, organized basic charity to provide food and shelter, but that could only have been temporary and is unlikely to have included much professional medical treatment for those suffering from burns and other injuries. It was no consolation to them that Nero was tramping through the ruins with his architects, planning a new inner city of wider streets, with easier access for fire-fighters and easier escape routes for the inhabitants.[2]

In future, the Emperor decreed, all tenement blocks were to be free-standing instead of leaning up against each other. Building regulations were to be tightened to ensure the use of as much flame-resistant material as possible. Each block was to have a special portico in front, to be erected at the Emperor's personal expense, on which firemen could stand when operating their bucket-chains and to make rescue easier from upper floors. These were important reforms, but they did nothing to alleviate current suffering. The fact that Nero had slashed the price of grain in the city by half was of value only to those who still had money to spend on buying back what the fire had taken from them. They focused instead on the Emperor's effective seizure of a huge area of fire-damaged property and land, much greater than the old palace complex, on which he intended to build himself a luxurious new imperial residence and lay out a pleasure park for his personal amusement.[3]

It did not take Nero long to realize that, in spite of his own losses in the fire and his unprecedented efforts for the welfare of his people, he had nevertheless forfeited their goodwill.[4] The sullen faces of the mob caused him both indignation and alarm, and it was fear that was to predominate. Protestations of love for his people fell flat when aimed at destitute men and women who had grown used to his capacity for deceitful as well as unconventional behaviour. The rumour of Nero's guilt in planning the fire would not go away.

To quash the rumour, therefore, Nero substituted other culprits, those commonly known as Christians, who were hated for their disgraceful activities – and he inflicted excruciating punishments on them. Christus, the originator of this name [of Christians], had been executed by the procurator Pontius Pilate during the reign of Tiberius. This deadly superstition, though repressed for a while, was breaking out again, not only in Judaea where the evil originated, but even in the city [of Rome], where all atrocious or shameful things flow in from all sides and flourish. So, at first, those who acknowledged it were arrested, and then by their evidence a great multitude were convicted, not so much for the crime of arson as for their hatred of the human race.[5]

This passage from the *Annals* of Tacitus has been subjected to more scrutiny than any other paragraph of secular historical writing that has come down to us from the ancient world. Not only have historians and classicists laboured over it, but also countless theologians representing every conceivable shade of Christian or Jewish belief – and, more recently, of unbelief or disbelief as well. In the post-Enlightenment quest for the 'historical Jesus', which has now been running for about 200 years, Tacitus' words, however uncomplimentary to Christians, provided a key item of documentary evidence in the case for the defence of the assertion that Jesus had been a real historical figure and not simply a figment of the religious imagination.

In considering it here as a vital document in the case for the prosecution against Nero, we need first to acknowledge that we do not know for certain the names or origins or other identifying features of any of the people who suffered in this Neronian persecution.[6] We know only that they were described as Christians and that they were apparently a 'great multitude'. This has often been assumed to mean that some thousands of them were executed, but the description is vague enough to apply to a much lower figure. To throw further doubt on the numbers involved, the third-century Church Father, Origen, writing of the total of Christian martyrs up to his own time, in Rome and elsewhere, states that there were not many – and that it was easy to count them.[7] The lack of an authentic and specific early Christian source for a mass persecution under Nero is also very odd.

The big questions are: who were the 'Christians' of Rome and why were they thought by Nero to be such appropriate scapegoats? To answer them, we need to look briefly at the troubled history of relations between Romans and Jews since Pompey effectively conquered them in 63 BC, but left them initially as a client state, under the Roman umbrella but not under direct rule. Even when direct rule was, from time to time, imposed over all or part of Palestine, the Senate and the emperors allowed them to live on terms that were not available to any other racial or religious group. Effectively, so long as they paid their taxes and kept the peace, they would be allowed to practice their religion under their own leaders and would not be recruited to serve in the Roman army; in imperial times, also, they were permitted to offer sacrifice to God, in their own Temple, for the benefit of the Emperor, rather than have to conform to the usual Roman rule of sacrificing directly to the divine spirit of the Emperor, which they would have considered sacrilegious, as a breach of the First Commandment to worship only the one God.

By the first century AD, their activities were monitored by a Roman prefect or procurator, appointed directly by the Emperor. This official, who was responsible for overseeing the collection of taxes, was based on the coast at Caesarea, sufficiently far from Jerusalem to maintain some diplomatic illusion of Jewish self-government. He had various small detachments of Roman legionary soldiers on call around the country, including a usually low-profile garrison near the Jerusalem Temple. The fragile nature of this policy of peaceful co-existence is sufficiently demonstrated by the report that when a garrison soldier bared his bottom provocatively during a Jewish procession outside the Temple, no fewer than 30,000 people were killed in the ensuing riots.[8]

However, the 'chief priests', so frequently the subject of uncomplimentary references in the New Testament gospels, undoubtedly did their best in normal times to prevent demonstrations against the colonial power, if only because it was in their material interests to do so. Jerusalem had become a rich city. Money flowed in from the absent Jews of the Diaspora, faithfully fulfilling part of their religious duty by contributing to the upkeep of the Temple, which Herod the Great had rebuilt on the site of Solomon's original structure. The *Pax Romana* ensured the uninterrupted flow of these pious contributions, just as it was to facilitate the spread of the Christian gospel around the Mediterranean world.

The chief priests and their extensive staffs, along with the dove-sellers and the money-changers whose stalls Jesus overturned in the Court of the Gentiles, formed part of a prosperous urban elite. Their authority in the city was enforced by armed guards, one of whom famously lost an ear to St Peter's impulsive sword-play. Elsewhere in Israel, life was very different for the Jewish peasants who formed the great majority of the population. They eked out a hand-to-mouth existence on their stony soil or, in the case of many Galileans, their land-locked sea. They, too, had to pay taxes for the upkeep of the distant Temple as well as to the Roman authorities, out of their subsistence-level incomes, and effectively got little or nothing in return. Yet at the same time they shared the national belief that they were God's chosen people, with all that this implied for their status in relation to the peoples of less favoured nations.

To point up the difference between their dream and the reality of their day-to-day existence, the men from among whom Jesus recruited his disciples had in their midst a large and prosperous Roman colonial city, full of ex-legionaries in receipt of state pensions and living on land seized from the Galileans. This city, Sepphoris, is never mentioned in the New Testament. Yet it was the administrative capital of its region and was situated 4 miles from the obscure village of Nazareth, where Jesus worked as a carpenter in his father's workshop.[9]

It is impossible to believe that there were not economic ties between the two places: the bustling Graeco-Roman city and the Jewish village on its doorstep. What language did they communicate in? Was it in Jesus' native Aramaic? Or was it, perhaps, in the simplified form of Greek which, at that era, was the lingua franca of the Hellenistic world – the very language in which the New Testament came to be written? We cannot be certain. An earlier generation of biblical scholars tended to dismiss the suggestion that Jesus knew any Greek. But the interesting consideration that the village carpenter Joseph and his son may often have worked to provide goods or joinery for local Romans must be quite high on the scale of probabilities. It would help to explain the ready response of Jesus to pharisaical questioning about the duty owed to Rome, when he held up a silver coin with Caesar's head on it and made the terse reply: 'Render unto Caesar the things that are Caesar's, and unto God the things that are God's.'[10]

It is a statement that encapsulates what the Romans demanded of the Jews, but which the Jews, understandably, did not always want to give. Among people who treasured a belief that God was about to send them a Messiah of the line of David to lead them against their enemies, there was an ever-present risk of revolt. When Jesus of Nazareth preached to them of the imminent arrival of God's Kingdom, it was no wonder that his peasant audience heard it as a political as well as a religious message. The Temple authorities moved to eliminate him when he brought his message to Jerusalem at Passover – and indicated its potentially violent nature by making a whip and driving out some of the money-changers.

The notion that Pontius Pilate would have dithered over the ethics of crucifying Jesus stretches credulity. Tiberius was ultimately to dismiss him for cruelty that was considered excessive even by Roman standards. In any case, it was Pilate's duty to suppress agitators. To have allowed Jesus back into the swarming and expectant city, packed with tens of thousands of Passover pilgrims, many of whom were sleeping in the streets, might have triggered an uprising led by his ecstatic supporters, threatening the control of the pro-Roman leadership of the priesthood. Such an outcome would have been badly received in Rome. Modern scholars tend to be sceptical about Pilate's reputed washing of hands and his disclaimer of moral responsibility on behalf of Roman officialdom. It fits too neatly with the desire of the later gospel writers to prove that it was really the Jews alone who were responsible for Jesus' death.[11]

Tacitus unequivocally confirms for us that Pontius Pilate had him executed, and makes no mention of any Jewish involvement in that decision. Thus, when Nero came to consider the evidence against the Christians, he was right to conclude that they were devoted followers of a man who had been legally crucified by a Roman official, acting on behalf of a previous emperor (Tiberius), for treasonable activity in leading what was clearly perceived to have been an anti-Roman movement. They were also 'atheists', as Roman jurists would have understood that term, in that they regarded as devils or demons the very gods and goddesses who were believed to protect the city of Rome, notably

Jupiter and his heavenly consort Juno. And, of course, they would not have wished to sacrifice to the divine spirit of Nero.

Any or all of these offences would have put them in danger of their lives if brought before a Roman court, whether or not they were guilty of arson as well. To compound their felonies, these Christians apparently believed that Jesus, as Messiah and Son of God (a title which Nero cherished for himself), had risen from the dead after crucifixion, and that true believers who called on his name could work miracles – or, as the Romans would have put it, work magic. The penalty for practising magic, even if you were a senator or a member of the royal family, was death.[12]

It is highly unlikely that Nero himself initiated the persecution of Christians. We do not know the precise sequence of events, but it seems natural to suppose that the first few of them would have been brought before a court by officials acting in the normal course of their duties, rather than on special instructions from the palace. If any of those early defendants had been inspired by their faith to defend themselves publicly in apocalyptic terms, incorporating prophecies of the destruction of Rome by heavenly fire, the outcome could hardly have been in doubt in the ravaged city. One can easily see how demands for the punishment of Christians would have mushroomed. Nero had no reason to protect them, but every incentive to acquiesce in a legal process of condemnation and punishment which would serve to reduce the level of superstitious public anger against himself.

It was not necessary, therefore, for a Roman magistrate to believe the wilder rumours of Christians eating babies at secret ceremonies and drinking their blood. The ceremony of the Eucharist, misunderstanding of which evidently gave rise to such bizarre reports, can scarcely escape falling within the definition of a magical rite. It is a procedure whereby natural substances, bread and wine, are supposedly changed, by the recital of a verbal formula by a suitably qualified person, into something supernatural, during the course of a sacred ritual. We do not know precisely how the Christians of Nero's Rome conducted their services, but it is an obvious supposition that some such ritual took place. Early Christians were also undoubtedly given to prophesying the imminent end of the world. Or, as Jesus himself is recorded as saying: 'I have cast fire upon the world, and see, I am guarding it until it blazes.'[13]

This quotation from the non-canonical 'Gospel of Thomas', attributed to the disciple Thomas Didymus – the 'doubting Thomas' who insisted on seeing before believing – raises a question that earlier generations of scholars perhaps thought needed only a short answer: who, in historical fact, were these Christians whom Nero was persecuting? The natural assumption, fostered by innumerable novels and films, is that the followers of Jesus Christ in Rome at this date were all members of a doctrinally uniform and mutually sympathetic group. That view, sadly, is no longer tenable. Even though only about thirty years had passed since the crucifixion, the new movement had already split into rival sects, not all of which had detached themselves from Judaism. The old, contentious question of whether or not St Peter was the first 'Bishop of Rome' is fading in importance under the weight of scholarly research into the nature of primitive Christianity, as the quest for the historical Jesus begins to merge with the quest for the historical church.

There is no space here even to summarize the many recent developments in a field being intensively investigated by hundreds of academics across the world, but it is vital to grasp the nature of the issues at stake. The two great discoveries of biblical archaeology in the 1940s – of the 'library' of Coptic manuscripts found at Nag Hammadi in Upper Egypt, and of the Dead Sea scrolls in Judaea – have finally led to a radical revision of what was previously known of first-century Judaism and Jesus' place within it.[14] They have also opened up strange new perspectives on the early church and its internal power struggles over such matters as leadership, gnosticism, apocalyptic prophecies and the central doctrine of the resurrection. It is not simply that an enormous amount of new information has had to be processed, but that its existence has caused scholars to question afresh some traditional interpretations of familiar passages in the canonical works as well.

The Nag Hammadi manuscripts have been dated to the late

fourth century, but have mostly been identified as Coptic translations of much earlier material. A minority of scholars believe that the Gospel of Thomas originated at about the same time as (possibly even earlier than) those attributed to Matthew, Mark, Luke and John. Thomas' seems to have been less a 'lost gospel' and more of a suppressed one. In the campaigns against heresy – especially after the formation of the later ruling system of bishops, priests and deacons – mainstream Christians sought out and deliberately destroyed such texts, which often conflicted sharply with the canonical accounts. Majority opinion among modern 'Jesus of history' scholars is that probably none of the gospels, canonical or otherwise, were actually *written* by any of Jesus' disciples. However, they may have been at least partly based on their oral testimony.[15]

The evidence is now overwhelming that the evolution of Christianity as a religion separate from Judaism was much more gradual than has traditionally been supposed. It is anachronistic as well as illogical to attempt to describe Jesus as the first Christian when he was quite obviously a Jew. He was not trying to found a new religion. He was trying to prepare the people of Israel for an imminent manifestation of God's power over the whole world. His message, although universal in implication, was one of restricted salvation. He compared those who were not fully practising Jews to dogs attempting to take bread from children. And the proverbial swine, before whom he deemed it inappropriate to cast pearls, were evidently to be found among the Gentiles.[16]

They can scarcely have been Jewish, since his declared mission was to the lost sheep of Israel, the sinners as well as the righteous. It becomes less of a mystery, therefore, that Jesus should have turned his back on the Graeco-Roman city of Sepphoris, just up the road from his home, to make the much longer journey to the Jewish villages around the Sea of Galilee, where he chiefly recruited his disciples. Those disciples, of course, were Jews. So were the people on whom the Holy Spirit is reported to have descended at the first Pentecost. Under St Peter, the Bible tells us, their numbers multiplied among those who worshipped at the Temple in Jerusalem.[17]

When St Paul saw the light on the road to Damascus it did not result in his conversion from Judaism to a new religion. He remained a Jew, even at the height of his activities as 'Apostle to the Gentiles'. He told members of his new flock in Galatia, Asia Minor: 'If ye be Christ's, then ye are Abraham's seed, and heirs according to the promise.' In other words, the message of salvation through Christ, which St Paul preached to both Gentiles and Jews, followed on logically from God's original covenant with Abraham, in whom 'all nations shall be blessed'. His missionary activities around Nero's Empire were designed at least partly to *add* to the number of God's chosen people, side by side with the Jews, not at their expense.[18]

But by the time the four New Testament gospels and the Acts of the Apostles were written the situation had changed. Now it had apparently become the turn of the Christians to be the favoured people of God, with the Jews often cast in the role of the main opposition. The Gospel of St John, almost certainly the last to be written, went even further and presented Christ as the co-eternal Son of God the Father and a participant in the creation of the universe, aeons before Abraham was born or the Jews were ever heard of.[19] That is a position utterly at variance with Jewish monotheism.

Perhaps the strangest thing is that none of the gospels, nor even the Acts of the Apostles, makes the slightest reference to the persecution by Nero of any Christians at Rome, let alone 'a great multitude' of them; these canonical writers all appear to go out of their way to be complimentary about the Romans as compared with Jews. It is a Roman centurion, for example, who is credited by St Luke with being the first to accord inspired recognition to Jesus at the moment of his death on the cross: 'He glorified God, saying, "Certainly this was a righteous man".'[20] Yet all four canonical gospels, with the possible exception of St Mark's, are now generally believed to have been written shortly *after* the reign of Nero, who also ordered the execution, according to church tradition, of both St Peter and St Paul, possibly in 67, the year before Nero's death.

Why are all these many martyrdoms, including two of such

significance, not mentioned? Several explanations suggest themselves. First, the overwhelming majority of world experts on the dating of New Testament writings may have got it hopelessly wrong, and the four gospels and Acts were written before Nero persecuted the Christians. Secondly, and more plausibly, it might have been Tacitus who was mistaken, and there was no substantial persecution of Christians; he is the only one who mentions a 'great multitude' of victims, and who connects their punishment with prosecution over the fire. Suetonius simply records: 'Punishment was meted out to the Christians, a class of men professing a new and wicked (*malefica*) superstition.'[21] If it were not for Tacitus' more detailed account, we would certainly interpret this passing reference by Suetonius as meaning that the Christians were being persecuted for their faith alone, but we would not be able to assume either that they were executed or that they were many in number.

A third possibility is that the victims were not members of that section of early Christianity which produced the canonical gospels and the Acts of the Apostles, and that went on to triumph over the other branches. They might, for instance, have been gnostic Christians,[22] whose bizarre beliefs are so strongly represented in the Nag Hammadi manuscripts, and whose early leader was the charismatic Simon Magus. They might have been Jewish Christians or Christian Jews, still practising male circumcision, of whom substantial numbers were still to be found in Jerusalem at this period, under the leadership of members of Jesus' own family, who had taken over there from St Peter.[23]

Far more Jews than Christians were living in Rome at the time of the Neronian persecutions. They had a number of Gentile supporters in high places, including the Empress Poppaea. Josephus, the Jewish historian, travelled to Italy to plead on behalf of a group of his fellow countrymen who had been arrested after a riot in Israel. Poppaea, whom he describes as a religious woman, received him sympathetically and pledged herself to save them. It has been suggested that she took such a partisan line in favour of Jews that she might even have persuaded the Emperor to begin the persecution of Christians. But there is no hard evidence – any more than there is for the romantic suggestion that Nero's first mistress, Acté, was a Christian who tried to convert him.

A measure of the difficulty of identifying precisely who was who in the seething religious underworld of imperial Rome is illustrated by an earlier brief reference by Suetonius, stating that Claudius expelled the Jews from the city for 'continual turbulence at the instigation of Chrestus'. This must surely be a reference to Christ, and almost all scholars assume that to be the case, but the wording of the passage makes it sound as if 'Chrestus' is a contemporary Jew who is stirring up his co-religionists in person. The author of the Acts of the Apostles, traditionally identified as being also the author of St Luke's Gospel, refers to Claudius' expulsion of the Jews from Rome but gives no reason for it. He certainly does not mention 'Chrestus' as being the inciter of the trouble.[24]

That leads us to a fourth possible explanation, which is that the later New Testament writers deliberately omitted mention of Roman persecution of Christians in order not to offend the masters of the secular world, whose co-operation they were anxious to win. By that time, after all, Nero was dead and it was the Jews who had just felt the full force of Rome's anger. Under the Emperor Vespasian and his son, Titus, who was also his successor, most of the population of Jerusalem was massacred after a long siege. The Romans destroyed and looted the Temple, expunged the name of Jerusalem from the map, and built a new city on its ruins.[25] Thus, the post-Neronian Christians had nothing to lose and everything to gain by seeking to ingratiate themselves with the Romans, and they had nothing to fear from attacking the recently crushed and decimated Jews.

If we do not, today, recognize the early Christians under such an unjust description as followers of a wicked superstition who hate the human race, that is because we are looking at them with the benefit of hindsight instead of through the eyes of Tacitus, Suetonius and Nero, who for once seem to be in agreement. If belief in Jesus Christ was the only route to salvation in a world that was on the point of being purged by divine fire, then it seemed to follow that those who did not share this belief were doomed, at best, to a horrible death, and at worst to everlasting torment in Hell. The offer of such saving belief might very well be freely available to all; but Romans would have to be prepared to repudiate the system of interlocking beliefs, traditions and practices that had raised their nation to its pre-eminent position and which continued to sustain it. Loyalty to the Emperor would have to be replaced by submission to an evidently fearsome and vengeful deity, who was personified in some mysterious manner by a corpse that got up and walked away after being executed in Rome's name by due legal process.

A strong element of ill-wishing is apparent in the apocalyptic beliefs of both Jews and Christians in the imminent destruction of secular Roman power. Whether they were an exploited subject people like the Jews, or whether they were socially despised or even enslaved, as so many of the earliest Christians seem to have been, their longing to triumph over their enemies is blatant and unashamed. Jesus may have taught some of them to love their enemies and turn the other cheek, but hatred, in the guise of righteous indignation, flows in waves out of the apocalyptic literature, including the canonical Revelation of John. These authors cannot wait for the ethical cleansing to begin.[26]

As for the Christian doctrine of the bodily resurrection of the dead, that would have seemed to Nero and most other Romans to smack of the most frightening and malevolent forms of black magic. They readily accepted the existence of incorporeal ghosts and other spirits, and they performed various rites to ward off or propitiate them. But the idea of corpses that walked and talked would have had for them a resonance similar to later generations' fears of necromancy, witchcraft and vampirism. This would have applied especially to a body that had been nailed to a cross, because Roman practice was to feed the corpses of crucified offenders to animals. It was part of the punishment that they should be deprived not only of their lives in this world but also of their chances of happiness in the next, which the sacred rites of burial were widely believed to confer.

An anecdote in the *Satyricon*, told as a flesh-creeping joke, underlines the point. A soldier, ordered to guard a newly crucified young man, hears strange cries at night from an adjacent burial ground and believes they are made by a ghost. But when he investigates he finds an attractive widow inside a vault, who is starving herself to death in mourning for her dead husband. As several days and nights pass, the soldier comforts her so effectively that she gives up the suicide plan and becomes his lover. But in his absence from his post, the parents of the crucified man steal their son's corpse from the cross to give it proper burial. The soldier, in despair, draws his sword to kill himself, but is stopped by the woman, who offers her husband's body as a substitute. Gratefully, he nails it to the cross, and they live happily ever after.[27]

This story demonstrates the security conscious routine of crucifixion, the pressing desire of relatives to bury a loved one in spite of the risks, and the soldier's preference for suicide over whatever form of physical and capital punishment would await him for the offence of losing a felon's corpse. It also shows the difficulty of being able to bribe the soldier to release the body. A grieving relative would need enough to bribe his superior officer as well, and any other officials whose duty it was to witness both death and appropriate disposal. Secrecy would also be required in order to avoid denunciation by any bystanders, who, under the Roman system, stood to receive payment for information leading to conviction. These are among the reasons why some scholars are rather less than certain about the authenticity of accounts of Pilate permitting Joseph of Arimathaea to take down Jesus' body from the cross and carry it openly to a tomb, watched by a group of women including Mary Magdalene.[28]

Nero's likely reaction to the resurrection story would have been either total disbelief or superstitious dread. In either case he would have considered it a fully justified act of his imperial authority to condemn such dangerous subjects to death, making a public example of them. 'The way they died served as an amusement,' Tacitus reports. 'Some were covered in the skins of wild animals and mangled by dogs. Others were nailed to crosses or set on fire, to be used as torches at night after daylight failed. Nero opened up his own gardens for this spectacle, and also provided games in his circus, fraternising with the common people while mounted on his chariot, dressed as a charioteer. Although they were guilty and deserved exemplary punishment, they were nevertheless pitied as if they were being killed not for the welfare of the state but on account of one man's cruelty.'[29]

Tacitus is surely mistaken in ascribing Nero's motives to cruelty, in view of the Emperor's lifelong record of seeking to avoid such displays, except where reasons of state required it. His primary motive was to shift the blame for the fire from himself, as Tacitus had acknowledged in an earlier sentence. Suetonius lists the punishment of the Christians among Nero's good deeds, not his bad ones;[30] that must indicate widespread support for the persecution. After all, if the world is about to end in flames from which only certain Christians will be saved, a rough guess would indicate that throughout Nero's Empire as many as ninety-nine people in every hundred could expect damnation. Although there is no surviving evidence to suggest that Christians actually started the fire, it would not have been unreasonable if the public had suspected them of helping it along once the flames had taken hold, believing they were accelerating the divine plan from which they alone expected to benefit.[31]

The punishments inflicted on the Christians were horrific but not unusual. Being burnt alive was the time-honoured penalty for arson, as it has been in many other societies. Juvenal asserts that people who offended Tigellinus, for whatever reason, could end up in a flaming shirt in the arena.[32] Criminals were regularly torn to pieces by dogs and other animals for public entertainment. Crucifixion was, of course, a normal punishment for slaves and lower-class non-citizens. The Neronian persecution of Christians was an isolated phenomenon, not repeated elsewhere in the Empire at that time; but it was the forerunner of later group martyrdoms, ordered by emperors who would not have Nero's justification of punishing them for arson. Even emperors who stopped short of persecution had no scruples about executing people if they were brought before a court and obstinately persisted in their 'disloyal' beliefs.

The classic position is set out in an exchange of letters between Pliny the Younger and the Emperor Trajan in about 112, at a time when both Tacitus and Suetonius were active.[33] Trajan says that Christians are not to be sought out for punishment, and that if they come up in court they must be given the opportunity of clearing themselves by formal denial, no matter how compromising their previous conduct may have been – so long as they also offer up the required prayers to the Roman gods. But refusal would mean death. It was easy in such times, therefore, to avoid martyrdom, for which they would have only themselves to blame. Yet untold numbers of anonymous individuals chose instead to embrace it. And it was their blood, quietly offered and brutally taken, which proved to be the seed of the church.

Whether or not the author of the Revelation of John intended to identify Nero as Antichrist, the beast with the number 666, that identification has been the popular choice among his readers ever since.[34] Both Greek and Hebrew, like Latin, use letters of their alphabets to represent numbers, and it has been confidently asserted that 'Nero Caesar', translated or transliterated into one or other of those languages, will work out to 666. The details of the calculation, however, remain obscure. What is beyond doubt is the excitement that the supposedly saintly author shows when contemplating the fate of all those sinners about to be trampled on by the Four Horsemen of the Apocalypse or plunged into a pit of everlasting fire.

Nero's decision, inspired by fear, to apply the laws of his country to a tiny, obstinate and deeply misunderstood minority, was by comparison neither malevolent nor deranged. Although cruel by most (but not all) modern standards, it was an attempt to restore public confidence in his government, inhibit future attacks of arson and placate the gods. There is no reason to suppose that any other Roman emperor before Constantine, faced with similar circumstances, would have treated them less severely. If the Second Coming prophesied by John of the Apocalypse, involving the immolation of almost the entire population of Rome, reflected the true aspirations of his fellow Christians in that city, Nero could quite reasonably claim to be acting in the interests of the vast majority of his subjects. They and their Emperor can hardly be blamed for wanting to go on living.

TWELVE

THE PLOT THAT FAILED

Persecution of the Christians as scapegoats may have helped to dampen down any stirrings of potential revolt among the population as a whole. But among a small and unrepresentative section of the elite a murderous conspiracy had long been ripening, and was about to come to a head. Its roots can be traced back to the aftermath of Seneca's removal (or retreat) from the Emperor's side. Late in 62 an informer, known only as Romanus, laid 'private accusations' (*secretae criminationes*) against Seneca, linking him with a prominent senator of distinguished lineage, Gnaeus Calpurnius Piso.[1] Because they were secret, we do not know what these accusations comprised, but Seneca was able to rebut them so convincingly that it was Romanus himself who was punished. Later events, however, were to indicate that the luckless Romanus had indeed stumbled upon treachery – if not yet by Seneca, then certainly by Calpurnius Piso.

One reason why Nero had been unable to believe that Seneca and Piso were in league against him was that they were such contrasting characters. Seneca quite obviously disapproved of Piso for much the same reasons that he had come to disapprove of Nero. The idea that he would support Piso in a bid for the imperial purple simply made no sense. It is true that both men were celebrated orators who wrote poetry in their spare time, and both had been exiled by Caligula, but there the resemblance ended. Piso had no time for the puritanical Stoic philosophy professed by Seneca. Far from being associated with the senatorial opposition, which certainly contained a Stoic leavening, he was outwardly a committed Neronian. As a boon companion of the young Emperor, he joined with enthusiasm in his disreputable parties and other social events, and was regarded as a pillar of the court.

According to Tacitus, this tall, good-looking, highly bred Roman aristocrat was a lover of 'frivolity, magnificence and sporadic debauchery'.[2] In imitation of Nero, Piso even took to the stage as an actor, performing numerous roles and revelling in the applause. The Emperor not only enjoyed his sophisticated company at court in Rome, but also went on holiday with him to Baiae, where Piso had a villa on the beach, not far from the imperial residence. They and their wives bathed together and played in the sun. Nero was so heedless of danger that he made a point of leaving his bodyguard behind when he and Poppaea visited the rich and fashionable Piso.

The Emperor's mistake was to misread the character of his 'friend' and believe that he shared his Epicurean outlook. He assumed that Piso's main interest in life, like his own, was to enjoy himself and to practise his art, which, for Nero, tended to amount to the same thing. In fact, the senator was seething with personal resentment against the imperial family; Caligula, for instance, had stolen his wife before exiling him. In a sense, therefore, Nero was being set up, at least in part, to pay for the undeniable sins of his mad uncle.

Romanus' warning about Piso was quickly forgotten as the day-to-day relationship between Emperor and senator continued to be so agreeable – at least on the surface. Nero never dreamt that Piso, having temporarily postponed his projected assassination attempt, was lulling him into a false sense of security, while patiently undermining his regime from within. The senator's ready smile concealed the long-term game plan of waiting until such time as it should prove safe to stab him in the back and step over his corpse to ascend the throne.

Seneca, of course, was not fooled. He had given up on Nero, but he saw no compelling reason to betray Piso to a regime he now despised. Equally, he refused to endanger himself by renewing an obviously dangerous liaison with such a man and such a cause. Piso, however, continued to hope for Seneca's support. The fire of Rome greatly increased the number of the

Emperor's opponents; and it is evident that in the latter half of 64 and early in 65 the senator was able to recruit among those members of the ruling class whose land had been requisitioned for the site of the new palace complex. They were being ruthlessly taxed to pay for the building work, even though they had lost their own homes. It was during this period that, in spite of earlier rebuffs, Piso made another serious attempt to recruit Seneca, too, in order to add political weight to his team – a quality that its membership conspicuously lacked.

Piso chose as his emissary a man well known to both of them, Antonius Natalis, a knight with a talent for backstairs intrigue. Seneca heard him out, and then invented an imaginary illness to explain why he had hitherto been unable to receive Piso in person and why he would be unlikely to manage to meet him in the foreseeable future. Nobody knows, of course, exactly what sort of proposition or alliance Natalis had suggested to him. The most that the diplomatic knight was able to take back to his patron was a verbal assurance, which reads rather oddly, to the effect that his (Seneca's) safety was dependent on that of Piso.[3] It may be that the old philosopher, at that stage, was simply hoping to ensure his own survival in the unlikely event of Piso's success.

Seneca's evident decision to take a hand in the affair was probably triggered by the actions of his nephew, Annaeus Lucanus (the poet 'Lucan'), who joined the conspiracy as an active and voluble partisan.[4] That put Seneca in some jeopardy. If the plot should fail and Lucan were to be arrested, Nero and Tigellinus would connect the young man's participation to the original allegation by Romanus of a compromising link between Seneca and Piso. Although he was only twenty-five, two years younger than the Emperor, Lucan had already amply demonstrated that he was the most talented and prolific poet of his era. Unfortunately, he had an ego to match. Posterity has judged him to have been second only to Virgil as a writer of verse epic in Latin. It is easy to understand the outrage he felt when Nero banned him from effectively 'publishing' his work by giving readings.[5]

The problem was Lucan's extreme republicanism, although

Tacitus is eager to blame Nero's jealousy. But the Emperor had been a keen admirer until Lucan began to peddle a political view, which, if taken to its logical conclusion, could only end with a latter-day disciple of Brutus and Cassius plunging a dagger into Nero Caesar's back. There had apparently been no suspicion of what Lucan's muse was inspiring him to do until the occasion of his first public reading of the opening books of what has proved to be his most celebrated surviving work, the epic *Pharsalia*.

This poem treats of the civil war between Julius Caesar and the senatorial forces, in which Pompey and the Stoic hero Cato the Younger are fighting to save the Roman Republic from Caesar's unprincipled attempts to destroy it. Nero and many of his courtiers came to the reading, and certainly approved of a brief early passage praising the young Emperor as Caesar's descendant;[6] but as the reading continued, and the emphasis on Caesar's tyranny was contrasted so strongly with the supposedly pure and noble cause of liberty, claimed to be represented by the old republican system, Nero got up and walked out, saying he had urgent public business to attend to.[7]

Lucan's response was to write a lampoon of Nero, which he carried with him around the city, reading out choice lines to friends. Any of the previous emperors would have banished or even executed him for that, so the decision to silence him in public was, by comparison, merciful. It was certainly a lesser penalty than the exile imposed for a similar offence on Antistius Sostius, who, it will be remembered, fortunately escaped a move by some senators to have him flogged to death. Nero did not try to stop Lucan continuing to write his offending epic, which ultimately stretched to more than 8,000 lines in 10 books, of which the later ones demonstrate a more extreme political position than ever.

If Seneca feared that Lucan's rage, allied to his anti-imperial opinions, might lead to the destruction of his own family, the old philosopher proved to be only too prescient. The poet's father, the wealthy knight Marcus Annaeus Mela, one of Seneca's younger brothers, either had no control over him, or may even have supported him. Fatally, Lucan had the backing of Mela's lively mistress, the Greek freedwoman Epicharus. Her misjudged intervention was to precipitate a crisis, but it was one that could not have been indefinitely postponed. In the event, she was to become the unforeseen heroine of the story. There were to be no heroes.[8]

Meanwhile, a disaffected Praetorian tribune, Subrius Flavus, had been sounding out fellow officers about their views of Nero's controversial behaviour. His chief success was to suborn his own commander, Faenius Rufus, who nominally shared control of the Guards with Tigellinus. Rufus had been a long-standing protégé of Agrippina. As a former Prefect of the Corn Supply of Rome, he had worked closely with both Burrus and Seneca in their days of unchallenged influence. He feared and hated Tigellinus, whom he believed was scheming to remove him from office. At some stage Rufus, Subrius and a handful of other officers, both tribunes and centurions, came into contact with Piso and his small senatorial and knightly group. Which group approached the other first is not known, but the subsequent intermediary may well have been Natalis, who, as a knight, was on the same social level as the prefect and his tribunes. Whereas it might have aroused suspicion for Piso to be seen conferring with Rufus, Seneca could safely dine with the prefect on the natural basis of their long professional association.

The fundamental problem for both groups, senatorial and Praetorian, was that neither could act without the guaranteed support of the other. The assassination of Caligula had shown that a guardsman who wielded the dagger would be executed by whoever became the next emperor – unless that person was the imperial candidate for whom the assassin could prove he was working. Equally, the candidate himself could not do it, and nor could any of his associates, without the armed protection of the Praetorian Guard. It would be impossible to reconcile these two imperatives without total trust between the two principals. The long gap between Piso's declared intention and his attempted coup shows by what measure that trust was lacking.

The stalemate was inadvertently broken by Epicharus, the former slave who was the lover of Annaeus Mela, the poet

Lucan's father. She can have had very little to gain in comparison with the potential rewards open to the men she served, but she had everything to lose. In March 65, eight months after the fire, she went to see a ship's captain, Volusius Proculus, who was based with the Roman fleet at Misenum, near the Bay of Baiae, where Nero was about to start his spring holiday by the seaside. One source claims that Epicharus was a former prostitute; if so, that would not necessarily be to her discredit, as slaves had no choice at all in the matter. It would, however, explain her 'cover', now that she was a favoured freedwoman, for fraternizing with one of the imperial sailors.

Proculus had played a supporting role in the murder of Agrippina six years earlier. He had been heard complaining that he had been passed over for promotion in spite of his valuable services. He may, indeed, have been one of the incompetent bunglers who had manned the collapsible boat – in which case it would not be surprising if Nero had been less than generous to him. Epicharus listened patiently to his complaints in order to draw him into her net. When she was convinced that he would be prepared to act against the Emperor for a large enough reward, she tried to recruit him to join the conspiracy. Presumably her plan, or that of her backers, was for Nero to be drowned at sea. That would certainly have been an act of poetic justice.

Neither Lucan nor his father would have known about Proculus' past villainy, because Seneca would scarcely have been so indiscreet as to tell even members of his own family such dangerous state secrets. In first-century Rome, careless talk could, and did, cost lives. It seems likely, therefore, that it was Seneca himself who had suggested targeting Proculus, although whether he had nominated Epicharus for the task must be open to doubt. She was plainly not up to the job. Either she exceeded her instructions or she was a bad judge of men. Proculus, calculating that it would be much safer and possibly just as rewarding if he stuck with Nero, reported her to the Emperor for treason.

Epicharus had not mentioned any names to Proculus and stoutly denied his accusations. Evidently Tigellinus had not been invited to accompany Nero to Baiae, or she would surely have been handed over to the torturers there and then. Nero simply ordered her to be held in custody in case evidence should turn up to corroborate this allegation of an aristocratic plot against his life. Proculus and Epicharus were so far from being aristocratic that it must have seemed to him to be a very unlikely story. He evidently did not know of the connection with Seneca's family, and she certainly never told him. But her detention caused shock waves among the two loosely connected groups of conspirators.

Seneca's secret involvement now faced the threat of imminent exposure; and it is clear that Epicharus also knew the identity of Piso and some of his associates, probably through the common link with Lucan. Very few people were ever able to withstand the attentions of the imperial torturers. Rufus and Seneca, who must have witnessed many such scenes of anguish, knew they could not safely wait in hope of Epicharus remaining silent once she fell into their hands. Usually the mere sight of the instruments of torture was enough to loosen a woman's tongue. An emergency plan was therefore proposed, for Piso to murder Nero the next time he came unescorted to his beachside villa. If Piso had been willing to attempt it, there can be little doubt that Nero would have died on the spot, probably along with Poppaea.

Why did Piso hold back? The excuse he gave to his fellow-conspirators was that, whatever the danger of delay, an assassination in such circumstances would constitute an unacceptable breach of the sacred laws of hospitality. The real reason, however, seems to have been his fear that, when Nero was safely dead, one of Piso's rivals in Rome would take advantage of his absence at Baiae to seize power and have him killed in his turn. Tacitus suggests that such a contender could have been Lucius Silanus (son of the 'golden sheep'), now the last living male descendant of Augustus, apart from Nero himself. One of the two current consuls, Marcus Vestinus Atticus, was also perceived by some to be enough of an opportunist to try and seize the Principate, ready to use the legitimate legal powers of his office to issue orders to the Praetorians, who would be divided at the top by opposing prefects.

But the strongest probability – a matter which Tacitus records as a rumour, while Dio asserts it as a fact – is that Seneca had already earmarked that role for himself, with the support of those sections of the Guards under Rufus that were led by Subrius and at least five other tribunes whom he had persuaded to join the conspiracy. They could easily have arranged for one of their number to ride post-haste from Baiae to Rome ahead of Piso with the news of Nero's death. Their first priority, after hailing Seneca as Emperor, would have been to dispose of the hated Tigellinus, and purge their ranks of his cronies. Seneca would have called on the Senate to ratify his elevation, while distancing himself from the assassins at Baiae. Piso's chances of survival in those circumstances would have been slim indeed. As Subrius was to say later: what would have been the point of replacing a lyre-player like Nero with a stage actor (*tragoedus*) like Piso?

In the event, Piso's refusal to strike down the Emperor at Baiae, where the crime might have been concealed for several hours, forced the plotters to opt for the much riskier alternative of stabbing him to death in public in Rome – like Julius Caesar and Caligula before him. They chose for the attempt the biggest and most crowded venue in the city, the Circus Maximus, which had been restored to new glory since the fire. The occasion was to be the final day of the Festival of Ceres, April 19, when everyone wore white and libations of milk and honey were offered to the fertile goddess of fields and crops. Piso did not intend to stain his own immaculate toga with blood. His role would be to wait in the Temple of Salus ('safety') until, as he hoped, Rufus should come to hail him as Caesar and lead him off with a triumphal escort to the Praetorian camp for formal acclamation. We may be confident once again, however, that Rufus had planned a different finale. He would find it much more profitable to leave the expendable Piso waiting at the altar of the temple while he proclaimed his old friend Seneca.

The chief active parts in this revised assassination plot were assigned by Piso to three senators. Plautus Lateranus, consul-elect and a former lover of the Empress Messalina, was to kneel down suddenly before Nero and clasp his knees in the traditional manner of someone entreating a favour. Flavius Scaevinus – a close friend of the writer Petronius and as dissolute as any character in the *Satyricon* – was to step forward as the muscular Lateranus threw Nero on to his back and stab him as he lay helpless on the ground. Afranius Quintianus, whom Nero had satirized in verse because of his paedophile tastes, would back up Scaevinus' attack, while the escort of disaffected guards would prevent the crowd or other soldiers from rescuing the Emperor.

The weak link among this louche trio proved to be Scaevinus. In a series of histrionic gestures, he took an antique dagger from the Temple of Fortune and handed it to his freedman, Milichus, on the evening before the planned assassination, with instructions to sharpen it – and to provide sets of bandages for the following day. As if these were not strong enough clues to his intentions, Scaevinus held an especially sumptuous dinner party that night, rewrote his will, freed several of his favourite slaves and gave a range of gifts to various other servants. After the rest of the household had gone to bed, Milichus sat up with his wife, anxiously discussing his dilemma while they prepared the bandages. He knew that if his patron intended to murder the Emperor, and if the plot failed, he would almost certainly be tortured for evidence and then executed for being the man who had sharpened the dagger.

His wife pointed out to Milichus that all the other servants were aware that something criminal was being planned, and that he had better tell the Emperor before someone else did so. That, at least, should ensure his survival. In addition, he would stand to get a big reward, which would set both of them up for life. So at dawn she and Milichus presented themselves at Nero's temporary quarters – his new palace was still being built – and talked their way in to see Nero's confidential secretary, Epaphroditus, who was a freedman like Milichus himself.

The Emperor was still asleep. Beside his bed was a doll, in the form of a little girl, which an anonymous hand had thrust into his own at the festive celebrations the previous day. Whatever the identity of the man who had handed the doll to him – and a search afterwards failed to track him down – he had said: 'Take it, Caesar! You need never fear a conspiracy while you keep it near you.' When Epaphroditus led Milichus and his wife into the imperial presence, displaying the antique dagger with its newly sharpened point, Nero began to wonder if the mysterious doll did, indeed, possess magical powers.

Scaevinus was immediately arrested, but lied so plausibly that matters remained in the balance until Milichus' wife reminded her husband that his patron had been closeted for some hours the previous day with Natalis, who was well known to be Piso's representative. This information led directly to the unravelling of the plot. When Natalis was brought in, he was questioned separately from Scaevinus. Their conflicting answers demonstrated their guilt, and on being shown the instruments of torture, Natalis named both Piso and Seneca as the chief conspirators.

The self-seeking treachery of Piso was a great shock to Nero. It made him question the loyalty even of those senators who had hitherto consistently behaved in a friendly way towards him. But the thought that Seneca had been plotting to have him murdered, if true, seemed the ultimate betrayal. The philosopher had been unofficially *in loco parentis* towards him during the most formative period of his life. If Nero had felt obliged to shake off his influence when he reached a certain stage of maturity, that had been no more than a natural reaction by a young ruler whose unique position virtually forced him to demonstrate his capacity to wield power without the constant help and advice of his childhood tutor. Nero had murdered his mother for a reason that was not dissimilar. Would he now be obliged to kill this father-figure, too?

The Emperor held back, at first, from striking down Seneca, but in his fear and anger he dispatched an execution squad to deal with Piso, without waiting to hear what the man might have to say. He may already have heard, through Tigellinus' network of agents, that Piso's friends had urged him – as soon as news of the first arrests emerged – to go to the Rostrum in the Forum and call on the people to rise up against tyranny. Even though he would probably fail, those friends had said, it would be better than waiting for the guards to arrest him, too; at least his name would then go down to posterity as one who had died fighting to restore republican liberty.

Piso, however, found he had no stomach for such an effort. His main motives had not included the restoration of the Republic but had been his own personal ambition and desire for revenge; these were not enough to sustain him in the crisis he had himself provoked. He simply abandoned those whom he had persuaded to risk their lives in support of his pretensions to imperial power. The man who had risen from his bed that morning hoping to become emperor, now went meekly back to it. When the Praetorian Guards hammered at his door he cut open the arteries in his arms and bled to death.

By now, both Tigellinus and Poppaea were at Nero's side, effectively constituting the sort of private law court behind closed doors that Nero had promised the Senate he would never employ. His two fellow 'judges' would naturally have called for Seneca's execution. Poppaea believed it had been chiefly Seneca's influence that had delayed her rise to become Empress. Tigellinus knew him as a formidable political enemy, but had hitherto been prevented from acting against him because of imperial protection. Both wanted revenge. Yet Nero still hesitated. He told a Praetorian tribune, Gavius Silvanus, to call on Seneca and ask what he had to say. If he was indeed guilty, as Natalis had claimed, he would no doubt commit suicide, without the need for a warrant. What the Emperor did not know was that Silvanus himself was one of the conspirators. At this stage of the inquiry, none of the civilian plotters had yet incriminated any of the guards.

Seneca, too, had been 'on holiday' in Campania, and it was only on the eve of the planned assassination that he had returned, and then only to the outskirts of Rome, where he had a property some 4 miles from the city. It provided him with a base to move quickly to the centre of affairs – or to remain at a safer distance if the plot should misfire. Nero's mistaken choice of Silvanus as his interrogator enabled Seneca to remain calm and composed while he sketched out a plausible reply. But by the time the Praetorian tribune brought it back to Nero, he found there had been ominous developments. The chief assassin, Scaevinus, realizing after Natalis' confession that he was in an impossible situation, had tried to save his skin by denouncing three of his senatorial associates: Lateranus, Quintianus and the poet Lucan.

The involvement of Seneca's nephew, Lucan, seemed to confirm the original accusation. Silvanus formally presented Seneca's defensive reply to Nero, Poppaea and Tigellinus, but the outcome could no longer be in doubt. They sent Silvanus back with a warrant for the philosopher's suicide or execution. Nothing demonstrates more clearly the Praetorians' intention to elevate Seneca instead of Piso than the fact that Silvanus risked his life by not delivering the warrant straight away. He made a detour to show it to his commander, Faenius Rufus, and ask if he should obey it. That in itself was a treasonable act. Rufus told him to carry out the Emperor's order; their priority now must be to avoid exposure. On receiving the warrant, Seneca observed bitterly: 'Nero murdered his mother and brother. Now he has nothing worse left to do than kill his foster-father and mentor.'[9] Then, surrounded by family and friends, he opened his veins.

By this time another prisoner had been brought before the Emperor's private court – one who had already been in custody for a month. Epicharus, the mistress of Seneca's brother Mela, was shown the instruments of torture but refused to say on whose behalf she had tried to suborn the naval captain, Proculus, at Misenum. Her continued silence – while the male prisoners vied with each other to betray their associates – was to bring her even worse sufferings than those inflicted on the persecuted Christians. First, she was brutally flogged; then, still recalcitrant, her limbs were racked to dislocation, and her flesh was burnt with red-hot irons.

Next day, unable to walk, this incredibly brave woman contrived to hang herself, using a strip of her own clothing as a noose, from the canopy of the covered chair in which she was being carried back to be tortured again. Throughout her ordeal she had not revealed a single name. Thus, as Tacitus acknowledged, a person who was an ex-slave and a woman, set an example that Roman senators and knights proved unable to match. Lucan avoided torture by denouncing his own mother. Nero showed his contempt by ordering that the mother should remain free and unpunished. He also prevented the suicide of Seneca's wife, Paulina, whose slashed wrists were bound up and who lived on for some years.

Throughout the first day, the conspirators among the Praetorian officers had successfully hidden their guilt. None of the civilian prisoners betrayed them at this stage because they were plainly still hoping that Faenius Rufus and his group would assassinate Nero during an unguarded moment. The tribune Subrius did on one occasion put his hand on his sword-hilt while standing behind the unprotected Emperor, but Rufus indicated to him by eye-contact and a shake of the head not to draw it and strike. Another of the military plotters, Statius Proximus, managed to maintain his cover even after being told to execute Lateranus, the senator who had planned to grab Nero treacherously by the knees. Statius hurried him outside and cut off his head without even giving him time to say goodbye to his children. When his complicity was finally established, the resourceful Statius received a pardon.

Rufus, however, overplayed his hand. His questioning of Scaevinus in front of the court was so harsh that the prisoner, in an outburst of rancorous sarcasm, threw the accusations back in his accuser's face. The prefect began to stammer, unable to deny his guilt coherently. His downfall led to the arrest of Subrius and the other officers in the group he had so patiently recruited. Before being led off to execution, Subrius was asked by Nero why he had plotted to kill him. 'Because I hated you,' the tribune retorted. 'None of the soldiers was more faithful to you than I was while you deserved to be loved (*dum amari meruisti*). I began to hate you after you murdered your mother and your wife – and flaunted yourself as a charioteer, an actor and a fire-raiser.'[10]

Whether or not he was still worthy of 'being loved' by his soldiers, Nero had evidently been feared by them. He was very lucky to be alive. There were only about a dozen tribunes (roughly comparable to colonels) in the Praetorian Guard at any one time, and half of them had joined the conspiracy. In all, a total of about forty individuals, mostly civilians, were involved, yet Nero enforced the death penalty in only seventeen cases. Tacitus' rhetoric about enormously long queues of waiting prisoners, and of the city being 'full of funerals', simply does not square with those basic statistics. It is hard to imagine any other Roman emperor, pagan or Christian, showing comparable restraint in such circumstances. Indeed, among absolute monarchs of any era – and certainly among totalitarian dictators of the twentieth century – Nero's clemency stands out as a notable exception to a general rule.

Two other plotters, including Gavius Silvanus, the tribune who had carried the death warrant to Seneca, committed suicide as a matter of honour, in spite of having been formally spared. The Consul, Vestinus Atticus, whose guilt was never officially proved, was nevertheless among those forced to take their own lives; it appears that he may have offered no direct help to Nero against the conspirators, but held aloof with his own private band of young supporters. Nero was so alarmed that he sent an entire Praetorian cohort of several hundred men to serve him the death warrant. Lucan died reciting snatches of his poetry as the blood ebbed slowly from his own severed veins. Scaevinus and Quintianus, too, as volunteers to carry out the actual assassination, could not be allowed to escape the supreme penalty. Most of the survivors were exiled, including Rufrius Crispinus, Poppaea's first husband.[11]

The knight Natalis avoided punishment through having been the first to confess and to name the leaders of the plot. Tigellinus and two other close allies of Nero during the crisis were awarded triumphal honours, as if they had won a great battle in the field against Rome's enemies. Faenius Rufus, who was beheaded, was replaced by one of his officers, Nymphidius Sabinus, as joint Praetorian Prefect. Ironically, it was Nymphidius who was to encompass Nero's death three years later. The ex-slave Milichus, who betrayed Scaevinus – the master who had freed him – was rewarded with a large sum of money and the official title of 'Saviour'. The Praetorian Guards were given a bonus of 2,000 sesterces each, as well as free bread rations for the indefinite future. The Emperor, it was said, made a practice of offering sacrifice and prayers to his magical protective doll three times a day.

The Senate responded to the bloodshed by voting to rename the month of April 'Neroneus', and even offered, in vain, to build a temple to Nero as a god. The Emperor was not to be so easily placated. If the year 62 had marked a turning point for his style of government, the year of the Pisonian conspiracy, 65, marked a watershed in relations between him and the senatorial elite. With the help of Tigellinus and an enlarged force of secret police, Nero now began actively looking for treachery in advance instead of simply reacting if it chanced to surface. It was in the ranks of the powerful that he sought it, not only among the senators and knights in Rome but at the top of the provincial administrations and armies as well.

The effect on morale needs no emphasis. Even those who had previously excused the Emperor's unconventional behaviour as youthful eccentricity, which greater maturity would overcome, now went in fear of investigation, which only too often led to exile and confiscation of property, even when it did not actually bring death. Early victims included some whose association with the failed conspiracy had not been immediately apparent. These included Seneca's brothers, Mela – whose relationship with Epicharus had presumably at last been uncovered – and Gallio (better known to us as the proconsul of Achaea who, according to the Acts of the Apostles, refused to sit in judgment on St Paul, when the apostle was accused of teachings incompatible with Judaism).[12]

The poet Lucan's puerile rebellion thus indeed ended in the destruction of his eminent family. But for the enterprise and merit of his grandfather, his uncles and his father, Lucan would no doubt have been brought up and educated, not in Rome and Athens under the best contemporary tutors, but in his provincial home town of Cordoba in Spain. Would his potential gifts have been nurtured there, so far from the capital and the only audience big enough and sophisticated enough to appreciate and encourage his art sufficiently to prompt the writing of a great epic? Early in 62, Seneca's word was effectively law throughout most of the Empire, Lucan was a court favourite with a dazzling career in prospect, his father was wealthy and indulgent towards him, and his Uncle Gallio was a senior proconsular member of the Senate. In little more than three years, all four had been forced to suicide, and their family name sank back into obscurity. It is a cautionary tale.

Another victim of the new dispensation was Nero's former 'arbiter of elegance', Petronius. Quite why the author of the *Satyricon* was marked down for death is not clear, but he had plainly aroused Tigellinus' jealousy. Given time to settle his affairs, he spent his last evening on earth chatting with friends in a light, gossipy way, thereby distancing himself from the Stoics, who characteristically engaged in deep philosophical discussions on their deathbeds, in imitation of Socrates.[13] That, in fact, was the manner in which the Stoic leader in the Senate, Thrasea Paetus, chose to meet his end after the inevitable warrant arrived. He had often risked Nero's anger in the past, showing considerable bravery and coolness. Now, in the radically different spirit of the times, his reproachful voice was finally silenced.[14]

Nero's changed mood became even darker as a result of personal tragedy. Poppaea had become pregnant a second time, giving him new hope of a child to continue the dynasty. Only about two months after Piso's conspiracy, however, she had a miscarriage, accompanied by haemorrhaging. The doctors had no effective means of stopping the internal bleeding. She died at the age of about thirty-three, leaving her husband desolate and the succession once again in doubt. To make matters worse, a rumour went around the city that Nero had kicked her in the abdomen in a fit of temper after she scolded him for coming home late from the chariot races.[15]

There is no reason to credit such an outrageous fabrication, which would make sense only at a much lower social level. That sort of domestic brawl no doubt occurred often enough in the urban slums, but is scarcely conceivable in the imperial household, where Emperor and spouse had separate apartments and sets of servants, and prided themselves on living in unparalleled splendour. It was also rumoured that he had poisoned her. When two such contradictory accounts are still circulating fifty years after the event – the period when Tacitus and Suetonius were writing – it is a clear enough sign that nobody knows the truth behind either of them.

In the circumstances, the obvious explanation of natural causes, allied with lack of medical competence, must be preferred. There is no mention of Nero ever raising either his hand or his foot against his first wife Octavia, even though he hated her for most of the ten years of their married life. Why should it be supposed that he suddenly abandoned a lifetime's restraint in his treatment of women at a personal, face-to-face level, in order to kick to death the one he loved above all the rest – and who, in addition, was carrying the child he so urgently needed for dynastic reasons? People who hated the pair of them were no doubt ready to believe whatever was to their discredit. As Tacitus states: 'Poppaea's death, although publicly mourned, caused rejoicing on account of her immorality and cruelty (*impudicitia saevitiaque*).'[16]

Poppaea's body was not cremated in the traditional Roman manner. Instead, as if she had been the consort of an Egyptian Pharaoh, it was embalmed, filled with costly oriental spices and laid in state in the Julian family tomb to facilitate her entry to the next world. Nero himself mounted the rostrum in the Forum to deliver the panegyric, emphasizing to the assembled mourners her radiant beauty while on earth and her divinity now that she was taking her place among the other goddesses in Heaven. The funeral is evidence of how far she and Nero had moved towards the Ptolemaic model of monarchy. Whether in life or death – whether in all seriousness or as public show – they seem to have aspired to the status of acknowledged divine or semi-divine figures, imbued with grace and power beyond the reach of ordinary mortals.[17]

Many of the senators and soldiers invited that day to believe in the apotheosis of Poppaea must have been reflecting less on heavenly consolations for their late Empress than on what was currently happening to the Roman constitution. In little more than half a century since the death of Augustus, his carefully balanced system of government seemed in imminent danger of degenerating into some form of oriental tyranny. For the three years that remained of Nero's rule, the recruiting slogan of the opposition would no longer be the restoration of a vanished Republic – which no one living had actually experienced – but the fight to hold on to what remained of the Augustan Principate.

THIRTEEN

THE THIRST FOR GLORY

The death of Poppaea isolated Nero to an extent that he had never experienced before. Any absolute ruler, of course, is ultimately 'on his own' by definition. That is the price of absolutism. But before the Pisonian plot Nero had always surrounded himself with people he believed he could trust. The plot had shown him that he could no longer trust anyone, especially not those of his own social background – with the sole exception of Poppaea. For a gregarious, talkative man like Nero, open to new ideas and experience, this was a terrible deprivation. Poppaea's death must have brought on unbearable feelings of alienation as well as the natural depression of bereavement.

We cannot know exactly what was going on inside Nero's head, but it has sometimes been alleged that he simply went mad – if he was not mad already. It is arguably true that some of his actions can be interpreted as displaying the sort of twisted logic associated with megalomania. Absolute power is proverbially believed to corrupt the mind of its possessor. But those who favour the diagnosis of outright insanity will need to account for the method that is clearly evident in so much of his supposed madness.

Nero's fundamental problem had always been one of status. Except for his dynastic connections, he lacked any of the recognized qualifications for holding down the position of Princeps in the Augustan constitution. He had none when he started as a boy of sixteen. He had acquired none in the intervening years. To be sure, he had learnt much about how to operate the levers of power, how to persuade capable men (but few senators) to serve him faithfully, how to get his own way. But

Nero had done nothing to justify his being treated by his fellow senators as supposedly *Princeps inter pares*, even if that description of 'first among equals' did not truthfully reflect the underlying division of power. In the quality that mattered most to them – the capacity to exercise military command – he was not even their equal, but conspicuously their inferior.

The Augustan system would be bound to break down without a minimum level of mutual respect between Princeps and Senate. Nero could not win this respect by becoming a valiant soldier, because the task was utterly beyond him. His actions over a number of years indicate clearly that he had been trying to gain this crucial senatorial respect by other means, notably by deploying his enormous spending power and parading his artistic gifts. The Pisonian plot should have taught him to moderate both these activities. Instead, it seems to have spurred him on to even greater efforts in the same fatal direction. This demonstrates an unusual degree of obstinacy and imprudence, but surely not mental derangement.

The more the Emperor distanced himself from his senators by out-spending them to achieve iconic magnificence, the more they grew inclined to hate him – especially as part of the money he was spending was being ruthlessly taken from their own pockets. His apparently absurd attempts to win musical and sporting laurels in 'fixed' competitions added derision to their hatred. Nero's expenditure, always inclined to excess, rose ever higher. The costs of recovering from the fire, along with the knock-on effects on revenue of the death or pauperization of so many hitherto reliable tax-payers, were already emptying the Treasury coffers, yet he pressed ahead with the construction of his vast new palace.

The methods he used to raise the necessary money were ruthless and effective. 'You know my needs,' he is reported to have told his Treasury officials, implying *carte blanche* for whatever action they might choose to take.[1] His agents around the Empire, under pressure to meet the raised targets, showed that they were ready in some cases to denounce reluctant payers as opponents of the Emperor, secure their conviction and seize their entire estates. Rich people were, in any case, expected to leave some of their money to the Emperor in their wills, in recognition of his role in maintaining the *Pax Romana* that enabled them to lead such comfortable lives. It was a sort of unofficial death duty, enforced by fear of possible imperial reprisals against their heirs.

In the new and difficult circumstances following the fire, such people were enouraged to amend their wills to bequeath him more. Even a freedman was now required to leave the bulk of his estate to his former master – and Nero happened to have more rich freedmen than anybody else. He also reduced the value of the gold and silver coinage by cutting the amount of precious metal in each coin, such that a fixed weight of gold would produce nine coins instead of eight, while a measure of silver would produce eight coins instead of seven. He did not, however, interfere with the copper coins used by poorer people for their everyday transactions.[2]

Part of this hard-won new revenue was spent on a 120-ft high statue of the Emperor as the Sun God, partly constructed of brass, with make-believe sunbeams jutting outwards in a dazzling aureole around its enormous head. This is Nero in his new Ozymandias mode: 'Look on my works, ye mighty – and despair!' According to Pliny, he commissioned a portrait on canvas of the same dimensions, which, erected in a garden, was struck by lightning and burned to ashes. That must have been the painted model from which the craftsmen-artists took their measurements. The claim that it was struck by lightning is probably no more than a way of suggesting divine anger at the Emperor's hubris. The statue itself was planned for the main vestibule of the new palace, from where it could be seen from many parts of the city, especially on clear days when it would reflect the real sun's rays into the uplifted and wondering eyes of his people. This, at least, seems to have been the theory behind it.[3]

Gold leaf and gems were lavishly applied to the ceilings and inner walls of the scattered groups of buildings that were rising up on the site of at least 250 acres which Nero had claimed for himself in the city centre.[4] On coming to power, he had inherited two separate sets of buildings and gardens: the eponymous palatial dwellings on the Palatine Hill and the smaller-scale urban villas on the neighbouring Esquiline Hill. Both hillsides had been extensively damaged in the fire, although a few properties had been at least partly spared.

Nero's master plan was to link these two ravaged areas by building across the muddy valley that separated them and through which at least one major road led into the adjacent Forum. He had already made a smaller scale attempt at such a connection before the fire, in the shape of the *Domus Transitoria*, but its destruction served only to increase his determination to surpass his earlier effort. Until modern times, the scale of Nero's building projects had to be taken on trust, because almost all had been buried beneath the works of his successors. Archaeologists have now succeeded in mapping most of the remains, although it has not always been possible, or even desirable, to expose them where they are inextricably mixed up with others.[5]

A notable success has been the excavation below the floor of the Flavian Emperor Domitian's banqueting hall, dating from about the year 92, which uncovered part of the original *Domus Transitoria* as well as foundations of the *Domus Aurea* (the Golden House), which replaced it. In this long-hidden space were porphyry columns supporting a roofed area over a central fountain. Several adjacent rooms were also uncovered, with floors of coloured marble and walls decorated with lively scenes from Homer. The plumbing indicated that water had been piped in to cascade decoratively down some of the surfaces.

The greater parts of the *Domus Aurea* that are most accessible today are the series of high-vaulted rooms and linking corridors which lie partly beneath the remains of the huge public baths built by the Emperor Trajan early in the second century. In an act of calculated vandalism or perhaps uncaring Philistinism, this section of Nero's palace was filled with rubble so that its walls could support the new superstructure as ready made foundations. Thankfully, the tightly packed rubble helped to preserve the buried frescoes through many centuries, so that when they were eventually cleared their colours were still remarkably bright.

Today, however, those frescoes which have not been removed to museums for protection have faded sadly from their earlier condition. It requires a considerable exercise of the imagination to visualize from these largely gloomy walls the true grandeur of the palace as it was when Nero built it.[6] The gap is at least partly bridged by a corridor in the Vatican, which was decorated in the early sixteenth century by Renaissance artists, copying with every refinement of detail those frescoes from the *Domus Aurea* that they had seen by being lowered on ropes through a floor into what at that time appeared to be ancient grottoes. Our word 'grotesque' derives from the Neronian 'grotto paintings', which artists such as Raphael saw, admired, copied and imitated.

The architects responsible for building the *Domus Aurea*, to Nero's instructions, were two master masons and engineers, Severus and Celer, who exploited the qualities of a recently discovered building material: concrete. Some unknown genius had had the idea of mixing small stones or hardcore rubble with cement to form slabs of any shape, including geometrically measured curves. The concrete could be faced with more attractive or durable materials, such as brick on the outside or marble panels on the inside. It could be pre-cast and used conventionally in a form similar to dressed stone blocks, but much greater flexibility was possible if the concrete was poured *in situ* between temporary retaining boards.

The result included, as part of Nero's great project, the first known example in the world of a large perforated cupola, placed above an octagonal atrium, allowing light to enter the interior through apertures in the top and sides of the dome-shaped roof. According to a description by Suetonius, a revolving dome was installed above Nero's main banqueting hall, apparently moving in synchronicity with the sun, moon and stars. Its mechanism may have been water-operated. There were also sliding panels in the ceiling, through which flower petals and sprays of perfume could float down upon the guests, either reclining at table or enjoying a leisurely orgy among these latest modern conveniences.

The architectural historian J.B. Ward-Perkins judges that the period of seventy-three years between the Great Fire of Rome and the death of the Emperor Hadrian in 137 saw 'all the essential stages of the revolution in architectural thinking which is Rome's great original contribution to the history of European art'. The first great public monument, he adds, in which we can deduce 'this ferment' in actual operation, is Nero's *Domus Aurea*.[7] Hitherto, builders and structural engineers had been forced to accept the limitations imposed by the stresses and strains involved in putting an ultimately solid roof, composed of many joined parts, on top of four walls. The Golden House represented a crucial step in the evolution of architectural methodology, whereby the concept of interior space began to take precedence over the problems of material mass.

Tacitus comments that Nero's two architects were clever enough to override the laws of nature.[8] But he adds that the remarkable character of the palace complex resided less in the materials and manner in which the actual buildings were constructed and decorated, than in the creation of a rural landscape in the centre of the city, with woods, lakes and meadows, and beautiful open vistas. Surrounded by groups of buildings linked by a full mile of colonnades, the enclosed rustic area must have seemed like an importation from the idyllic world of Virgil's *Eclogues* and *Georgics*, with their singing shepherds, their contented animals and bees, their sunny fields and shady groves.[9] The central feature was a lake – where Vespasian's Colosseum now stands – complete with water fowl and surrounding shrubberies.

However much it may have cost in material terms and sweated labour, Nero's concept of *rus in urbe* (country in town) was inspired and inspirational. 'At last,' he exclaimed, when it was ready for his occupation. 'At last I can begin to live like a human being!'[10] He could also entertain in unprecedented magnificence – and to that extent, at least, the Golden House had a role to play in the interests of the state. When the suppliant King of Armenia, Tiridates, came to Rome in 66 to accept his crown from Nero, the display of wealth and power impressed the visitors to an extent that was to pay a long-term diplomatic dividend.

Tiridates was the younger brother of King Vologaeses of

Parthia, who had been waging intermittent war for ten years over the succession to the Armenian throne. In that era, Parthia was the only bordering state that could be considered a substantial long-term threat to Roman arms. Parthia and Rome had treated each other as hostile neighbours for more than a century, since Julius Caesar's fellow-triumvir, Crassus, had attempted an invasion of Parthia for motives of personal aggrandisement and had been massacred along with his legionary army at Carrhae. King Vologaeses had in reality won the ten-year encounter over Armenia, but Nero wisely held back from committing himself to all-out war with Parthia in order to recover it.

Instead, having annexed the neighbouring territory of Pontus (bordering the Black Sea), which had hitherto been ruled by a client king of Rome, Nero offered peace terms to Vologaeses. These involved a degree of humiliation for his brother Tiridates but allowed them to keep Armenia without having to fight Corbulo and his legions, who at that moment were massed on the Euphrates border in the mountainous region east of Cappadocia, threatening invasion of Parthia itself as well as Armenia. First, Tiridates had to enter the legionary camp and lay down his crown in front of Nero's statue, which was set on a rostrum in a Roman magistrate's curule chair. The crown was then taken to Rome, where Tiridates was invited to get it back.[11]

The journey of Tiridates and his escort of 3,000 Parthian cavalry took nine months, there and back, and all the while he was in Roman territory Nero paid him a subsidy of 800,000 sesterces a day. When he reached Rome, every available soldier was drawn up in gleaming armour to greet him – and to overawe him. In front of vast crowds, Tiridates had to make his way up a sloping platform to where Nero was sitting in state, surrounded by his senators and guards. He fell down in obeisance at the feet of the Emperor, who graciously raised him up again and kissed him.

A second ceremony took place at an open-air theatre, where a huge embroidered curtain, showing Nero in a chariot surrounded by golden stars, was raised above their heads to keep the sun off. Tiridates, on his knees, referred to himself as Nero's slave, and said he had come to worship the Emperor in the way that he worshipped Mithras, the Persian god of light. Then he got his crown back. Nero formally closed the doors of the Temple of Janus, signifying that Rome was everywhere at peace. So far as relations with Parthia were concerned, that peace was to last for the next fifty years.[12]

Meanwhile, Nero had been looking for another wife. He needed a new empress to provide him with an heir. His first choice was Claudius' only surviving child, Antonia, the elder half-sister of Britannicus and Octavia. This demonstrates the strong political imperative to ally himself once more with dynastic legitimacy; he was no longer seeking a love match. But, not surprisingly, Antonia gave him a stony refusal. He had, after all, killed her husband, Faustus Sulla, as well as her sister and, she believed, her brother, too.

It was rumoured that, at the time of the Pisonian plot, Antonia had participated to the extent of being prepared to stand publicly at Piso's side when he came to claim imperial power after the projected assassination of Nero. This is hard to believe. Nero would scarcely have wanted to welcome to the centre of his domestic household – where he would be most vulnerable to sudden and secret attack – a woman he suspected of having already plotted to kill him. In any case, Piso had been devoted to his own wife. It may well be that the rumour of Antonia's supposed treachery was spread by Nero's own agents to justify what happened next. Antonia was denounced and put to death. Nero would not have wanted people to think he had killed her simply for refusing to marry him.[13]

Nero could not safely have allowed her to marry anyone else. The general public no doubt saw her demise as the completion of his long-term aim to rid himself of all of Claudius' children. His eye now fell on another woman whose husband he had forced to suicide – Statilia Messalina, widow of the consul Vestinus Atticus, whose conduct during the Pisonian crisis, as we have seen, did not appear to the Emperor as sufficiently loyal. There is some evidence that the four-times-wed Statilia had once been Nero's lover. Perhaps persuaded by Antonia's fate, she agreed to become his third wife. Although older than the Emperor, she was still of child-bearing age. Nero, however, was to have no more legitimate children.

There is a widespread belief that Nero must have left his bride behind when he finally set out on his long-postponed visit to Greece in the early autumn of 66. The reason is that during this overseas adventure Nero went through a form of marriage with the slave-boy Sporus, whom he called Sabina because of his close resemblance to Sabina Poppaea. Tigellinus was there to give the 'bride' away. By castrating Sporus, presumably just before puberty, he undoubtedly turned him – according to the modern perspective on such matters – into a 'sex-object'. But that was not his primary motive – if, indeed, it figured in his thinking at all. Nero's daring and brilliant concept involved a further inversion of the laws of nature, this time going far beyond the realm of architectural and scenic illusion. It was nothing less than the creation of a living work of art, symbolizing the ultimate divine power to defeat death itself.[14]

The imperial wardrobe mistress, the sophisticated and aristocratic Calvia Crispinilla, was put in charge of Sporus for the whole of the Greek tour. Her daily task was to dress him up in only the most beautiful of female clothing, such as Poppaea herself might have worn. Perfumed, coiffeured and painted with make-up, Sporus was required to appear to *be* Poppaea rather than merely resemble her. Any direct sexual contact between Nero and Sporus would either have been highly ritualized or entirely incidental, and in any case infrequent. The Emperor may only ever have pretended to have sex with his Poppaea-substitute, as part of the protocol sustaining the fantasy.

Suetonius says that Nero frequently and publicly smothered Sporus/Poppaea with kisses.[15] Extravagant public demonstrations of that sort are not the mark of someone who is privately enjoying a sustained sexual relationship with an established partner. They are, however, characteristic of actors greeting their leading ladies in a social context. All serious transvestism requires some degree of acting a part. And as Anthony Storr points out, elaborate rituals of cross-dressing are *symbolic substitutes* for the sexual act.[16]

Nero's earlier pretended 'marriage' to Doryphorus or Pythagoras, when he himself played the transvestite role by dressing and behaving as a bride, may have involved only simulated sex. Most male transvestites, including Nero, are heterosexual. They derive intense pleasure from dressing up in women's clothes. They are not inviting rape.

The records of the 'Arval Brothers', covering centuries of emperor-worship in pedantic detail, indicate that in Rome on 25 September 66 they offered prayers and sacrifice for the safe journey and hoped-for safe return of both Nero *and* Statilia. It is true that this does not prove that she actually reached Greece, but it seems reasonable to suppose that either Suetonius or Dio would have mentioned it if she had flounced back on her own in a jealous rage. The probability that she accompanied her husband to Greece and travelled back with him supports the supposition that his relationship with Sporus was not necessarily pederastic.

Before setting out for Greece, the Emperor delivered a calculated rebuff to the Senate, by nominating a former slave, Helius, to rule the city in his absence.[17] 'Helius' is a Latinized version of the Greek 'Helios', the name of the Sun God, whose colossal statue with Nero's head on it was to tower over the city. There is no indication in the sources that the choice of this freedman, of probable Greek origin, had depended on the coincidence of his name, but the irony would not have been lost on the Roman aristocrats who would now be obliged to defer to him.

Helius had been promoted under Claudius and Agrippina, and he had continued to work his way upwards. But even Claudius, who had been bitterly criticized behind his back for empowering so many freedmen, had appointed a senior senator, Lucius Vitellius, as his representative in Rome when he was absent during the conquest of Britain. Dio claims that Helius was given the power to banish or execute Roman citizens, including Senators, without needing to consult Nero by courier. As Tigellinus accompanied his master to Greece, Helius must have controlled the Praetorian Guard through its other joint prefect, Nymphidius Sabinus, who was thereby given ample scope and opportunity to start building up a personal following of his own.

The huge Neronian convoy of carriages, wagons and horses, carrying soldiers and slaves, actors and heralds, mistresses and musicians, imperial chefs and a few favoured senators, along with thousands of paid cheer-leaders and their noisy assistants, hogged the road for miles as they made their uproarious way along the same route as before – south to Naples, then across the lower knee of Italy to Brindisi. Dio says sarcastically that there were so many men armed with lyres and buskins and other accoutrements of their trade, that if they had been carrying weapons instead they could have beaten the entire Parthian army.[18]

The members of this bizarre expeditionary force once again quartered themselves and their camp-followers in the hill town of Beneventum for a night or two – and once again treason was uncovered. Unfortunately, the whole of Tacitus' account of the last two years of Nero's reign has been lost, so few details of what happened are available. We must presume that another group of conspirators was planning to assassinate the Emperor, and we know that the chief of those who were put to death was Corbulo's son-in-law, Annius Vinicianus, who had formally conducted Tiridates from Armenia to Rome.[19]

This Annius Vinicianus was the son of the former senator of the same name who had conspired successfully to murder Caligula a quarter of a century earlier. He was also the brother of one of the minor conspirators involved in the recent Pisonian attempt. In addition, he had links with leading political Stoics who were known to be morally opposed to the regime. It may well have been fortunate for Nero that Tigellinus was on hand to advise him. They could not have believed otherwise than that Annius Vinicianus had been acting on Corbulo's behalf. The problem, of course, was that one false move on their part might unleash a civil war – which they could easily lose.

The great general was still in command of the main eastern army, which had been brought together to intimidate King Vologaeses of Parthia. Corbulo had been leading many of these battle-hardened legionary soldiers for more than a decade;

offered a choice, they would probably follow him rather than Nero. He was a disciplinarian but a cautious tactician, never exposing his men to danger without a compelling reason. Unlike some of his subordinate commanders, who ranged over the huge territory for which he was nominally responsible, he had never personally lost a battle in the field.

In his letters to Corbulo from Rome, Nero had been in the habit of writing as if he were a son addressing a father. From Beneventum onwards, he continued to do so, but only in order to lull his suspicions. Although there is no record of a specific letter to Corbulo on the subject of his son-in-law's downfall, Nero must have sent one to reassure him that he was not being blamed in any way for the younger man's treason. Otherwise, Corbulo might have seen that his only hope of survival would be to put himself at the head of his legions and march on Rome to seize power by force. Had he made such a move while Nero was singing in Greece, he would have stood a good chance of securing the Senate's endorsement, incensed as they were by being forced to subservience by the freedman Helius.

Even if it had come to a vigorously contested civil war, Corbulo would very likely have won support among other military leaders on the fringes of the Empire. It is probable, in fact, that he was in correspondence already with the two brothers, Rufus and Proculus Sulpicius Scribonius, who commanded the armies of upper and lower Germany. But that chance was lost. Corbulo accepted at face value an apparently cordial invitation to join his Emperor in Greece now that the frontier was so peaceful. On arrival, without sufficient escort to defend himself, he was handed a suicide warrant by a military death squad.

'Serves me right!' he said, stabbing himself with a sword.[20] Whether he meant these laconic last words to stand as a confession of his involvement in the Beneventum plot, or whether he was commenting on his naivety in trusting the imperial invitation, is not recorded. The brothers Rufus and Proculus received similar invitations and suffered the same fate. For the moment, Nero and Tigellinus may have congratulated themselves on outmanoeuvring three disaffected generals. But other army commanders and proconsular governors around the Empire must have wondered if it might not be their turn next – and what steps they might need to take to prevent it.

Nero, however, among his thousands of travelling supporters and with the cheers of the Greeks ringing in his ears, was having the time of his life. He had finally crossed the Adriatic in a fleet of ships to the island of Corcyra (Corfu), just off the coast of modern Albania, where he gave his first performance beside the altar of the ancient temple of Jupiter at Cassiope. What he sang or declaimed is not recorded, but we know enough of his repertoire to hazard a guess. Although he was a passionate Graecophile and enjoyed a fluent command of the Greek language, he wrote his poems and songs in Latin. For his dramatic performances, however, he would presumably have used the original Greek of the plays from which his monologues were extracted.

During his tour of Greece Nero's own effort at rivalling Homer and Virgil would have been a staple of any concert programme. This, of course, was the account of the fall of Troy which he had been accused of singing while Rome burned. It had taken him between two and three years to write and was commensurately long. Not a single manuscript copy survived the Middle Ages, but from various references to it we know that the leading character was not one of the conventional heroes such as Achilles or Odysseus on the Greek side, or even Hector or Aeneas among the defending Trojans, but the unwarlike anti-hero Paris.

It was Paris, Hector's good-looking and philandering younger brother, who had caused the ten-year Trojan War by abducting the most beautiful woman in the world, Helen, wife of Menelaus, one of the Greek leaders. 'Helen of Troy', possessor of the face and body that launched a thousand ships, had effectively been Paris' illicit prize for awarding the golden apple to Aphrodite (Venus), goddess of love, in her nude contest with Juno and Athene for the title of most beautiful of the immortals. Nero plainly agreed with the judgment of Paris – and strongly identified with him. In Homer's version, when Paris does venture on to the battlefield, he is humiliated and has to be rescued by Aphrodite. Nero's Paris gives as good as he gets when it comes to a fight, and while in disguise he even beats his brother Hector on the games field.

After completing his poem on Troy, Nero had gathered materials for a mammoth epic celebrating the history of Rome from its foundation in as many as 400 books. Lucan's Stoic tutor, Cornutus, a member of Seneca's household, protested that nobody would read so many. When someone reminded him that the Stoic sage Chrysippus had written many more than 400 volumes, Cornutus replied, even less tactfully, that those had been for the benefit of mankind. For this observation, Cornutus was banished – but we do not know whether Nero ever started his great project.[21]

We know, however, that Nero wrote many shorter works, including a song in honour of Poppaea's beautiful auburn hair. As we have seen, he wrote some satirical stanzas about the paedophile senator, Afranius Quintianus, which nearly got him killed, and he also ridiculed in verse another aristocrat, Claudius Pollio. A more serious work was a poem about 'Mithridates', but it is not known which of the several pugnacious kings of Pontus of that name he was referring to. At the Youth Games of 59 he had sung verses about Attis, son of the mother goddess Cybele, who ritually castrates himself in a fit of divine madness and, like Adonis, is supposedly reborn or resurrected once a year. It sounds excessive enough for Nero's taste, but it is not known if he actually wrote the lyrics.

A few lines, or half-lines, of Nero's poetry have survived through being quoted by some other ancient writer. Seneca, for instance, praises a passage five words long: '*Colla Cytheriacae splendent agitata columbae.*' It certainly has rhythm and grace. (When saying it aloud, bear in mind that the probable pronunciation of Latin 'c' is always hard like English 'k', and that the 'g' is hard, too). 'Cytheriacae' is a designation of Aphrodite, one of whose birth-legends has her stepping out of the foam on to the shore of Cythera, the large island off the south-eastern tip of the Peloponnese; Nero's words may therefore come from his poem on Troy. Out of context, it is difficult to offer a satisfactory translation. The doves (*columbae*) of Venus seem to be ruffling their feathers, or perhaps arching their necks (*colla*), in flight; at the same time they or their necks are shining (*splendent*), presumably reflecting the sun. They may be carrying a message from the goddess to Paris at some point of crisis in the poem, or it may be that the manner of their flight bears some divinatory meaning.

As for his theatrical roles, Nero is reported to have acted women's parts as well as men's, including those of the Sophoclean heroine Antigone and of the pregnant Canace from the *Aeolus* of Euripides, holding his 'womb' and groaning in labour. More conventionally, he trod the stage dressed up as such famous protagonists as Antigone's father, Oedipus, and as Orestes, Hercules, Alcmeon and Thyestes. It needs to be emphasized that Nero did not take part in full productions of the plays in which these characters appear, but in dramatic extracts, with appropriate props. He did not merely stand still declaiming the words, but portrayed them in action – so realistically that on one occasion a soldier, who had just entered the theatre, seeing him in chains, rushed on to the stage to set him free. An earlier incident demonstrating the Roman taste for theatrical verisimilitude occurred when Nero, as a spectator, seated as close as possible to the action, was spattered with blood when a man playing the role of Icarus came to grief after launching himself too enthusiastically into simulated flight.[22]

Three of the male roles the Emperor is said to have performed involve situations that mirror real or reported incidents from his own career, so the information may have been incorporated into the historical record purely for rhetorical effect. On the other hand, Nero was quite robust enough to act as Alcmaeon or Orestes, each of whom killed his mother to avenge his father and was pursued by the Furies, or as Oedipus, who unknowingly killed his father and went to bed with his mother. He seems sometimes to have worn an actor's mask, in the traditional Greek fashion, and sometimes not. When he played female roles he wore a mask in Poppaea's likeness, so that she should in some sense take part in the performance, although dead.

It would have been towards the end of October, at the earliest, when Nero resumed his slow journey from Corcyra. That would have been much too late in the year to risk sailing around the Peloponnese, so we can be sure that he took the safer route along the narrow Gulf of Corinth, a voyage of more than 100 miles after turning east at the offshore island of Ithaca. The various ships' captains would have wanted to stop at Ithaca's deep-water harbour, to take on supplies or perhaps shelter from a storm, and it is hard to believe that Nero would not have relished the opportunity to walk around the mountainous island home of Odysseus. That was where Homer's 'man of many wiles' had returned to liberate his faithful wife Penelope from the unwelcome attentions of the many suitors who had wanted to usurp his throne. The Emperor's interest in Odysseus is evidenced by his later seizure at Olympia of a portrait of the wandering Ithacan hero.

The route through the Gulf of Corinth would have taken Nero past Delphi, on the northern shore, and it is even more likely that he stopped there, too. Not only was it the site of the most venerated oracular shrine in the Hellenistic world, but it was also indelibly associated with the art of poetry. Drinking from the Castalian spring below Apollo's shrine on the slopes of Mount Parnassus was popularly believed to aid poetic inspiration. Visitors were required to purify themselves in its waters before ascending the Sacred Way, carrying a ritually baked cake and leading a sacrificial animal, which together constituted the price of admission.

Nero might not have appreciated the carved injunction above the door – 'NOTHING IN EXCESS' – but he would have loved the ancient ceremonial involved in consulting the elderly priestess, whereby his question would be put to her by a bardic acolyte, who would render and interpret her gnomic reply in the form of Greek hexameters. He would also have gazed with deep interest at the *Omphalos*, or navel-stone, said to mark the absolute centre of the (flat) earth, and on which Orestes himself had reputedly sat while awaiting advice about his act of matricide.

The shrine gets its name from Delphos, the legendary son of a dolphin that had received the amorous attentions of Poseidon (Neptune). Delphos was ruling the area when Apollo – with whom Nero identified closely – arrived to displace him, killing the python guarding the shrine, which since Mycenaean times had been sacred to a cthonic mother goddess. She, too, had to leave, clearing the way for an unbroken succession of 'Pythian' priestesses that was to last for more than a millennium, and for the Pythian Games, in which Nero was to compete in 67. The Emperor had, in advance, persuaded the organizers of these contests, along with the authorities responsible for the Olympic, Isthmian and Nemean Games, to hold all of them in that single year – for the first and only time in history – so that he could compete in all of them without having to go through the traditional four-year cycle.

Nero did in fact consult the Oracle at least twice during his stay in Greece. The first of the Pythia's prophecies was apparently little more than conventional flattery to a visiting notable, and pleased him sufficiently to reward her. The last was perhaps too 'delphic' in its ambiguity, and he appears to have carried out some sort of reprisal.[23] It is possible that Nero also went there during the three months of winter, when Apollo was absent, leaving the shrine under the control of Dionysus, whose grave was said to be in the inner sanctum. The orgiastic rites of the god of wine and ecstasy would no doubt have been celebrated in the sacred grove of myrtles and olive trees, from which the crowns of victory in the games were plucked.

Much of the Emperor's first winter in Greece was spent at Corinth, on the narrow isthmus, barely 4 miles wide, separating the Ionian and Aegean seas, and marking the boundary between the Peloponnese and mainland Greece. Athens lay less than 50 miles to the east. For reasons that are unclear, he never visited Athens, nor its historic rival Sparta. It is likely that this omission was a calculated attempt to raise the status of Corinth. The Romans had destroyed the former Greek city of that name more than 200 years earlier, when the consul Lucius Mummius killed or enslaved its inhabitants at the end of the war against the Achaean League. The new city, founded by Julius Caesar, was essential to their strategy of control, placed as it was at one of the great crossroads of the ancient world, and defended by the impregnable hill fortress of Acrocorinth.

St Paul had recently founded a church there. Judging from his two letters to the Corinthians, they were a difficult flock to control, having apparently split into a number of rival factions. Nevertheless, there is no report of any persecution of Christians. According to church tradition, St Paul had left Rome after being taken there under guard for his 'appeal to Caesar', and spent at least part of the year 66 in Macedonia (or possibly in Spain). It is quite likely, therefore, that he did not return to Rome until after Nero had left the city to go to Greece. If so, his martyrdom may have occurred under the temporary regime of Helius.

Christianity as a way of life faced an especially difficult moral challenge in Corinth, which had become notorious throughout the Mediterranean world for its sexual licence. It was on the direct slaving route from the Levant as the first port of call after the island of Delos, where much of this human cargo was assembled and classified by wholesalers, before being sent to auctions in Italy. Corinthian brothel owners had the opportunity of running their eyes over the new slaves as they walked the 4 miles across the isthmus from the Saronic Gulf, and could bid for the prettier girls – and boys.

The city must have been a home-from-home for Nero, who, as well as immersing himself in Greek culture, was able to while away his lighter moments. But with the spring, he geared himself up for the challenge that lay ahead: the winning of musical and sporting events at the series of pan-Hellenic festivals that had been specially rearranged for his convenience. He gave the self-imposed task everything he had. Evidently he could not see that by doing so – and by relinquishing his day-to-day role as ruler of his great Empire – he was in danger of exchanging the imperial laurel crown for garlands that would rapidly wither.

FOURTEEN

WINNER LOSES ALL

Because all forms of artistic endeavour are essentially voluntary – they are not necessary for the maintenance of life – many people believe them to be trivial. For Nero, they were integral to his policy of achieving personal greatness and making the world a happier and more beautiful place. The fourteen months he spent in Greece clarified for his traditionalist opponents at home the terms of this long-incubated struggle for the soul of Rome. Nero now emerges as the Messiah of his own cult of aesthetic divinity, proclaiming a new golden age of peace and plenty, in which there would be no more wars.

The practice of his art also represented Nero's vindication of his earlier conduct as Emperor. How else could he justify clinging to a power he had consistently refused to exercise in the manner expected of him by the Senate and People of Rome? How else could he justify killing his mother? Or his wife? Or various of his close relatives and political opponents? It would not be enough for him to say: 'I had to do all those things if I wanted to stay alive.' Survival is always a problem for an absolute ruler, but much less so if he rules in accordance with accepted standards.

Had Nero behaved with at least an outward show of propriety he would not have lost the support of Seneca, whose own career constituted in itself a lesson in the usefulness of hypocrisy. Nor would he have lost the acquiescence of the Senate as a whole, or the goodwill of the army. Nero did not need to lead his troops into battle – or even from behind. He needed only to pay an occasional visit to one or other of the far-flung legionary camps in order to demonstrate an interest in the officers and men, and to acknowledge the truth that it was they who guarded him while he played and slept.

Every iconoclast needs an alibi, if only to assuage an inner sense of guilt about overturning the most cherished beliefs of his ancestors. Nero believed he had found salvation in an aspect of Greek civilization, which he was ready to exploit for the benefit of Rome. For hundreds of years, the Greeks had conferred a status not far short of divinity on those rare athletes who, from time to time, became the *periodonikes* – a man so outstanding that he won the chief prizes at all four of the great pan-Hellenic festivals, held in successive years. Such a person was held to have won also the greater prize of immortality, and to be exempt from the revenge of Nemesis, whose task it was to bring ultimate disaster on those humans who were too conspicuously successful in life.

Nero intended to be crowned the greatest *periodonikes* of all time, and to return to Rome in triumph like a conquering general, with all his leafy garlands to prove it. He believed that such an achievement would represent a complete and final answer to his growing number of critics, as well as enhancing his popularity among the common people. The tour of Greece was planned with all the seriousness and attention to detail of a military invasion. The Greek judges had made their position clear in advance, bringing him prizes before he had even crossed the Adriatic. 'Only the Greeks appreciate my music,' he had exclaimed.[1] Tigellinus and his detachment of Praetorians were on hand in Greece to make sure they continued to do so. The huge troop of well-paid *Augustiani*, trained by numbers to applaud rhythmically in time to the commands of their cheer-leaders, did their utmost to justify the Emperor's expense in bringing them all the way from Rome and Naples. In the face of such a display of imperial excess and partisanship, the local Greeks fell into line and enjoyed the shows and the perks.

Nero was not an athlete of the physical type that embodied the Greek ideal. He was evidently not a great runner or discus thrower. But he was an expert charioteer and, of course, a professional musician. Many Greek games included musical contests along with the track and field events, and where they had not previously existed, as at the Olympic Games, Nero insisted on introducing them for himself to win. And Nero 'won' whenever and wherever he entered a contest. At the Olympics he won the chariot race in spite of falling out of his vehicle and having to be picked up from the track, dusted off and put back on board.[2]

People tend to laugh when they read of all these victories, numbering 1,808 in total, but that may be partly because they assume that 'winning' is the sole, or main, object. Certainly Nero loved getting each prize, but it was the actual participation in the contests that fed his obsession. Games and contests are ritualized activities with their own distinctive rules of behaviour, and an order of precedence often far removed from that of ordinary social life.[3] Nero liked pretending not to be Emperor. He always took pains to conform to these game rules as if he were just another competitor. At the end of each contest, he knelt down among his rivals on the stage, holding up his hand, like them, in mute appeal to the massed ranks of spectators, as if he, too, doubted the outcome. When each victory was inevitably confirmed, he rejoiced with apparent spontaneity as if it had been a great surprise as well as a great achievement. He always announced that he dedicated it to the people of Rome, conspicuously omitting to mention the Senate in the usual formula of *Senatus Populusque Romanus*.

As well as competing in the four major games, Nero also performed at venues all over the Greek mainland, wherever a local festival could be arranged. Then he could bask in the applause and indulge his pleasure in giving extended encores. It was evidently at events such as these that our sarcastically humorous sources tell us of spectators, who had been forced to sit in the audience, shamming death in order to be carried out on stretchers, and thereby avoid having to listen any longer to the Emperor's voice, or of women giving birth in the aisles because the guards would not let them leave.[4] We need not give credence to these old jokes.

Some of the festivals lasted for more than one day. The crowds who came to watch and listen in the arenas and sacred groves were enjoying a break from their usual tasks or duties, and sat around amusing themselves like the mass audiences familiar to us today from modern pop festivals. Nero had a backing group of long-haired boy dancers, whose role was apparently to sway rhythmically on stage on either side of him while he sang. It would not be surprising if they had a 'warm-up' role as well, dancing to other musicians before the Emperor's star turn.[5]

There were no artificial means of amplifying Nero's voice, but it is no coincidence that our word 'acoustic' comes directly from Greek; by experimentation and design, the Greeks had, over many centuries, placed their stages where the conditions for sound were as helpful as possible to the performer. Today's visitors to the ancient open-air theatre at Epidauros – where Nero must surely have performed during his stay in the Peloponnese – can hear for themselves the remarkable clarity of the slightest word spoken on stage, even if they happen to be listening from the most distant row of seats.

Senatorial visitors from Rome, who called to see Nero during breaks in performances, were shocked to find him wearing excessively long, wavy hair and flowery tunics, instead of the regulation toga. He did not want to hear about bad news, either from home or abroad, and became doubly impatient when messages arrived from Helius, advising his return. But he had been unable to ignore entirely the crisis which had arisen in Judaea, that can serve us as one example, among many, of the risks that an absolute ruler like Nero runs when he neglects to take the time to assess how best to exercise his unique constitutional powers, while refusing to delegate some of those powers to the most competent and suitable people, for fear of setting up a rival.

Judaea had always been a problem area for the Romans, but the situation had deteriorated alarmingly since the appointment – on Poppaea's recommendation – of Gessius Florus as procurator in 64.[6] That was the year of the Great Fire of Rome, and Florus was evidently given orders, like the rest of Nero's tax-collectors around the Empire, to raise as much money as possible. In April 66, six months before Nero left Rome for Greece, the Jews rioted

in Caesarea and paraded through Jerusalem with an effigy of
Florus dressed as a beggar, asking for alms. The Procurator's
response to this insult was to lead an utterly inadequate force to
Jerusalem with the intention of punishing the ring-leaders. Faced
down by thousands of angry Jews, he promptly retreated back to
Caesarea, leaving one cohort and the small permanent garrison
behind. The cohort negotiated its own terms of departure, but
when the garrison troops finally emerged, on the promise of
being allowed to march away, they were massacred. Only their
commander, Metilius, survived – by agreeing to be circumcized.

News of the massacre and the treachery provoked bloody
reprisals in many towns and cities in the East where there were
significant Jewish enclaves. No fewer than 20,000 are said to have
been slaughtered at Caesarea by the majority Greek population.
At Alexandria, where there was an especially large and
prosperous Jewish community, they were expelled by the
governor's fiat, with an order to Roman troops to kill on sight any
Jew who tried to stay in the city. In some towns, however, the
Jews came off best, killing many Gentiles. News of most of these
events must have reached Nero before he left Rome on 25
September. The Jerusalem massacre had occurred in August,
and the pogroms within a few weeks of it.

What, if anything, Nero did at this stage is not recorded. The
emergency was not allowed to interfere with his plans to visit
Greece. The obvious answer would have been to instruct
Corbulo to take charge of the entire Palestine region, quell the
unrest and restore Roman pride; but perhaps Corbulo's loyalty
was already suspect. Instead, the legate of Syria, Cestius Gallus,
set out from Antioch with a force of 30,000 men, in which
auxiliary troops clearly outnumbered fully trained legionary
soldiers. There seems to have been no serious attempt at
diplomacy, aimed at detaching the moderates from the hard-line
revolutionaries. Gallus marched through Galilee, ravaging and
slaughtering as he went, while Nero was still on the road to
Brindisi with his courtiers and cheer-leaders.

By the time the Emperor was giving the first of his
entertainments on the island of Corcyra, the punitive army of

Gallus was storming Jerusalem. But the Jews proved to be tougher fighters than the Romans had expected – and winter was not far off. After seven successive days of frontal assaults against Jerusalem's defences, Gallus lost heart and, like Florus before him, began a retreat towards Caesarea, intending to wait until the spring to mount a full-scale siege. The defenders, however, thought they had defeated the hitherto invincible Roman army. The moderates hastened to join the rebel ranks and harry the retreating soldiers.

More freedom fighters streamed down from the hills, including many who had sheltered in fortified positions in Galilee, which Gallus had foolishly left untaken in his eagerness to reach Jerusalem. The struggle became so desperate that he abandoned his artillery and other siege equipment, and tried to escape by forced marches at night. As a final measure, he left behind a doomed rearguard of 400 men, who fought to the death in their stockaded camp while the main column reached the comparative safety of Caesarea.

This humiliation for Roman arms occurred as Nero was making his leisurely way towards Corinth. He may already have arrived at the Isthmus by the time the news reached him. He could not pretend that his quest for musical and sporting renown took precedence over a situation where his soldiers had been effectively chased out of an entire province, retaining just a precarious toe-hold on a hostile coast. If he lacked the spirit to cross the Aegean himself, he had to send a truly seasoned professional with the necessary ability to reconquer Palestine and restore it to the Empire. In a decision that was to have momentous and entirely unforeseen consequences, he chose the elderly Titus Flavius Vespasianus,[7] whose last conquest had been of the Isle of Wight in the aftermath of Claudius' invasion of Britain. Within three years of his appointment by Nero, this coarse-tongued former mule-trader had taken over not merely Palestine but the entire Roman world – as the Emperor Vespasian.

Nero returned with relief to his idealized world of Greek pleasures. Vespasian sailed east through the Saronic Gulf and island-hopped over the wintry sea to the Asian mainland, leaving behind him a story that an imperial freedman had once shaken him roughly awake when he fell asleep during one of Nero's longer concerts. With the aid of his elder son, Titus, who would eventually succeed him as emperor, he commandeered three legions, the 5th, the 10th and the 15th, and spent the rest of the winter training them for siege warfare. He also recruited as many auxiliaries as he could attract to the colours with promises of easy bloodshed and loot.

In the spring of 67, when Nero started the rounds of the festivals, cithara in hand, singing to cheering crowds, Vespasian entered Galilee. He did not make Gallus' mistake of rushing ahead to Jerusalem. Patiently, he laid siege to one Galilean fortress after another, crucifying any Jews who resisted. The local commander in Galilee was Josephus, later to become the celebrated historian of the Jewish war. To escape crucifixion, Josephus and the last of his men decided to stab each other to death when their position became hopeless. When only Josephus and one other were left alive, he persuaded his companion to let him try talking to Vespasian. Immediately on being taken in front of the Roman general, Josephus, claiming to have the gift of prophecy, hailed him as a future emperor. Vespasian took care not to pass this prediction on to Nero, and retained Josephus as his interpreter.[8]

The young Emperor, meanwhile, having surveyed the Isthmus of Corinth with his engineers, decided to revive Julius Caesar's old project of digging a canal across it so that ships could pass through without risking the long sea voyage around the often treacherous waters of the southern and western Peloponnese. Curiously enough, many Greeks objected to the idea, chiefly on religious grounds. Nero, having put the Roman moralists in their place, was not one to be dissuaded by the votaries of Poseidon. He set the example by digging the first spadeful of soil and carrying it away on his back, in spite of groaning noises and blood that witnesses claimed to perceive coming out of the violated earth.[9]

The town and fortress of Taricheae, at the southern extremity of the Sea of Galilee, surrendered conveniently to Titus at the end of August after a naval battle, and Vespasian sent 6,000 of the able-bodied male Jewish prisoners to Corinth to help dig more of the canal. The rest of the population, some 30,000, were sold into slavery. At the end of the campaigning season, Vespasian retired to winter quarters in Caesarea, having garrisoned his Galilean conquests and secured the whole of the Mediterranean coastline. Thousands of refugees from Galilee made their way to Jerusalem, more than replacing those who had left the Jewish capital while escape routes to the south and east remained open.[10]

In Corinth, Nero – like the poet Byron 1750 years later – had 'dreamed that Greece might still be free'.[11] Disregarding the current serious loss of revenue from Judaea, coupled with the high cost of provisioning and paying the troops there, he announced at the Isthmian Games that the entire province of Achaea was to be granted its freedom from that moment, including freedom from paying tax to Rome.[12] This did not mean that the Greeks need no longer regard themselves as part of the Roman Empire; but it placed Greece on a level roughly equivalent to that of Italy so far as taxation and degrees of local autonomy were concerned. To compensate the Senate for the loss of Achaea, Nero handed over control of the Italian offshore island of Sardinia, whose prestige and revenues were lower.

The grant of freedom to Greece was a quixotic gesture. It won him great popularity in Hellenic lands, but enraged taxpayers in other provinces, who perceived that they would now have to pay proportionately more to support Nero's free-spending regime. It also confirmed, in a material way, the Emperor's partiality for Greeks and their way of life. From the perspective of the hungry mob left behind in the city of Rome, whose corn-dole had become uncertain and irregular during Nero's absence, it must have seemed as if he was in the process of deserting the land of his ancestors – as if, indeed, it was no longer good enough for him.

Helius, the freedman who had been left in charge of the capital, had no doubt of the urgent need for Nero's return. After the Emperor had rebuffed several pleading messages from him, Helius travelled to Corinth in the dead of winter to confront him personally with the truth. Opposition to Nero had reached a dangerous level, and the punishment of the handful of disaffected aristocrats whom Helius had put to death had not eased the problem.[13] He may well have named those he chiefly suspected of plotting; but whatever the details of Helius' confidential report, they were serious enough to persuade Nero to abandon Greece and go home.

Tigellinus can be presumed to have had a share in this decision. The sinister prefect controlled an effective spy network, with agents in every province; and as we know from hindsight that the most immediate danger to Nero was currently festering in Gaul and Spain, rather than in Rome itself, it is curious that news of it had apparently not already reached him, too. Even Vespasian, in far-off Judaea, had become aware of a Gallic conspiracy at about this time, according to Josephus. But Tigellinus now mysteriously disappears from the historical record, to re-emerge only after the crisis has passed. Had he deliberately withheld certain information from his master? Or had he simply been taken ill?

On his way back through Italy, Nero stopped at Naples to enjoy a formal triumph, in the manner of a Roman general as well as of a pan-Hellenic champion. A ceremonial breach was made in the walls for him to drive through in a chariot drawn by four white horses. The crowds, of course, were only too delighted to see him back in their largely Greek-speaking city. It was effectively a dress rehearsal for the major triumph that he now went on to celebrate in Rome, this time driving Augustus' own triumphal chariot, which hitherto had been used only for celebrating significant military victories.

Presumably he had taken the advance precaution of seeing that plenty of free corn was available again, because the rapturous mob threw flowers in his path, and released flocks of song-birds as his procession passed. With their emperor back in Rome, they no doubt felt they need not fear hunger any more. He stood upright in the chariot, wearing a star-spangled Greek-style military cloak, with an Olympic victor's crown on his head. In front of him, marching attendants carried placards setting out details of his artistic and sporting achievements. 'O Zeus! O Apollo! O Divine Voice!' the cheer-leaders cried, encouraging the plebeians to join in.[14]

Nero made a circuit of the Circus Maximus before a capacity audience, then on to the Forum and up the hill to the Temple of Apollo, where he dedicated his 1,808 fading victory wreaths of laurel, bay and olive leaves, and the even more wilted ones of parsley and wild celery. Afterwards he had them arranged around his rooms in the completed main section of the Golden House. For the Senate, Nero's 'triumph' was a blasphemous insult to their ancestors. The Emperor does not seem to have made the slightest attempt to mollify resentful senators. Having assured himself that his word was still law throughout the city, he retired once more to the Bay of Naples for his customary spring holiday.

It was there, in March 68, that he received news that the governor of one of the 'unarmed' Gallic provinces, Gaius Julius Vindex, had revolted and was raising an army of Gauls against him.[15] Nero was so little concerned that he did not even trouble to write to the Senate about it until a week had passed. He knew that the untrained Gauls would be no match for his legions, and is said to have remarked that putting down the rebellion would provide a great opportunity for confiscating property. When the Emperor did eventually return to Rome and summoned senior senators to the palace, he spent much of the time talking about, and tinkering with, a new type of water-operated organ that he had just been given.

The Emperor, although suspicious of particular individuals, was still unaware of his true peril. By spending so much time away from his power base in order to follow his own desires, he had effectively allowed a widespread revolutionary situation to develop. His many enemies were simply awaiting a lead – so they could all strike safely together. Vindex, although only a Romanized Gaul, provided it. The first significant figure to follow him was Servius Sulpicius Galba, the 73-year-old governor of northern Spain – the patrician whom Agrippina had once targeted as a potentially suitable step-father for Nero, before she married Claudius. He was a former governor of

Aquitania, in South-West Gaul, from whose royal family Vindex claimed descent.

On 2 April 68, with Vindex's evident agreement, Galba placed himself at the head of the armed opposition to Nero by declaring that he was the legate not of the Emperor but of the Senate and People of Rome. He had only one legion at his disposal, but he began immediately to enrol a second. The governor of southern Spain joined him in revolt, along with Poppaea's ex-husband, Marcus Salvius Otho, whom Nero had sent to Lusitania (Portugal) ten years' earlier. The Emperor was shocked but his fears were now being soothed by the other Praetorian Prefect, Nymphidius Sabinus, in Tigellinus' absence.

Nero's best chance at this stage would have been to call on all his immediately available forces and lead them in person against the still small group of declared rebels. Instead, he pronounced himself sole consul for the length of the emergency and relied on three of his other generals to do any actual fighting that might be required. Three of the legions from upper Germany, under Lucius Verginius, were already marching, albeit very slowly, towards Vindex's estimated 100,000 Gaulish irregulars, who were besieging the Roman colony of Lugdunum (Lyons) at the head of the Rhône Valley. Petronius Turpilianus, the former governor of Britain, and Rubrius Gallus were put in charge of the Italian-based legionaries, and sent north – some to guard the line of the River Po, others to move up into Gaul.

The Emperor had briefly considered going with them, to the extent of loading wagons with musical instruments to entertain the soldiers, and mobilizing a troupe of concubines, for whom he ordered short haircuts and an issue of light-weight axes so that they could play the part of Amazon warriors, presumably at a decorous distance from the fray. According to Suetonius, he also talked of appearing unarmed and alone in front of the rebel forces and restoring them to loyalty by the sight and sound of his reproachful tears.[16]

Ironically, it was the defeat and death of Vindex that revealed the extent of the forces ranged against him. Verginius, at the head of his three Rhine legions, faced Vindex in May near Vesontio

(Besançon), but did not launch an immediate attack. The two men are said to have met, presumably under some form of truce, and to have reached an agreement to co-operate against Nero. If there was, in fact, such an plan, it was repudiated next day by the Rhine soldiers in the most brutally effective way possible. They fell upon the hapless Gauls and killed 20,000 of them. Vindex committed suicide.

It was claimed that the slaughter was inadvertent, due to lack of communication with the forward troops, who were mostly non-Roman auxiliaries. An alternative explanation, however, is that the aggressors had no intention of taking third place behind Galba's legion from Spain and Vindex's despised Gauls. Having broken away from their unprofitable border duties, they wanted the lion's share of any reward for making a new emperor, especially if it involved a summer campaign in Italy, where many of them originated.

Verginius refused to lead them there even though they repeatedly hailed him as Emperor. He could no longer pretend to be acting on Nero's behalf, or the only agreement he could legitimately have made with Vindex would have been for the Gauls' surrender. He sent a formal message to the Senate proclaiming that he awaited their orders. A further irony was that Galba, on receiving the news of Vindex's defeat, thought that it was Nero who had won. He left the main body of his small army, accompanied by a few close associates, apparently to settle his personal affairs and prepare to commit suicide. It was the arrival of a messenger from Rome that stayed his hand.

What had been happening to Nero during these weeks of confused military manoeuvring? He had spent the time in Rome, alternately depressed and exhilarated by the reports coming out of Gaul and Spain. Both Suetonius and Dio suggest that his head was full of wild schemes, which he discussed with his dwindling band of cronies. Should he take reprisals against all the Gauls in the city? Should he go to the East, where he had recently planned to lead a major expedition through the 'Caspian Gates', and earn his living as a travelling singer instead? Perhaps he ought to compose a stirring march to put heart into his soldiers? Would he be sure of finding refuge in Parthia? Should he have all the senators murdered while he still had the chance? Or should he set fire to the city a second time?

It is highly unlikely that Nero entertained any such notions. The non-violent ones form part of the secondary legend of him as a cowardly buffoon and are designed rhetorically to counterpoint the primary legend of Nero as a monster of cruelty and depravity. The truth is that until the last 12 hours of his life, Nero had every reason to suppose he would easily defeat Galba – and, if it proved necessary, Verginius, too. Galba obviously thought so, or he would not have prepared to kill himself. Most generals around the Empire had demonstrated their loyalty by passing on to the Emperor the treasonable invitations they had received from Vindex. Galba allied himself publicly with Vindex because he knew that Nero had already given orders for his death – perhaps because he had kept quiet about Vindex's plans.

If Galba, less than 500 miles from Besançon, thought that Verginius had already put down Vindex's revolt on Nero's behalf, it is scarcely credible that legates in more distant provinces would have taken a different view. In any case it would have needed a month or more for any message from Verginius to reach those furthest away, and he would not have wanted to commit anything treasonable to paper. It is beyond any reasonable doubt that when his message to the Senate arrived in Rome, the Emperor believed that he himself was still in control of most of the frontier legions – and was probably correct in thinking so.

With the exception of forces controlled by Clodius Macer, the maverick governor of Africa (not the continent, but the area once ruled by Carthage), Nero could justifiably have counted on mobilizing, in whole or in part, at least fourteen legions in addition to the troops he had already sent to northern Italy and Gaul – and not counting those in Britain in Verginius' rear. By the last week of his life, early in June, he had made preliminary moves to do so. His plan was to go to Alexandria and muster an army sufficient to protect Italy against invasion from the north-west. He could confidently have applied to Vespasian for help. At that stage the old general would not have considered himself to be a plausible contender for the throne. As the son of a mere equestrian tax-collector, he knew he would have been scorned in a Rome that had not yet learnt submission to any imperial candidate other than a blue-blooded dynast.

Nero naturally thought that Nymphidius, as Praetorian Prefect, was busy helping him make the necessary security arrangements in connection with his projected voyage to Alexandria. But Nymphidius was in daily contact with Galba's agent, Icelus, who was in his custody in Rome but whom he evidently allowed to meet selected senators. Convinced that Galba would advance his career to new heights, Nymphidius devised a plan to destroy the Emperor that avoided the risk of assassination.

The crucial first step was to persuade Nero to send his German bodyguard on ahead to Alexandria, along with various of his freedmen, to prepare a suitable welcome for him in Egypt. Once this advance party had sailed away, the only soldiers left in Rome to guard Nero were under Nymphidius' direct command. When, on 8 June, the Emperor ordered the relevant group of Praetorian officers to get themselves and their men ready to conduct him to the port of Ostia, some made excuses while others simply refused. One of them even quoted from a line of Virgil: 'Is it really so great a misery to die?'[17]

After the officers left, Nero was clearly unable to face the implications of this unprecedented disobedience. It may well be that he had been drinking – scarcely an unusual occurrence for him – and that would help to explain both why the officers had been quite so direct in refusing his orders and why he himself went off to bed after supper, instead of taking action to keep his hold on power. He went to sleep guarded, as usual, by a small detachment of Praetorians outside his bedchamber. When he awoke at about midnight they had gone. So had most of the servants.

Sleep had cleared his head. He knew now that Nymphidius must have betrayed him – and he feared that assassins might come for him at any moment. Still in his night clothes, he ran from his quarters in search of help. Several of his more prominent senatorial supporters had been staying at the palace.

He hammered at their doors but got no reply. He did not know they had been summoned to stand by for a torchlight session of the Senate at the Praetorian camp, where Nymphidius was mustering all the available guards. Running back helplessly the way he had come, Nero met two of his most senior freedmen, Epaphroditus and Phaon, both of whom held ministerial posts in his Administration. They advised him to leave the city at once, hide out somewhere for the rest of the night, and ride on to the port of Ostia in the morning.[18]

Nero paused only to make a quick search for a phial of poison which Locusta had prepared for him against an emergency. He failed to find it. But he found Sporus asleep in a neighbouring room, and made him come, too. The four of them, with perhaps one or two others, went to the stables to find horses. Nero was still in his slippers, with a cloak flung over his nightshirt. Phaon, who owned a small villa a few miles outside the city walls, offered it as shelter for the night. The panic-stricken Emperor agreed to ride there even though it was the opposite side of the city to the road that led to Ostia and the ships waiting to sail to Egypt. He may have thought his enemies would be less likely to look for him in that direction, or that in the morning he might be able to catch a boat inconspicuously down the Tiber.

Nero covered his face with a cloth as he rode through the darkened streets. They could see lights and hear shouting from the nearby Praetorian barracks as they passed through the city gates. It looked and sounded very ominous. Before clearing the outskirts of Rome, a veteran soldier hailed him as Emperor when the cloth slipped briefly from his face. Rumbles of thunder, interspersed with vivid lightning flashes, made their nerves jangle and upset the horses. They dismounted to leave the road where Phaon guided them. For some reason they were unable to enter the villa by the front door. Nero had to crawl on his belly through dense undergrowth to reach a side entrance. On the way he slaked his raging thirst by lapping from a puddle. Finally, after pulling dozens of thorns out of his cloak, he crept inside and lay down on the nearest bed, in a slave's room. Phaon did not join him, but rode back to Rome in search of news.

The freedman evidently went to the Praetorian barracks, because later that night a messenger arrived at the villa to tell Nero that he had been deposed as Emperor in favour of Galba, and that the Senate had declared him a public enemy. Search parties would be sent out to look for him, to bring him back to Rome for punishment in the 'ancient manner'. When Nero asked what exactly this punishment comprised, he was told that he would be stripped naked, forced to walk through the streets with his head clamped in a forked branch, and then beaten to death with staves. After a long pause, Epaphroditus suggested it would be better if he committed suicide. Nero retorted, no doubt sarcastically, that Epaphroditus or one of the others should stab themselves first to show him the way. Perhaps he had begun to suspect that they and Phaon had all along been part of the cunning plot against him.

Such a suspicion would certainly have fitted the facts. News of Nero's flight had been taken at once to Nymphidius, who announced to the assembled Praetorians that Nero had shamefully deserted both them and Rome. Then he promised that Galba would pay each guardsman 30,000 sesterces once he became Emperor. With little hesitation, they hailed Galba, in his absence, as *Imperator*. The senators who had been standing by quickly convened a meeting to ratify the choice and condemn Nero to death. It had been in all their interests that Nero should seem to have abdicated by running away before their decisions were taken. Thus, a future emperor would not have grounds to accuse any of them of treason.

Nymphidius, of course, had never had the slightest intention of risking the possibility of Nero's escape to Alexandria. He knew that, as the reigning Emperor, Nero would have been able to command the loyalty of the legions of the East, in the huge arc stretching from Egypt, around the Levantine coast and Asia Minor, to the primitive frontier areas of the Danube. In Egypt he was already worshipped as a god. As the great-great-grandson of Mark Antony, who had once ruled the eastern half of the empire beside Cleopatra, and had dreamed with her of ruling the West as well, Nero would be perceived as reincarnating that iconic hero of a cause that once was lost but could now at last be won. Whether or not Phaon and Epaphroditus had intended to destroy Nero's last hope, their actions fitted perfectly with Nymphidius' agenda. By following their advice, the former Emperor had sacrificed any chance of getting clear away. And now Nymphidius knew exactly where to find him.

Just before dawn, Nero went outside the little villa and watched as the remaining freedmen dug his grave. He had been transformed, in the space of a few hours, from the master of the civilized world to a dirty, sweating fugitive. He pulled himself together sufficiently to test the points of two daggers. 'How base and shameful that I'm still alive,' he said. Even now, he could scarcely believe how quickly his world had collapsed. It was absurd and, to him, unfair, and yet it was happening and he could think of nothing to stop the seemingly inexorable course of events. He had had such magnificent plans for Rome, for the people, for himself. '*Qualis artifex pereo!*' he exclaimed through his tears – 'What an artist dies here!' He begged the freedmen, as a last favour, not to let his head be cut off for his enemies to gloat over and pass around.

Dawn was breaking. As mounted soldiers approached, he quoted in Greek a line of poetry from the *Iliad*: 'I hear the noise of swiftly running steeds.'[19] Aptly enough, these words by Homer herald the arrival, in the poem, of the callous Diomedes, who savagely wounds Aphrodite, the goddess of love, during the siege of Troy. Nero, her disciple, now raised one of the daggers and, with the help of Epaphroditus, plunged it into his own throat. As he slid towards the ground in agony, he was grabbed and held up by a centurion who had leapt from his horse, trying to stem the flow of blood. He was still capable of whispering a few words. 'You're too late,' he told the man, whose only concern had been to capture him alive. 'So this is your loyalty.' His voice failed. His blue eyes protruded and became fixed in a glassy stare. Nero was dead. It was the morning of 9 June, and he was thirty years and six months old.

Nero's final request was granted. Nymphidius and his associates wanted his body disposed of quickly and with the minimum of fuss. They did not want it to become a focus for potential rioters, like the blood-soaked corpse of Julius Caesar a century earlier. His first love, Acté, faithful to the last, claimed his body. She and his two old nurses, Ecloge and Alexandria, washed off the blood and dressed him in a white robe, embroidered with gold thread. His widow, Statilia, seems not to have participated. In accordance with immemorial custom, he was placed on a funeral pyre and cremated. The few mourners transferred his bones and ashes to a porphyry casket and laid it before the altar of the Domitian family tomb, near the Campus Martius, among his illustrious ancestors.[20]

No Roman now proclaimed his divinity. His memory was officially damned, and his statues were removed from public places. The month of 'Neroneus' reverted to being the month of April. Less sensitive, more business-like men took over his Golden House and his Empire. Rome no longer needed to fear being renamed Neropolis.

EPILOGUE

THE BEAST OF THE APOCALYPSE

Nero's death brought disaster in its wake. The senators thought they were preventing civil war by repudiating him in favour of Galba. Events were to prove them wrong. Galba had no better claim to supreme power than a hundred others, now that the old dynasty had died out. Around the frontiers of the Empire, other army commanders began to ask themselves: 'Why Galba? Why not me?' As Tacitus was to write later: 'The secret of empire stood revealed: the Emperor could be made somewhere other than Rome.'[1]

By deposing Nero, the Senate effectively rejected heredity as a qualification for the Principate. But far from throwing the succession officially open to all the competing talents – at least among the senatorial order – it merely ratified the choice already made for it by the Praetorian Prefect. The guards, under the influence of Nymphidius, 'were led to transfer their allegiance from Nero more by deceitful art and pressure than by their personal inclination'; and he was deposed 'more by messages and rumours than by actual force of arms'. Galba accepted the Senate's support but repudiated the dubious preliminaries which had brought it about. He refused to pay the bribe of 30,000 sesterces which Nymphidius had promised, on his behalf, to each guardsman. 'I choose my soldiers,' the new Emperor retorted. 'I don't buy them!'[2]

Galba followed up the sarcasm by replacing Nymphidius as Praetorian Prefect while still on the march to Rome from Spain. The city was stunned. Without Nymphidius' support against Nero, Galba would probably already be dead. With the backing of a consul, Nymphidius went to the Praetorian camp, claimed to be the natural son of Caligula, and asked the guardsmen to make him Emperor instead of Galba; they would then get the money they were owed. The soldiers promptly killed him. They believed, quite wrongly, that Galba would now feel sufficiently grateful towards them to pay the outstanding bribe.[3]

Galba had failed to grasp another great 'secret of empire': if he wanted Praetorian support he would have to pay for it, as both Claudius and Nero had done. He also needed a powerful, legally designated heir. The distinguished senator was over seventy, childless and homosexually oriented. He was so crippled by arthritis in feet and hands that he could scarcely walk more than a short distance, and could not swing a sword. He also had an extensive hernia, which needed to be strapped up. There could be no realistic prospect of such a man marrying a woman of child-bearing age, fathering a son and surviving until the child should be old enough to succeed him. 'Galba's age drew scorn and derision from those who had been used to Nero's youthfulness,' Tacitus writes. 'As is the way of common people (*mos vulgi*), they judged emperors according to their shapeliness and beauty.'[4]

Soldiers and senators judged Galba, rather, by his early mistakes. He executed Nero's general, Turpilianus, for no better reason, it would seem, than that he had followed his master's orders. He sent assassins to murder the Governor of Africa, Clodius Macer, for displaying doubtful loyalty; Vespasian, still at the head of his large army in Judaea, believed that Galba intended to do the same to him. Verginius was abruptly dismissed from his Rhine command and replaced by the unreliable drunkard Aulus Vitellius, son of Claudius' former chief adviser. The Gallic tribes that had fought against Verginius were rewarded. Worse was to follow. As Galba approached the gates of Rome a group of former sailors, whom Nero had recruited as soldiers, came out from the city to petition him about their conditions of service. He rebuffed them haughtily. When they failed to move out of his way fast enough, he ordered his troops to kill them. Galba's partly Spanish army then marched on into the city over their bodies.[5]

On the first day of 69,[6] the Rhine legions that had tried, and failed, to revolt under Verginius, now did so definitively under Vitellius. Galba made his ultimate mistake by hastily adopting as his heir an inexperienced young aristocrat, Lucius Calpurnius Piso Frugi Licinianus, instead of a seasoned commander. This arrangement lasted five days. Poppaea's ex-husband, Otho, outraged at being passed over in favour of a blue-blooded nonentity, had them both murdered by the Praetorians in return for agreeing to pay the long-delayed bribe. Galba had reigned for seven months: Otho was to reign for three. He failed to win the support of Vitellius, whose legions defeated his scratch troops in April near the River Po. Otho's suicide cleared the path to Rome for Vitellius, who was welcomed slavishly by the Senate, many of whose members narrowly escaped being massacred by his troops.

But the East was already stirring. By July, Vespasian and his supporters had put together a massive alliance. He did not need to move any troops from Judaea. He was hailed as Emperor, first by the two legions in Egypt, then by the four in Syria. The Balkan legions, which had been searching for a leader against their rivals on the Rhine, joined up enthusiastically under his banner. It was a Balkan army that now set out, as an advance force, to recapture Rome. By the time they arrived, their opponents had lost thousands of men to disease, thanks to the malarial swamps near the capital, during the long, hot summer; others had simply melted back into the population, determined never to return to the German frontier. The civil war ended in December in vicious street fighting, as the Temple of Jupiter went up in flames on the Capitol Hill, from which Vespasian's eighteen-year-old younger son, the future Emperor Domitian, escaped by disguising himself as a priest of Isis. Eventually, Vitellius was dragged from his hiding place and tortured to death in front of his former subjects.

Nobody knows how many people died in the war. The three men chiefly responsible for starting it – Vindex, Galba and Nymphidius – were early victims. Soldiers of all sides slaughtered, raped and robbed civilians, as well as killing each other. Otho's troops, for instance, ravaged the Gallic area that is now the Italian Riviera, culminating in the destruction of the coastal town of Albantimilium (Ventimiglia), close to the present French border. After their victory in the Po Valley, the Rhine legions looted farms and rural settlements all along the route of their southward march to Rome. Later, the Balkan troops committed the biggest single atrocity of the civil war, by sacking the city of Cremona, leaving it a heap of smoking ruins. 'It was never more clearly proved by terrible disasters and signs,' Tacitus writes, 'that the gods do not care about our well-being but vengefully want to punish us.'[7]

Vespasian had postponed the reduction of Judaea while the conflict raged in Italy. Now he handed over the task to his elder son, Titus. The new imperial dynasty of the Flavians needed a convincing military victory against Rome's declared enemies rather than her own citizens. The Jews refused to surrender Jerusalem, which fell after a long and bitterly resisted siege. Titus granted no quarter. The heavily populated city was put to the sword and the great Temple demolished. The historian Josephus, who was present, reported that more than a million people were killed in the siege – in addition to those who died elsewhere in Judaea and Galilee during the rebellion. That is almost certainly an overestimate, but if it is anywhere near the truth it must surely rank as the worst single massacre in Jewish history until the twentieth century.[8]

Would Nero have been equally ruthless in punishing these rebellious subjects? We cannot know for certain, of course. But if it is reasonable to judge by his treatment of the British rebels a decade earlier, it is arguable that he would have preferred to avoid such a holocaust. The irony is that Titus, who succeeded his father as emperor in 79, is celebrated in one of Mozart's operas, *La Clemenza di Tito* ('The Mercifulness of Titus'), as a ruler of noble magnanimity. Suetonius describes him as 'very benevolent by nature', while Dio affirms that Titus never put a single senator to death during his mild reign of only two years.[9] Nobody since their day seems to have pointed out that, in the context of a historical tradition that praises Titus while demonizing Nero, the life of one Roman senator is evidently worth much more than the lives of a million Jews.

Nero's reputation see-sawed during the Year of Four Emperors, depending on the outlook of successive rulers. Galba, naturally, defamed him and also punished numbers of his former supporters. These included Helius, the freedman who had been left in charge of Rome for more than a year during Nero's absence in Greece, and the ageing poisoner, Lucusta. They were paraded through the streets in chains before being executed, to great public satisfaction. But Galba mysteriously refused all demands for Tigellinus to be put to death, which may indicate that there had been collusion with him at an early stage before the death of Nero. It was Otho who forced Tigellinus to cut his own throat – after the former Praetorian Prefect had enjoyed a last fling in a provincial brothel.

Otho, surprisingly, in view of his long-buried resentment over Poppaea, assiduously cultivated his former rival's memory. He was happy to be hailed as 'Nero' by his troops; he replaced his statues and made funds available for resumption of work on the Golden House. His last act before suicide was to write a letter to Nero's widow, Statilia Messalina: he was sorry he would not now be able to marry her. Vitellius gave Nero's cold remains a lavish new funeral, followed by a banquet at which he called upon a flute-player to perform a number 'from the maestro's book'. Sporus, the fastidious transvestite, killed himself during Vitellius' reign to escape a plan to exhibit him on stage as a woman being raped – thus lending strength to the argument that his role at Nero's court was primarily decorative and symbolic rather than sexually submissive.[10]

The new Flavian dynasty of Vespasian, Titus and Domitian consistently denigrated Nero's memory. Vespasian stopped the work on the Golden House, drained the ornamental lake in its central gardens, and began building there the huge gladiatorial arena that later became known as the Colosseum. At the inaugural series of daily 'games' during the reign of Titus, no fewer than 9,000 animals, both wild and domestic, were slaughtered for entertainment. Domitian executed Epaphroditus for having helped Nero to cut his throat, but this was to protect himself from potentially over-zealous freedmen.[11] Early in the second century, the Emperor Trajan built his huge baths directly on top of a section of the *Domus Aurea* after filling its beautiful salons and corridors with rubble.

Nevertheless, a widespread belief lived on among the common people that Nero had escaped from Rome in disguise, and would one day come back to reclaim his throne. The first to take advantage of this legend was an anonymous young man who was 'accomplished both at singing and playing the cithara' (*'citharae et cantus peritus'*). These skills, according to Tacitus, gave plausibility to his imposture – a fact that should surely lay to rest the traditional sneer that Nero was a poor performer. This first of a line of bogus Neros caused great alarm among the Roman authorities in Greece and Asia, where he recruited deserters from the legions during the Year of Four Emperors. After he was tracked down and killed on the island of Cythnus, where he had armed the slaves, his corpse was taken on a provincial tour and finally shipped to Rome so that the plebs could be assured that, whoever he really was, he was not Nero and he was unquestionably dead.[12]

Nineteen years later, during the reign of Domitian, a more dangerous pretender arose in the East. He also looked like Nero and sang like Nero, while playing the cithara; more importantly, he convinced the Parthians that he really *was* Nero. For a moment it seemed that the King of Parthia might be about to go to war on his behalf. Fortunately, the Romans were able to identify him as a confidence trickster named Terentius Maximus, but it was only with great reluctance that the Parthians agreed to hand him over to imperial justice. Ever since the visit of Tiridates of Armenia, the Parthians had been admirers of Nero, and when they sent ambassadors to Rome to renew the peace treaty he had sponsored, they asked for Nero's memory to be formally honoured.[13]

When too many years had passed to make it plausible that Nero himself could ever return to Rome, his inveterate admirers subscribed to the legend that he would enjoy a second coming from beyond the grave. Each spring and summer, according to Suetonius, they continued to place seasonal flowers upon his tomb in the Campus Martius, and, in spite of the evident risks, to display his edicts in the Forum 'as if he were somehow alive [*quasi viventis*] and just about to return to inflict great evil on his enemies'.

The prophecy was given sustenance from an unexpected quarter – as influential as it was hostile – which ultimately took over entirely from the original legend and transformed its purpose. The persecuted Christians were about to get their revenge in this bizarre contest of reputations and destinies. Nero was predicted to be about to come back to earth as Antichrist, lose the final battle of Armageddon and be submerged alive in a lake of fire and brimstone – there to suffer for all eternity along with the Devil and anyone else whose name 'was not found written in the book of life'.[14]

The best known of all these apocalyptic writings of the first and second centuries of the Christian era are the twenty-two chapters of what has come down to posterity as the 'Book of Revelation' in the canonical New Testament. For most of Christian history it was firmly believed that the Book of Revelation was written by St John the Evangelist, author of the Fourth Gospel, which bears his name. Few scholars would be prepared to take that view today. St John's Gospel is possibly the most sublime work of religious literature ever written. Although it contains a number of beautiful and moving individual passages, the Book of Revelation, considered as a whole, is a radically different work – often shockingly different.[15]

Towards the end of the 1st century, a Christian author named John, writing in the Jewish apocalyptic tradition, announced to the scattered communities of the Christian Church that, from his hill-top home on the Aegean island of Patmos, he had been granted a series of visions. In one of them, he claimed to have seen a strange beast, partly in the shape of a leopard with seven heads, rise out of the sea uttering blasphemies.[16] This 'first beast' has traditionally – and surely accurately – been identifed as symbolizing Rome itself, which is built on seven hills. John later sees a 'second beast', with two horns and the voice of a dragon, which he says is identifiable by the number 666. It is this beast, which, by the same tradition, has been identified as Nero.[17] Whether John of Patmos intended it to represent Nero is a separate issue. What is important for posterity's view of Nero is that early Christian tradition says he did. That tradition pre-dates by a thousand years or more the splitting of Christendom into Catholic, Orthodox and later Protestant strands, and is therefore common to all of them.

John of Patmos' second beast exercises 'all the power of the first beast', and makes people worship it. He also makes fire come down from heaven on to the earth in the sight of men – supposedly a reference to the Great Fire of Rome. His subjects receive 'the mark of the beast' on the forehead or hand. John of Patmos warns all Christians that anyone who worships the beast and his image 'shall be tormented with fire and brimstone in the presence of the holy angels and . . . of the Lamb: and the smoke of their torment ascendeth up for ever and ever: and they have no rest day nor night . . .'.[18]

If the tradition is correct, and the beast is indeed meant to symbolize Nero, then the reference to the worship of his image can only mean the ceremony that the Roman courts used as a test of loyalty to the Emperor. Those men and women who refused to make this formal acknowledgement of his claim to some degree of divinity, by sacrificing (or merely swearing an oath) in front of a bust or plaque representing the Emperor, automatically doomed themselves to prolonged death by torture in a public arena, typically involving braziers and red-hot implements. It is an open question how many credulous believers refused the test of loyalty to Rome for fear of this imaginary fate of eternal punishment by fire and brimstone, conjured up by John's powerful language – and suffered instead the horrifyingly real fate of earthly torture.

Leaving motives to one side, it is arguable that, in terms of consequences, John of Patmos has been responsible for more suffering inflicted on innocent Christians than Nero was. At this remove of time, it is impossible to be sure whether some or all of

Nero's Christian victims were held to be guilty of offences against the state apart from their religious beliefs. But those who died in agony in order to keep faith with John's visionary warnings were guilty of nothing worse than superstitious dread, combined with the pious hope of ascending direct to Heaven as privileged martyrs. It is only in modern times that most Christian theologians have come to see that this kind of morbid rhetoric about everlasting punishment, without mercy and without hope, is incompatible with belief in a loving and omnipotent God.

If the Book of Revelation is treated like any other historical document of its time instead of continuing to shelter behind the fig-leaf of supposedly divine inspiration, then few today would want to take an unqualified stand in favour of John's Apocalyptic Lamb, who has no obvious connection with the peaceful and suffering Lamb of God, who takes upon himself the sins of the world for humankind's salvation. Or, rather, the only connection between the two is in the vengeful and probably deranged mind of its very unsaintly author. His Apocalyptic Lamb, as we have seen in the passage quoted above, oversees the unending torture by fire and sulphur of those who have failed to make it into the exclusive pages of the 'Book of Life'. This is a picture not of Heaven but of Hell-on-Earth. There is a prophetic whiff of Auschwitz about the smoke that rises night and day from this sinister Lamb's brimstone incinerators. And there is a foretaste of modern chemical warfare as his angels hurl dishes of deadly plagues to earth, causing the victims underneath to 'gnaw their tongues for pain', and killing 'every living thing' in the sea.[19] In the face of this genocidal ethical cleansing, who would not be tempted to take sides with Nero if forced to choose between him and the Apocalyptic Lamb?

Another mystical seer, Plutarch (who wrote religious works as well as his famous *Lives*), visualized Nero's soul after death being prepared for reincarnation. While it was being changed in shape so that the former Emperor could be reborn as a viper, a heavenly voice ordained his rebirth, instead, as a frog, to sing among ponds and marshes. This favour was granted him in recognition of his gift of 'freedom' to Greece, the land that the gods most loved. Plutarch was living in Greece at the time of Nero's concert tour, and may very well have attended a performance. He does not suggest that Nero should remain a frog for ever.[20]

Plutarch's contemporary and fellow-Greek, Dio Cocceianus (also known as Dio Chrysostom, 'the golden mouthed'), was devoted to the memory of Nero 'whom still even at this time all men long to be alive, and most men verily do believe at this day that Nero is still living'.[21] This was probably written at roughly the same period as Tacitus wrote his *Histories* and *Annals*. Cocceianus was a wandering philosopher who claimed a divinely appointed mission for the cure of souls, but it is likely that his respect for Nero derived from the same short-lived grant of freedom that swayed Plutarch's heavenly spokesman.

Christendom of the Middle Ages preferred the apocalyptic version. As Bernard Henderson wrote in his 1903 biography of Nero (still the longest in English): 'To be devoured by wolves was his customary fate from the fifth century onwards, though the Devil supped off him at times, and in milder moments he was impaled.'[22] Today we have largely lost our belief in the Devil, but our faith in the monster that was Nero lives on. It is hard to suppress a suspicion that the myth of Nero appeals to something in human nature at a level resistant to truth, if not largely impervious to it.

Nero's hold on the contemporary imagination is demonstrated by the crowds drawn to the recently reopened section of his Golden House – 'the unchallenged favourite for public interest', according to Andrew Wallace-Hadrill in a millennium 'Letter from Rome', published in April 2000. 'To visit the cavernous sequences of the pleasure pavilion of the playboy Emperor, with patches of freshly restored fresco gleaming out . . . is an experience that must move the most jaded tourist.'[23] Meanwhile, in the Vatican City, on the very spot where Nero executed at least some of his Christian victims, pilgrims were arriving from all over the world to celebrate the official 2,000th birthday year of Jesus of Nazareth, and worship him at the shrine of St Peter beneath Michelangelo's great dome.

It is not a mere curiosity of history that Nero and Jesus had things in common, but a vital piece of knowledge about the society in which Christianity sowed its early seeds. Once outside the confines of strict Judaism, the Gospel fell upon ears already conditioned to belief in the potential or actual divinity of various particular human beings. Battle chiefly raged over which of them were appropriate contenders for belief, rather than concerning itself with our modern dilemma of whether any form of supernatural belief is possible at all. That ancient battle was eventually won by those who regarded the books of the New Testament, without exception, as 'holy writ', which it would be heresy to challenge.

The *Annals* of Tacitus cannot lay claim to such exalted status, but generations of scholars have admired his work to an extent that makes it rather a rash enterprise to challenge his time-honoured portrait of Nero as an especially loathsome tyrant, although many have been happy enough to quibble about particular details. The result leaves Nero still stuck anachronistically between the Rock of St Peter and the hard-line classical tradition. To liberate him fully will require the patient demolition of both those entrenched positions. That may need to be the work of more than one generation. But in the immensely long perspective of the history of religious ideas, it is certain we have not yet heard the last word in the supposed cosmic conflict between the Beast and the Lamb. Nero awaits his apotheosis.

APPENDIX ONE

THE CHIEF LITERARY SOURCES

Nero's reign is more abundant in the quality and extent of surviving ancient literary sources – whether written during it or about it – than that of any of his successors as Roman Emperor, throughout the rest of antiquity. Even so, it is far less rich than the period covering the closing years of the Roman Republic and its replacement by the Augustan Principate. The reason for these successive declines remains a matter of debate. There seems to have been a tailing-off of good writing in the generation after the death of Tacitus, as well as a mystifying disappearance of manuscripts. Christians have attracted some of the blame, for censoring, altering and frequently destroying any texts of which they disapproved, and also for creating a society in which religious writing gradually overshadowed other forms of literary endeavour.

The growing absolutism of imperial rule was also an important factor, making work especially difficult for historians. During the Republic, decisions on important affairs of state were taken in public, after debate in the Senate and speeches to citizens in the Forum. As the Principate developed, more and more decisions were taken behind closed doors in the palace, and less and less information about what was really happening was made public. People became sceptical of the truth of all government statements, whether made honestly or not. This process did not fully mature until well after Nero's reign, during which the system of government was still partly open, especially during the first eight years, before the retirement of Seneca. A lot of fairly reliable, factual material was therefore available for ancient historians to work on, but they had to be very careful not to offend the reigning Emperor. Caligula had an obscure playwright burnt alive simply for writing one ambiguous line, which was interpreted, in performance, as a reflection on him.

Ancient historians differed in a number of ways from their modern counterparts, both in outlook and methodology. Two differences are especially important. They were inclined to regard the writing of history less in terms of an accurate and dispassionate reconstruction of the past as in terms of a work of art that provided moral lessons for the present, especially as exemplified in the careers of certain prominent individuals whom they designated as either heroes or villains. Having decided that Nero was a villain, for instance, they would have been reluctant to cloud the issue. 'Good' decisions during his reign would tend to be attributed to the actions or influence of someone else (such as Seneca); 'bad' ones would be blamed on him.

The second significant difference was their attitude to sources. Even if they had an original document in front of them – for instance, the actual wording of a speech – they would be extremely reluctant to quote from it directly. As a matter of professional pride, they would seek to create their own, more eloquent version. It was their metier to refashion the banal actuality of a particular event so that it became, in a sense, more true than ever – so that it was elevated to the level of *poetic* truth.[1] And that, after all, is a very good reason why most of us prefer to read Tacitus than any of the erudite commentators upon his work.

In addition to these general reasons for treating Tacitus with caution – and his *Annals* are by far the most important source for the life and reign of Nero – it is imperative to take into account the great historian's bitter personal experience of imperial rule. Under the 'reign of terror' of the Emperor Domitian, Tacitus had to acquiesce in the judicial murder of numbers of his fellow senators, in order that he himself should survive. He was ashamed of his moral failure. When he was no longer personally in danger he evidently tried to purge his feelings of guilt by writing a moralistic account of his own era (the *Histories*) and of the period which immediately preceded it (the *Annals*). He claimed to be writing without anger or prejudice, but his selection of material focuses on the vices of previous emperors, and his inimitable brand of sardonic misanthropy pins them, writhing, to the page. 'Like so many great artists,' Ronald Mellor writes, 'Tacitus was trying in a healing work of self-revelation to exorcise his own demons; his books are to some degree a study of his own troubled soul.'[2]

Fortunately, unlike most ancient historians, Tacitus will sometimes indicate an occasion where his primary sources are in conflict. These included historical works now lost, such as those of Pliny the Elder, Cluvius Rufus, Fabius Rusticus, Aufidius Bassas and even Agrippina herself, who wrote her memoirs when she was out of favour some time after her son's accession. At least some of those lost works were available to Suetonius and Dio, accounting for similarities in parts of their otherwise very different extant texts. Tacitus also uses the rhetorical contrivance of innuendo to suggest that certain events occurred, when he is not really sure if they did. An example is the scene where Nero, dressed up as a bride, goes through a form of marriage with one of his freedmen. Tacitus indicates that, after the ceremony, events appropriate to the married state took place in public instead of in private. The reader concludes that Nero submitted to public anal intercourse – an assumption which, if true, would surely have cost him his throne very much earlier than the date on which he was in fact deprived of it. Nevertheless, that is the usual supposition, which long ago attained the status of a generally accepted 'fact'. Apologists for Tacitus point out that he can *rarely* be caught out in a direct lie. But how many times is that necessary? Once is surely enough to make it mandatory to treat every statement with the utmost caution.

Our knowledge of Tacitus' background and career is sketchy. We know that his name was, in part, Cornelius Tacitus, but there is uncertainty about his *praenomen*, which may have been Publius. He was born into a prominent equestrian family in southern Gaul in, perhaps, 56. When he was about twenty-one he made a shrewd career move by marrying a daughter of Agricola (Governor of Britain), whose patronage helped him to become a senator under Titus. He held various public appointments under Domitian, and may at one stage have commanded a legion. He became consul the year after Domitian's assassination, and some years later served a term as Governor of Asia. His first extant work, a biography of his father-in-law, contains a denunciation of Domitian. His 'Histories', written in the first decade of the second century, covered the twenty-eight years after Nero's death, but only the narrative to 70 is extant. The *Annals*, his undoubted masterpiece, were published about ten years after the *Histories*, spanning the period from the accession of Tiberius to the suicide of Nero.

Only two (incomplete) manuscripts of the *Annals* survived the Middle Ages, each bearing a different portion of the precious text. The first, a copy made in Germany in about 850, contains books 1–6; the second, copied in the eleventh century, *Annals* 11–16. The missing books had covered the whole of the reign of Caligula and the early years of Claudius, and therefore the period of Nero's birth and early schooldays; also lost are the closing chapters, covering roughly the last two years of Nero's life, and therefore the whole of the tour of Greece and the events leading to his downfall. The accounts by Suetonius and Dio Cassius are vital for plugging some part of these huge gaps, but neither is an adequate substitute.

Gaius Suetonius Tranquillus was a biographer and antiquarian rather than a historian. Much of his work is lost, but he is believed to have written as many as 100 lives, most famously the 'Twelve Caesars', from Julius to Domitian. For part of his career he was in charge of the palace library under the Emperor Hadrian, who dismissed him for apparent over-familiarity with the Empress Sabina. This seems to have occurred when he was about half-way though his researches on the first twelve emperors, so that the later ones get rather less extensive coverage than their predecessors. His coverage of Nero, sixth on his list, is comparatively quite substantial, but much less detailed than that of Tiberius, who of course reigned longer.

Suetonius' selection of material has struck some of his later readers as trivial, even bizarre, considering what he leaves out; and it is arranged chiefly according to themes rather than chronologically, so that it is often impossible to date events with precision. The works, however, are immensely valuable for personal details about their subjects, of a sort that Tacitus would probably have thought beneath the dignity of a serious historian to record. Suetonius is not too proud, either, to quote directly from original documents. He was born a year or two after Nero's death. His father, an equestrian, fought on Otho's side as a senior officer in the 13th Legion in the losing battle beside the River Po against the troops of Vitellius during the Year of Four Emperors.

Dio Cassius (or Cassius Dio), writing about 100 years after Tacitus and Suetonius, compiled in Greek an eighty-book history of Rome from its foundation. It is pedestrian, lacking in particular that mastery of telling detail that distinguishes the work of the two earlier writers. The section dealing with Nero survives only as epitomes drawn up in the eleventh and twelfth centuries at Byzantium, which are believed to be mostly selected extracts rather than summaries, and are prone to error. As a consul, and the son of a consul, Dio tends to judge previous emperors by the extent of their co-operation with the senatorial order, and he follows the tradition of hostility to Nero. Unlike Tacitus, however, he does not reminisce about the Republic as a time of lost 'freedom', but accepts the need for a strong ruler.

Flavius Josephus, who started life as Joseph ben Matthias, was a Pharisee who changed sides in the Jewish rebellion of 66–73. He was the commander of a force of rebels in Galilee who decided to stab each other to death rather than surrender to the Romans, who would probably have crucifed them anyway. When only Josephus and one other remained alive in their besieged stronghold, he persuaded his subordinate to surrender, after all. On being taken in front of Vespasian, he prophesied that the old general would become Roman Emperor. After the prophecy was fulfilled, Josephus stayed on in Judaea long enough to witness Titus' destruction of Jerusalem; then he went to Rome where he lived rent-free for the rest of his life as an imperial pensioner and Roman citizen, writing voluminous historical works, chiefly about the Jews. Naturally, he was careful to show Vespasian and Titus in a favourable light. His *Jewish War*, published in the late 70s and subsidized by Titus, is fascinating and indispensable, but seeks to minimize Titus' responsibility for the sack of Jerusalem. Book 19 of his later *Jewish Antiquities* covers the assassination of Caligula in detail because of the role played by Herod Agrippa in the subsequent accession of Claudius.

A few scattered references to Nero survive in the extant works of Pliny the Elder, who was active as a lawyer in the Roman courts during his reign. His history of his times is lost, but his massive *Natural History* served as a sort of encyclopedia throughout the Middle Ages. As commander of the fleet at Misenum, he ventured too near the erupting Mount Vesuvius in 79 and succumbed along with most of the population of Pompeii and Herculaneum. His nephew, Pliny the Younger, was a friend of Tacitus and the patron of Suetonius. His letters give an interesting picture of his times, and include a few invaluable references to early Christians.

The Greek biographer Plutarch was about eighteen when Nero visited Greece. He almost certainly wrote a life of Nero but it has not survived, unlike his brief lives of Galba and Otho. He was a mystical Platonist, critical of both Stoicism and Epicureanism, and he spent the last thirty years of his life as a priest of the Delphic Oracle. In the next generation Pausanius, a Greek from Asia, wrote a tourist guide to the monuments and places of interest in Greece, which confirms Nero's exertions in the games of 67 as well as his seizure of precious objects to take back to Rome.

Among Latin poets, work written during Nero's reign survives from the pens of Lucan, Persius and Calpurnius Siculus, but with little direct reference to contemporary events. A much sharper picture of urban society emerges from the brilliant, often scabrous verses of Martial, who wrote under the Flavians, but had lived in Rome from about the mid-60s. The later satirist

Juvenal, writing at about the same time as Tacitus, preserves much pre-Flavian material, but in a heavily embroidered form, which is of doubtful value to historians.

As for Seneca, his nephew Lucan and Petronius, author of the *Satyricon*, they are important actors in their own right in Nero's story as told here, and it would be otiose to repeat what has been said about them and their writings, in appropriate context, in the main part of the book.

APPENDIX TWO

WAS NERO A MASOCHIST?

Masochism is not an especially uncommon psychological disorder. Although its name derives from a man who needed to be whipped in order to achieve sexual gratification, its definition has been widened to include less seriously afflicted people who suffer from an addictive desire for physical or verbal abuse, or other forms of humiliating treatment, which are linked in some way with sexual response, not necessarily at a level of complete self-awareness. It is enough for some to be 'under strict orders' in order to derive pleasure from serving a person in superior authority – somebody whose approval is worth more than the degree of humiliation that might be involved in obtaining that appreciation.

Nero is popularly believed to be a sadist – even, perhaps, the most sadistic tyrant who ever lived. Almost all the surviving evidence, however, indicates that he was not a sadist but a masochist. This evidence has been presented at various different points in the book, but without being drawn together until now. The following list is heavily abbreviated, and therefore lacks any of the qualifications that appear in the main text. Individual points may not appear very significant, but in total they reveal a strikingly different personality to the one hallowed by legend.

1. He was dominated by his mother, from whom he was separated for an extensive period before the age of three. It is not known if she inflicted corporal punishment to obtain obedience (normal for Roman boys), but who else would have dared to risk beating a possible future emperor?

2. He deferred to both Seneca, his tutor, and Burrus, his guard commander, for several years after becoming Emperor. Burrus spoke to him peremptorily on a number of recorded occasions.

3. When he transferred his affection from his mother to the freedwoman Acté, he was sufficiently anxious to please her that he tried to marry her, even though such an action could well have cost him his throne.

4. He dressed as a slave to go out at night incognito with other young men, coming back with facial bruising.

5. He was dominated by Poppaea, who subjected him to scornful reproaches in order to get him to murder both his mother and his first wife, Octavia, so that she could become empress. Under her tutelage, he changed his lifestyle from easy domesticity with Acté to the sort of extravagant magnificence characteristic of Hellenistic 'God-Kings'.

6. Acté, Poppaea and his third wife Statilia Messalina were all older than him. So was the only other woman he asked to marry him, his step-sister Antonia, who was about ten years his senior.

7. Octavia was a child when he was forced to marry her. They had no children in ten years of marriage. As she was unable to dominate and excite him as the older women plainly did, it may be that he found it difficult to achieve or sustain intercourse.

8. He played submissive roles on stage, including that of a man in chains.

9. At court, he dressed up as a bride and pretended to submit sexually to one of his freedmen, who played the role of bridegroom.

10. He submitted to extreme dieting and had lead weights placed on his chest while preparing for concerts.

11. He showed excessive deference to the judges of contests that he entered, pretending to fear loss of points or even physical punishment, although he knew he was bound to be judged the winner.

12. He knelt in supplication to audiences after competitive stage performances, in a mute plea for their applause.

13. In order to assure maximum applause, to which he was evidently addicted, he paid as many as 5,000 people to clap and cheer his performances.

14. His chief motive in the persecution of Christians was to shift on to them the blame for the Great Fire of Rome that otherwise fell on him, hoping thereby to restore himself to public favour.

15. He tried to stop the practice of fights to the death between gladiators in the arena.

16. He protested at having to sign death warrants.

17. He spared a number of conspirators who had plotted to kill him.

18. Unlike his predecessors, he declined all opportunities to acquire military glory by using (or attempting to use) his highly trained legions to slaughter 'barbarians' beyond the frontiers, preferring peaceful diplomacy to war.

19. He appeared strangely apathetic in the last weeks of his life, when he lacked the support of any obvious authority figures, to whose advice he could have deferred.

20. On his last night, he allowed himself to be led in the opposite direction from the obvious route to safety, accepting the suggestions of his former slaves, crawling on his hands and knees through a thorn hedge to a hide-out, and further abasing himself by drinking from a puddle.

21. Instead of trying to escape abroad while he was still at liberty, he waited supinely while his servants dug his grave, before cutting his throat.

NOTES

References to ancient sources follow conventional numbering except in the case of Dio Cassius, where the traditional notation of the Greek text can baffle even experienced researchers; readers are therefore referred to volume and page number of the only readily available and complete English translation, the nine-volume Loeb edition.

Preface

1. Nero was 'Son of God' through deification of his predecessor, Claudius, who was also his step-father and uncle; the appellation appeared on his coins as *DV* (short for *DIVI FILIUS*). Latin differentiates between *divus* (a god who was once human) and *deus* (always a god); Greek uses one word, *theos*, to cover both. In the eastern part of the Empire, where god-kings were traditional, Nero was worshipped unequivocally as *theos*, *deus* or *filius dei*. For his triumphal procession through Rome, see Suetonius, *Nero*, 25. For his last night and suicide, Suetonius, *Nero*, 47–9; Dio, *Histories*, 8.187–93.

2. See Chapter Eleven, 'Saving Rome from the Christians'. The state of 'Jesus of history' studies is conveniently summarized in Mark Allan Powell, *The Jesus Debate* (Oxford, 1999), originally published in the USA as *Jesus as a Figure in History* (Louisville, 1998).

3. Both men arguably had 'twelve disciples', Nero's being the inner circle of a religious brotherhood, '*Fratres Arvales*', devoted to the cult of emperor worship; on a number of special days throughout the year they offered up blood sacrifices of animals and birds in a Roman temple to him, his family and his deified ancestors. These 'Arval Brothers' were chosen from among the Roman elite to run what seems to have been a sort of glorified masonic lodge.

4. '*O Néron, laisse-moi vénérer ta mémoire!*', quoted in Mario Praz, *The Romantic Agony* (Oxford, 2nd edn, 1951), p. 190.

5. For Nero's first 'professional' performances, in Naples, see Chapter Ten; for his concert tour of Greece, chapters Twelve and Thirteen.

6. In Caesar, *Gallic War*, e.g. Book 4.15 on the massacre of a reported 430,000 of the migrating Usipetes and Tencteri tribes. Michael Grant summarizes Caesar's own claims to have fought more than 30 pitched

battles in the Gallic War, captured more than 800 towns, killed a million men and taken prisoner a million more. Grant, *Caesar* (London, 1974), p. 101.

7. He liked to watch the faces of the dying. Once, outside Rome, when an executioner could not be found to beat some criminals to death, he sent for one from the city and waited until nightfall to witness the punishment. Suetonius, *Claudius*, 34.

8. Suetonius, *Claudius*, 28.

9. Poppaea Sabina, as Empress, secured in 64 the release of some Jewish priests who had been arrested in Palestine for political agitation. Josephus, *Autobiography*, 13–16.

10. Notably the late Sir Ronald Syme, OM. See his exemplary *The Roman Revolution* (Oxford, 1939) and his lengthy *Tacitus* (2 vols, Oxford, 1958).

11. Jás Elsner and Jamie Masters (eds), *Reflections of Nero* (London, 1994), Introduction.

Introduction

1. Julius Caesar was hailed as '*imperator*' many times by his troops, but at that stage of constitutional development it signified 'commanding and victorious general'.

2. Augustus published a list of his achievements, including his rise to power, in the *Res Gestae Divi Augusti*. The most accessible edition, with Latin text, English translation and notes is that edited by P.A. Brunt and J.M. Moore (Oxford, 1967, and many reprints).

3. Demographic estimates about ancient Rome inevitably involve much guesswork. For a recent attempt, see Walter Scheidel, 'Emperors, Aristocrats and the Grim Reaper: Towards a Profile of the Roman Elite', *Classical Quarterly* (No. 1, 1999; Vol. 93 of continuous series), 254–81. Scheidel refers to the 'statistical fluke' that enabled Augustus 'to outlive both his rivals and their memory', in spite of the 'aggressive germ community' in Rome, where malaria was endemic.

4. A few examples among many: in spite of being a serial adulterer he introduced the death penalty for adultery; he hired assassins to murder Mark Antony, but after making a deal with him he fled from the field of the first Battle of Philippi (against Brutus and Cassius) and hid in a marsh for three days, leaving Antony to win without him; he enforced the deaths of hundreds of his political enemies in proscriptions; in 40 BC he burnt the ancient Etruscan city of Perusia to the ground, slaughtering many civilians while sparing the lives of the defending garrison (who surrendered to avoid starvation) because he wanted them to increase the size of his army in order to seize even more power. Suetonius, *Augustus*, 10, 13, 15, 62, 69; Elder Pliny, *Natural History*, 7.147–50; Plutarch, *Antony*, 22; Appian, *Civil Wars*, 5.46–7; Seneca, *De Clementia*, 1.9.

5. Caligula marched an army to the Channel to invade Britain, but (for reasons that are unclear) failed

to do so. Claudius conquered south-east Britain and incorporated Mauretania into the Empire. Suetonius, *Gaius* (Caligula), 46; *Claudius*, 17; Dio, *Histories*, 7.415–27.

6. Suetonius, *Nero*, 10.

7. Suetonius, *Nero*, 12.

8. The estimated number of slaves in Italy in Augustus' reign was about 2 million, possibly as many as 3 million, forming 35 to 40 per cent of the population. Keith Hopkins, *Conquerors and Slaves* (Cambridge, 1978), p. 8. This estimate would mean that 500,000 new slaves were 'needed' each year for the Roman Empire as a whole between about 50 BC and AD 150 (compared with an annual average of 28,000 over 350 years of the Atlantic slave trade between Africa and the Americas, with a peak period average of 60,000). Keith Bradley, *Slavery and Society at Rome* (Cambridge, 1994), p. 32.

9. 'The mass eviction of the poor by the rich underlay the political conflicts and civil wars of the last century of the Roman Republic', Hopkins, *Conquerors and Slaves*, p. 5.

10. In AD 47 Claudius decreed that any sick slaves abandoned by masters on the islet of Aesculapius in the Tiber would automatically become free, and that any master who killed a slave just because he was sick would be liable to face a murder charge. Suetonius, *Claudius*, 25.

11. Tacitus, *Annals*, 14.42–5.

12. 'Formal manumission' conferred citizenship. The more usual informal version 'meant that the liberated slave enjoyed only a *de facto* freedom at the pleasure of the owner', Bradley, *Slavery and Society*, p. 155.

13. Captured 'barbarian' warriors often ended their days killing each other for entertainment in the arena. Even women were sometimes made to fight as gladiators. See Michael Grant, *Gladiators* (London, revised edn, 1971), pp. 27–35.

14. Tacitus speaks for the senatorial class when he asserts that the inferior status of freedmen in relation to that of free-born citizens and nobles is a guarantee of *libertas*, associated with the former Republic. Under the monarchical system of the Principate, however, these ex-slaves rise above their appropriate station in life and 'get power in the state'. Tacitus, *Germania*, 25.

15. 'The heyday of the power of freedmen coincides with a period of intrigue and influence among the female members of the imperial household', Andrew Wallace-Hadrill, 'The Imperial Court', in *Cambridge Ancient History*, Vol. 10 (1996), p. 302.

16. Yann Le Bohec points out that whereas in our day soldiers, such as those of the United Nations, are sent to keep the peace, 'such an idea would have appeared absurd' to the Romans. They fought to win. Nero, he alleges, was 'incapable of embarking upon reform or conquest; the fact that all his wars were defensive differentiated him from the other emperors'. Yann Le Bohec, *The Imperial Roman Army* (London/New York, 1994); English translators of *L'Armée Romaine, sous le Haut-Empire* (1989), pp. 120, 186.

272 *Notes*

17. Julius Caesar was planning to leave Rome to invade Parthia when Brutus and Cassius stabbed him. Suetonius, *Julius*, 79–80.

18. Nero did hold 'orgies', but they were stylish events in which members of the imperial family are more likely to have dressed up in gorgeous clothes than to have doffed them, and would have featured voyeuristic entertainment rather than imperial participation in front of their courtiers. See Chapter Ten.

19. Suetonius, *Nero*, 34.

20. Juvenal, *Satires*, 6.114–32.

21. Dio, *Histories*, 7.413.

22. Suetonius, *Tiberius*, 42–5.

Chapter One

1. Suetonius, *Nero*, 5.

2. Before adoption by Tiberius, he was Nero Claudius Germanicus; afterwards he became Germanicus Julius Caesar. His daughter Agrippina the Younger, Nero's mother, therefore became Julia (Agrippina) instead of merely Claudia (Agrippina), in line with Augustus' dynastic plans to be succeeded ultimately by an heir of his blood, because Agrippina the Elder was his grand-daughter. All Roman girls took the name of their paternal *gens*. Thus, if a *Pater Familias* of the *gens* Cornelius had seven daughters, all seven would be named Cornelia. This can lead to insoluble problems of identification in the ancient texts.

3. Tacitus, *Annals*, 3.1–6.

4. 'Germanicus . . . claimed major victories – and accomplished very little. Despite, or rather because of,

that fact, he enjoyed lavish honours', Erich S. Gruen, 'The Expansion of the Empire under Augustus', *Cambridge Ancient History*, Vol. 10 (1996), p. 186. 'Germanicus was what would be called today a "charismatic leader", especially if we take the cynical attitude that charisma means that image takes precedence over substance', Anthony A. Barrett, *Agrippina* (New York, 1996), p. 22.

5. Suetonius, *Augustus*, 23.

6. Lucius Aulus Sejanus was Praetorian Prefect and later also Consul when he plotted to overthrow Tiberius to become emperor himself. Claudius' mother, Antonia, warned Tiberius in a letter smuggled from Rome to Capri. Sejanus was executed along with his children and many of his followers.

7. Tacitus, *Annals*, 5.3.

8. He had Phidias' statue of Zeus brought to Rome from Olympia so he could replace its head with his own. Another statue of himself, life-sized and covered with gold, was set up in a shrine to be dressed each day in whatever sort of clothes he happened to be wearing. He ordered a bust of himself to be placed in the Temple at Jerusalem to be worshipped by the Jews, but fortunately for the *Pax Romana* he died before this directive was enforced. Suetonius, *Gaius*, 22; Tacitus, *Histories*, 5.9; cf. Anthony A. Barrett, *Caligula: The Corruption of Power* (New York, 1989), pp. 140–53.

9. Suetonius, *Gaius*, 14.

10. Suetonius, *Gaius*, 24. But see

the 'highly sceptical' analysis by Barrett, *Agrippina*, p. 54.

11. Suetonius, *Nero*, 6.

12. The motives, movements and locations of those involved in this series of incidents are impossible to establish definitively. cf. Barrett, *Agrippina*, pp. 61–70.

13. Under Augustus' moral legislation, a complaisant husband of Gnaeus Domitius' status could have been arraigned before the Senate, with doubtful hope, under Caligula's malign influence, of survival.

14. The general case is exhaustively set out in John Bowlby, *Attachment and Loss* (3 vols, London, 1969, 1973, 1980).

15. Suetonius, *Nero*, 6.

16. Suetonius, *Gaius*, 37–9.

17. Ibid., 54.

18. Ibid., 36.

19. Ibid., 27–33.

Chapter Two

1. The version of events given here is based chiefly on the Jewish historian Josephus' detailed account in Book 19 of *Jewish Antiquities*, which is open to a radically different interpretation of Claudius' actions and intentions than the traditionally accepted one based on the much briefer treatments by Suetonius and Dio, in which he comes to power by chance rather than design.

2. At this period the Palatine Hill, south-west of, and overlooking, the Roman Forum, was still occupied by many private dwellings of the aristocracy as well as the imperial household, and was a maze of narrow alleyways in some parts and large gardens in others.

3. Josephus, *Antiquities*, 19.96–8. The senator is named in the text as Minucianus, but has been identified as Lucius Annius Vinicianus, one of the 'Arval Brothers'. See T.P. Wiseman, *Death of an Emperor* (Exeter, 1991), pp. 47–8.

4. Valerius Asiaticus, from southern Gaul, survived to become consul in 46, but was forced to suicide by Claudius a year later for alleged treason.

5. Cassius Chaerea was a long-serving officer, who may have come up through the ranks. He served as a centurion in Germany in AD 14. Caligula had forced him, to his shame, to torture an actress who refused to betray a lover accused of slandering the Emperor.

6. German bodyguards were evidently chosen by Caligula because he did not fully trust his own Praetorians.

7. Milonia Caesonia, Caligula's fourth wife, was about thirty-five. She and Caligula had been married only a short time. Suetonius repeats a story that she had given him a love potion which sent him insane; Suetonius, *Gaius*, 50.

8. Ordinary Praetorian guardsmen received an annual salary of 3,000 sesterces, compared with only 900 for a legionary foot-soldier. Information on the pay of individual higher ranks is scarce.

9. The Urban Cohorts were basically a militarized police force, responsible for the safety of the city of Rome, whereas the Praetorians' special responsibility was the safety

of the Emperor. Their salary level was half that for Praetorians, but they were on a higher level than the Vigiles, the third component of the Rome garrison, who had duties including police work and fire-watching.

10. Capitol Hill was the original fortified stronghold of Rome, from whose Tarpeian Rock traitors were hurled to their deaths in the early Republic. It towers above the Forum, opposite the Palatine Hill.

11. Tacitus, *Annals*, 11.1.

12. The imperial 'palace' complex of Caligula had grown from a number of different buildings used successively by Augustus and Tiberius, and which Caligula extended towards the Forum, where there was an official, guarded entrance.

13. Agrippa is better known as 'Herod Agrippa' because he is given that name in the Acts of the Apostles. As a boy he was brought up alongside Claudius in the house of his mother, Antonia (Mark Antony's younger daughter), who was a friend of his family. He was briefly imprisoned by Tiberius, who was impatient of his intrigues, but his career was advanced by Caligula and then by Claudius, who made him King of Judaea. According to Acts, he beheaded the disciple James (brother of John) and put St Peter in jail, from which he was rescued by an angel who arranged for his chains to fall off; Herod then executed the unlucky prison guards. At Caesarea in 44, speaking from his rostrum, Agrippa was hailed as a god by the crowd and was at once struck down by an angel, was 'eaten up by worms' and died. Acts of the Apostles 12.1–23.

14. Tiberius Claudius Caesar (41–55) gained the *cognomen* Britannicus after his father's conquest of Britain in 43.

15. Suetonius, *Galba*, 5.

16. Crispus may have been rather older than Claudius and even more eccentric. Pliny the Elder records a curious story of his apparent dendrophilia, in which he pours libations on a favourite beech tree and embraces it lovingly.

17. 'Stock characters in the romantic plays of Shakespeare, such as the ghost, the nurse and the barbarous villain, were transmitted from the Greek through the medium of Seneca', *Oxford Companion to Classical Literature* (2nd edn, 1989), pp. 517–18.

18. Laws of 18 BC imposed the death penalty for adultery and some homosexual acts, and confiscation of half the estate of a man who seduced a virgin or a respectable widow. Bachelors had to pay heavier taxes, but married men with children were rewarded with incentives. To inhibit displays of wasteful luxury, upper limits were placed on the amount of money a host could spend on dinner, but were habitually ignored.

19. St Paul had to be rescued by the Town Clerk of Ephesus after preaching that gods and goddesses that were made by craftsmen were not divine at all.

20. Under the Republic, two consuls were appointed to serve together for a whole year. The

emperors found it convenient to appoint consuls for only six months or so, in order to spread their patronage more widely.

21. Suetonius, *Nero*, 6.

22. This was the 'Game of Troy', open to aristocratic boys. Suetonius, *Nero*, 6.

23. Suetonius, *Claudius*, 17; Dio, *Histories*, 7.421–3.

24. Tacitus, *Annals*, 11.26–38.

25. Tacitus, *Annals*, 11.12.

26. Ibid., 11.27.

27. Tacitus, *Annals*, 11.30.

28. Ibid., 11.31. However, Suetonius (*Claudius*, 29) suggests improbably that Claudius himself signed the marriage contract, having been led to believe that the wedding was a pretence for his benefit, in order to thwart a prophecy that an unfortunate fate would befall Messalina's husband. Anthony A. Barrett thinks this is 'perhaps the least unsatisfactory explanation' (*Agrippina* [New York, 1996], p. 91).

29. This was the actor Mnester, whom Claudius had firmly instructed to do whatever Messalina told him to do. The law discriminated against actors, who were classed as *infames*, along with prostitutes and gladiators.

30. Tacitus, *Annals*, 11.38.

Chapter Three

1. In addition to Pallas as keeper of the accounts, the other leading freedmen's areas of authority were: Narcissus, *ab epistulis*, in charge of correspondence; Callistus, *a libellis*, in charge of petitions.

2. Tacitus, *Annals*, 12.1–2.

3. Ibid., 12.3.

4. Lucius Vitellius is said to have been the first senator to prostrate himself in front of Caligula as if worshipping a god. Claudius trusted him so much that he put him in charge of the capital when he left Rome for the British campaign in 43.

5. The praetorship was the second highest regular magistracy in the state, immediately below that of consul. It carried important judicial functions, although fewer than under the Republic. Ex-praetors could expect to be sent out to govern provinces or command legions.

6. Tacitus, *Annals*, 12.7.

7. Dio, *Histories*, 8.17

8. Suetonius, *Nero*, 52.

9. 'Roman moral superiority was a guarantee of the divine favour which assured Roman military successes . . . Idealised Roman forefathers gave authority to the moral precepts enjoined on their descendants', Catharine Edwards, *The Politics of Immorality in Ancient Rome* (Cambridge, 1993), pp. 21–2.

10. Tacitus, *Annals*, 12.56–7; Suetonius, *Claudius*, 32.

11. Tacitus, *Annals*, 12.64.

12. Tacitus, *Annals*, 12.64–5.

13. Suetonius, *Claudius*, 42.

Chapter Four

1. Tacitus, *Annals*, 12.66–8; Dio, *Histories*, 8.29–33. Dio's version includes Nero's joke about mushrooms being the food of the gods, since they led directly to Claudius' deification.

2. Suetonius, *Claudius*, 44.

3. For Nero's first few days as Emperor, see Tacitus, *Annals*, 12.69, 13.1–5; Suetonius, *Claudius*, 45, *Nero*, 8–10; Dio, *Histories*, 8.37.

4. Tacitus, *Annals*, 13.1. One of the assassins was an imperial freedman, Helius, then a tax official in Asia, whom Nero later put in charge of Rome for more than a year when he toured Greece in 66 and 67. It is difficult to think of a comparable career ladder: from slave to tax inspector, to secret agent with a licence to kill, to direct executive authority, including the power of life and death, over all the senators and people of the city of Rome.

5. The *Apocolocyntosis*. Claudius' many distinguished victims put him on trial at the bar of Heaven, but Caligula steps up to claim him as his runaway slave.

6. Suetonius, *Claudius*, 46.

7. Seneca, *Apocolocyntosis*, 4. Professor Sullivan says the play establishes 'a Neronian ideology' early in the reign: 'an image had been created by Seneca, which aspirants to fame, fortune and power had to incorporate into their more personal flattery of Nero's good looks, godlike presence or poetic skills', J.P. Sullivan, *Literature and Politics in the Age of Nero* (Cornell, 1985), p. 51.

8. The cithara was an ancient instrument even in Nero's day, having been in use in the Greek world since about the middle of the second millennium BC. It differed from the lyre in that its sound box was made of wood instead of the shell of a tortoise, and it was usually larger and heavier. It had, typically, seven strings stretched over a bridge low down the face, which were adjusted along a bar near the top. The performer held it up against the left shoulder and chest by a short sling over the left forearm or wrist, leaving the fingers of the left hand free to pluck the strings from behind, while the right hand used a plectrum at the front of the instrument, facing the audience. A skilled performer could thus play a bright, clear note with the plectrum while simultaneously producing softer tones with his finger ends. Aristocratic, amateur musicians preferred the lyre. Mastery of the cithara required long and arduous professional training, especially for a performer, like Nero, who wanted to sing at the same time. cf John G. Landels, *Music in Ancient Greece and Rome* (London/New York, 1999), pp. 47–61.

9. Tacitus, *Annals*, 13.4.

10. Ibid.

11. Ibid., 13.5.

12. Evidence for the nature and activities of the *Consilium* in the early Principate is sparse. Its membership can ony be a matter of conjecture; it would have caused a scandal if a woman's name (Agrippina's) had been listed, as women were officially barred from the political process. For a recent discussion, see A. Wallace-Hadrill, 'The Imperial Court', in *Cambridge Ancient History*, Vol. 10 (1996).

13. Control of the kingdom of Armenia had long been a source of contention between Rome and the neighbouring Parthian Empire, with each side promoting its own

candidates for the throne. Hostilities rumbled on for much of the reign, until Nero eventually achieved a long-term diplomatic solution.

Chapter Five

1. The acute accent placed here on the final letter of 'Acte' is not strictly in accordance with classical orthography, but it takes account of the less-than-perfect transliteration from the Greek version of the name. The Greek letter *eta*, which converts to Latin 'e', is always long, suggesting that the probable pronunciation of the name is 'Ack-tee' (or possibly 'Ack-tay').

2. Tacitus, *Annals*, 13.12.

3. Dio, *Histories*, 8.49.

4. Suetonius, *Nero*, 28.

5. *The Oxford Classical Dictionary* (Oxford, 1949), p. 108.

6. Dio says that Acté, through winning Nero's love, was actually adopted into the Attalid family; Dio, *Histories*, 8.47.

7. Tacitus, *Annals*, 13.13.

8. Tacitus, *Annals*, 13.13.

9. Ibid., 13.13–15.

10. Suetonius, *Nero*, 33.

11. Anthony A. Barrett, *Agrippina* (New York, 1996), p. 171.

12. Tacitus, *Annals*, 14.15.

13. Ibid., 13.18. Antonia Minor was mother of Germanicus and Claudius.

14. Rubellius Plautus was notionally a sprig of the Julian clan. His mother got her name of Julia from the fact that her paternal grandfather, the Emperor Tiberius, had been adopted by Augustus. This dynastic legal fiction from a vanished era was enough to endanger Augustus' supposed great-great-grandson Rubellius Plautus, whenever plots were suspected by his genuine great-great-grandson Nero.

15. Tacitus, *Annals*, 13.20.

16. Faenius Rufus went on to become a joint Praetorian Prefect, and was executed by Nero for his leading role in the so-called Pisonian conspiracy of 65.

17. Faustus Cornelius Sulla was a descendant of the dictator Sulla (138–78 BC), who seriously considered executing the young Julius Caesar, but eventually spared him, with justifiable misgivings.

18. For a pithy assessment of this report of a golden quinquennium, see Miriam T. Griffin, *Nero: The End of a Dynasty* (London, 1984), pp. 37–8; she helpfully quotes the relevant Latin passages from the two obscure fourth-century texts in which the references to Trajan appear: Aurelius Victor's *Liber de Caesaribus*, 5.2–4, and the *Epitome de Caesaribus*, 5.2–5.

19. Tacitus, *Annals*, 13.31.

20. Ibid., 13.50–1. It would be anachronistic to suggest that Nero's proposal shows he favoured 'free trade' as a policy concept.

Chapter Six

1. 100 million is a convenient round figure, but an earlier generation of demographers greatly underestimated how populous the Roman Empire was when they guessed about 50 million or 60 million. Roman Britain, for

instance, once thought to have fewer than a million inhabitants, is now believed to have had 4 million. Colin Wells comments: 'Throughout the empire new archaeological evidence suggests that we should revise population estimates drastically upwards.' Colin Wells, *The Roman Empire* (2nd edn, London, 1992), p. 305.

2. Seneca, *De Clementia*, l.l.

3. Ibid., 1.5.

4. Miriam T. Griffin, *Nero*, p. 47.

5. Tacitus, *Annals*, 14.16.

6. 'If a man were called to fix the period in the history of the world during which the condition of the human race was most happy and prosperous, he would, without hesitation, name that which elapsed from the death of Domitian to the accession of Commodus.' (i.e., 95–180), Edward Gibbon, *The Decline and Fall of the Roman Empire*, (1776–88), Chapter 3.

7. For a recent assessment of the Stoic opposition, see David Shotter, *Nero* (Lancaster Pamphlet, London/New York, 1997).

8. Veterans were entitled to a gratuity and housing after discharge from the legions. In some cases they were placed in specially built *coloniae* to provide a Romanized leaven in particular provinces. Only too often, provincials were evicted from their land to make way for them. cf Graham Webster, *The Roman Imperial Army* (London, 1969).

9. Suetonius, *Nero*, 19; Dio, *Histories*, 8.149; Tacitus, *Annals*, 15.36; Seneca, *Naturales Quaestiones*, 6.8; Pliny, *Natural History*, 6.181, 184.

10. Tacitus, *Annals*, 13.6–8. Vespasian, the future Emperor (69–79), was the son of a peripatetic equestrian tax-gatherer. Corbulo was the half-brother of Caesonia, Caligula's last wife.

11. Tacitus, *Annals*, 13.2.

12. Ibid., 13.25; Suetonius, *Nero*, 26; Dio, *Histories*, 8.51–5.

13. Tacitus, *Annals*, 13.47. Tacitus implausibly presents the story of this encounter as if it was a fabrication designed to get Faustus into trouble; but clashes between rival gangs of young men after dark are only to be expected.

14. Tacitus, *Annals*, 13.45–6, *Histories*, 1.13; Dio, *Histories*, 8.61, 135; Suetonius, *Nero*, 35, *Otho*, 3; Plutarch, *Galba*, 19.

15. Tacitus, *Annals*, 13.46. A woman who spent three nights away from her husband was giving grounds for divorce.

16. Ibid., 13.45.

17. J.P.V.D. Balsdon, *Roman Women* (London, 1962), p. 125; Sallust, *Catiline*, 25.

18. Seneca, *Epistulae Morales*, 19.

19. Catharine Edwards, *The Politics of Immorality in Ancient Rome* (Cambridge, 1993), p. 88.

20. Tacitus, *Annals*, 14.1.

21. On Octavia as victim see Tacitus, *Annals*, 60–4.

22. Ibid., 14.2.

23. Some historians doubt that Poppaea was involved at all, suspecting that the date order might have been rearranged, perhaps by one of Tacitus' sources, to provide a cogent motive for the murder. Thus Michael Grant: 'It looks probable that he and other historians

antedated her influence over Nero in order to provide a tidy, somewhat novelettish course of events to explain the murder of Agrippina', Grant, *Nero* (London, 1970), p. 48.
24. Tacitus, *Annals*, 14.1.

Chapter Seven

1. The narrative here of Agrippina's murder chiefly follows that of Tacitus in *Annals*, 14.3–8, with contributions from Suetonius (*Nero*, 34) and Dio (*Histories*, 8.63–7). An account written only a few years after the events described is contained in the anonymous short play (fewer than 1,000 lines) known as *Octavia*, once mistakenly thought to have been by Seneca; it contains a description in verse of the shipwreck and murder (lines 310–76) and features a blood-curdling monologue by Agrippina's ghost (593–645). As this is tragic poetry its value as history is limited. It does, however, fit well with what Tacitus reports.
2. Dio, *Histories*, 8.83.
3. Ibid., 8.55.
4. Elder Pliny, *Natural History*, 9.172.
5. Tacitus, *Annals*, 14.7.
6. Anthony Storr, *The Dynamics of Creation* (London, 1972), p. 53.
7. 'Mothers can be fatal to their sons . . . She that gives life also blocks the way to freedom', Camille Paglia, *Sexual Personae* (Yale UP, 1990), p. 14.
8. Tacitus, *Annals*, 14.9; Suetonius, *Nero*, 34; Dio, *Histories*, 8.67.
9. Suetonius, *Nero*, 34.

10. Dio, *Histories*, 8.71.
11. Publius Clodius Thrasea Paetus was a well-known Stoic, credited with being an opposition leader within the Senate. His walk-out may have been less in reaction to Nero's murder of his mother than to the Senate's response in sycophantically voting an official thanksgiving for it.
12. Considering that she is supposed to have played such an important role in persuading Nero to kill his mother, it is strange that Poppaea is not mentioned again in the sources until after the Emperor returns to Rome some months after his crime.
13. Tacitus, *Annals*, 14.13–14.
14. cf. J.P. Toner, *Leisure and Ancient Rome* (Cambridge, 1995), pp. 1–10.
15. Professional actors were usually slaves or freedmen. They were considered to lack integrity because they pretended to be somebody else and declaimed lines that they did not believe.
16. In Greek mythology, Zeus becomes King of the Gods after overthrowing his murderous father Kronos ('Old Father Time'). In Roman mythology, Jupiter deals similarly with Saturn.
17. Dio, *Histories*, 8.93–5.
18. Tacitus, *Annals*, 14.14.
19. The Field of Mars was where soldiers had trained in the early years of the Republic, but by Nero's time it was the site of numerous family tombs and temples.
20. Tacitus, *Annals*, 14.15.
21. His voice was '*exigua et fusca*', Suetonius, *Nero*, 20.
22. Suetonius, *Nero*, 11.

23. Dio, *Histories*, 8.81; Suetonius, *Nero*, 20; Tacitus, *Annals*, 14.15.

24. Calpurnius Siculus, *Eclogues*, 1.42, 59.

Chapter Eight

1. This force comprised more than one-eighth of the entire Roman army, bottled up in about one-quarter of a primitive offshore island. Paulinus had a reputation as an intrepid and adventurous commander: he had been the first Roman general to cross the Atlas mountains in North Africa with his troops and reach jungles 'swarming with elephants and snakes', Elder Pliny, *Natural History*, 5.14.

2. The chief ancient sources are Tacitus, *Annals*, 14.29–39 and Dio, *Histories*, 8.83–105. 'The course of the rebellion has been often told, yet the horror of the events does not pall', Peter Salway, *Roman Britain* (Oxford, 1981), p. 117.

3. It would have taken at least a fortnight for a message from Britain to reach Rome, and even longer for an individual messenger who could be questioned about events there.

4. Dio, *Histories*, 8.23. Caratacus was pardoned by Claudius; afterwards he lived in exile in Italy with his wife and family.

5. Suetonius, *Nero*, 18.

6. Dio, *Histories*, 8.57, 83.

7. 'Tu regere imperio populos, Romanae, memento; Hae tibi erunt artes; pacisque imponere morem, Parcere subjectis et debellare superbos.' Virgil, *Aeneid*, 6.852–5.

8. Tacitus, *Annals*, 8.31.

9. The Trinobantes (or Trinovantes) occupied the area north of the Thames Estuary, which later became Essex. When Julius Caesar invaded for the second time, in 54 BC, they had allied briefly with the Romans, in order to gain an advantage over rival tribes.

10. Tacitus, *Annals*, 8.30.

11. It was presumably not far from Watling Street, which crosses the Midlands, south-west of Leicester and north of Birmingham, on Paulinus' line of march between London and Wroxeter.

12. Accurate copies of Roman arms and armour are widely available in England, where they are used by enthusiasts for reconstructing battles. Today, in the city of Chester (whose name derives from Latin *castra* = army camp), occasional 'legionary soldiers' in full fig may be seen mingling with tourists during the holiday season.

13. Tacitus, *Annals*, 14.37.

14. Ibid., 14.38–9.

15. Cerialis, who had lost much of the 9th legion when fighting Boudicca, was made governor by Vespasian in 71, and pushed the boundary of the Roman conquest as far north as the Pennines. His successor, Frontinus, edged further to the west; Agricola, governor from 77, conquered (temporarily) half of Scotland.

16. Martial, *Epigrams*, 7.34.

17. See Chapter Five, note 15.

18. On Roman attitudes to public baths, see J.P. Toner, *Leisure and Ancient Rome* (Cambridge, 1995), pp. 53–64.

19. Suetonius, *Nero*, 20, 24.

20. Ibid., 11.

21. The Circus Maximus, situated in a valley between the Palatine and Aventine Hills, held up to 250,000 spectators. Racing was visible from part of the palace complex.

22. Suetonius, *Nero*, 22.

23. Dio, *Histories*, 8.105.

24. Tacitus, *Annals*, 14.51–6.

Chapter Nine

1. This process seems to have occurred earlier in Sicily than it did on the Italian mainland. That was why, in the closing years of the Republic, the gladiator Spartacus was able to recruit a slave army so rapidly in the rebellion that bears his name. After defeat, while trying to escape north through Italy, the survivors were the victims of a horrifying mass crucifixion by Crassus, Julius Caesar's colleague in the First Triumvirate. Ever afterwards, the Romans were especially watchful in Sicily to avoid a repetition; few can have wanted to live there.

2. Dio, *Histories*, 7.335.

3. The evidence derives from anonymous marginal notes on the *Satires* of Juvenal made by a scholiast, perhaps several centuries later. The lines on which he comments are those portraying Tigellinus as a tyrannical figure, who has his critics burnt to death in the arena. Scholiast, Juvenal, *Satires*, 1.155.

4. Ibid.

5. Dio, *Histories*, 8.105.

6. Tacitus, *Annals*, 14.48–9.

7. Ibid., 14.52–6.

8. Ibid., 14.57–9.

9. Ibid., 14.60; Dio, *Histories*, 8.105–7.

10. Tacitus, *Annals*, 14. 61–4.

11. *Octavia*, lines 403, 438, 441, 504–13.

12. Ibid., 530. '*Nos quoque manebunt astra*' (Us, too, the stars shall await!). By 'us', Nero means 'me', an early example of the royal plural.

13. Ibid., 530–43.

14. Ibid., 89–90: '*Odit genitos sanguine claro, Spernit superos hominesque simul.*'

15. Ibid., 593–645; 712–39.

16. St Matthew 16.16. The AV gives 'Thou art the Christ . . .'; the NEB has 'You are the Messiah . . .'. Like Nero, Jesus had readily interchangeable divine titles, conferred on him by others through guesswork.

17. Epicurus (*c.* 341–270 BC) taught in the garden of his house in Athens from about the age of thirty-five until his death, the first philosopher to have female as well as male pupils pursuing an organized course of study. He and his followers lived communally in order to enjoy the benefits of mutual friendship and simple pleasures. His views were partly set out for Romans in the long but unfinished Latin poem *De Rerum Natura* (*On the Nature of Things*) by Lucretius. For a modern treatment of both Epicurean and Stoic philosophy, with translated texts, see A.A. Long and D.N. Sedley, *The Hellenistic Philosophers* (Cambridge, 1987), Vol. 1.

18. Known as the *Domus Transitoria*, it was shortly to be destroyed in the Great Fire of Rome in 64.

19. Tacitus, *Annals*, 15.23.

Chapter Ten

1. Suetonius, *Nero*, 30.

2. It was from these Alexandrian Greeks that Nero's cheer-leaders learnt techniques of rhythmic applause: 'the bees', presumably a buzzing sound; 'the roof tiles', clapping with hands hollowed like the typical Roman *imbrex*; 'the bricks', clapping with flat palms. Suetonius, *Nero*, 20; Tacitus, *Annals*, 15.33–4.

3. One of a series of earthquakes to affect the Naples area in the years building up to the catastrophic eruption of Vesuvius in 79, which buried Pompeii and Herculaneum.

4. 'Monstrous births were a sign that the sacred *Pax Deorum*, or "covenant with the gods", had been broken. Prodigies of this kind were recorded on a yearly basis in the pontifical records . . .', Robert Garland, *The Eye of the Beholder: Deformity and Disability in the Graeco-Roman World* (Cornell UP, 1995), p. 67.

5. Tacitus, *Annals*, 15.34–5.

6. Suetonius, *Nero*, 30.

7. Tacitus, *Annals*, 15.36.

8. Tacitus, *Annals*, 15.36; Suetonius, *Nero*, 19.

9. Tacitus, *Annals*, 15.37.

10. Tacitus, *Annals*, 15.37; Suetonius, *Nero*, 27.

11. Dio, *Histories*, 8.109–11.

12. Gaius (or Titus) Petronius is generally identified as the same Petronius who wrote the celebrated 'novel' in prose and verse, *Satyricon*. 'Arbiter' may have been his *cognomen*.

13. Suetonius, *Nero*, 29.

14. Seneca, *De Vita Beata*, 7.3.

15. Cicero, *Philippics*, 2.45.

16. Petronius, *Satyricon*, 25–6.

17. Suetonius, *Nero*, 28.

18. Ibid., 29.

19. Tacitus, *Annals*, 15.37; Suetonius, *Nero*, 29. 'The distinction between "active" and "passive" roles in sex between males was profoundly implicated in the distinction between free and slave', Catharine Edwards, *The Politics of Immorality in Ancient Rome* (Cambridge, 1993), p. 72.

20. Eva Cantarella, *Bisexuality in the Ancient World* (Yale UP, 1992), p. 97.

21. Dio, *Histories*, 8.153; Suetonius, *Nero*, 21.

22. '. . . the charge of arson has been universally disbelieved by modern scholars', B.H. Warmington, *Nero: Reality and Legend* (London, 1969), p. 124.

23. 18 July 64, the 454th anniversary, to the day, of the burning of Rome by invading Gauls in 390 BC, when the youngest and strongest of Rome's population looked down from the impregnable Capitol Hill while the old and sick, who would have consumed too much of the limited food and water supplies, were left to their fate below. Thus Roman values were preserved for later ages.

24. The sort of run-down neighbourhood that would have attracted poor immigrants. If they included Jewish Christians, with their own cooked-food shops, that might help to explain their later denunciation as fire-raisers.

25. Tacitus, *Annals*, 15.38–40; Suetonius, *Nero*, 38; Dio, *Histories*,

8.111–13; Elder Pliny, *Natural History*, 1.

26. Tacitus, *Annals*, 15.40–1; Dio, *Histories*, 8.117.

27. Suetonius, *Nero*, 38; Tacitus, *Annals*, 15.39; Dio, *Histories*, 8.115.

Chapter Eleven

1. Tacitus, *Annals*, 15.44.

2. Ibid., 15.43; Suetonius, *Nero*, 16.

3. Tacitus, *Annals*, 15.42.

4. Dio says the people were cursing Nero – but without actually naming him (which would have been too dangerous, because cursing the Emperor was a capital offence); Dio, *Histories*, 8.117.

5. Tacitus, *Annals*, 15.44. 'No other writer, Christian or pagan, in the following centuries refers to Nero using the Christians as scapegoats, although Christian tradition knew of Nero as a persecutor . . .', Warmington, *Nero: Reality and Legend* (London, 1969), p. 126.

6. According to church tradition, St Peter was the leader of the Christians in Rome, but that is not mentioned in the New Testament, which is equally (and mysteriously) silent on the specific Neronian persecution of 64 reported by Tacitus. The *Acts of the Apostles* records St Paul's journey to Rome, where he arrived in about 60, but not his martyrdom. Tradition indicates a possible date of 67 for the beheading of St Paul and the crucifixion, upside-down, of St Peter, both in Rome, but it seems equally possible that one or both of them died among their fellow Christians in 64.

7. Quoted by the French scholar G. Walter (from Origen, *Contra Celsum*, 3.8.) in his detailed survey of church sources (or lack of them) on the Neronian persecution, in *Nero* (London, 1957), pp. 159–74. He discusses the possibility that part of the reference in Tacitus is a later 'pious interpolation' by Christian apologists.

8. Josephus, *Jewish War*, 2.223–33. The incident took place at Passover during the procuratorship of Cumanus (48–52). The soldier allegedly farted. When the Jews hurled stones in retaliation, Cumanus sent in reinforcements, and many of those who died were trampled and crushed in the panic to escape through the narrow streets of the city. The figure of 30,000 dead is plainly exaggerated. Josephus himself revises it down to 20,000 in his later *Jewish Antiquities*, 20.12.

9. Professor E.P. Sanders claims that Sepphoris was 'solidly Jewish' with 'some Gentiles as well', but that hardly seems to square with either the lack of any reference to Jesus having been there or the fact that in the Jewish revolt of 66 the Sepphorians, after some initial hesitation, were the only people in the whole of Galilee to side with the Romans, and to ask for and receive the protection of a Roman garrison, of 6,000 infantry and 1,000 cavalry. Sanders, *The Historical Figure of Jesus* (London, 1993), p. 105; Josephus, *Jewish War*, 3.30–4.

10. Matthew 22.21; Mark 12.17; Luke 20.25. Mark Powell reports that of all the sayings of Jesus in St

Mark's gospel, 'Render unto Caesar . . .' was voted the most authentic by members of the American-based Jesus Seminar, in which more than 200 scholars have so far participated since its foundation in 1985. Powell, *The Jesus Debate* (Oxford, 1999), p. 78.

11. e.g. 'His blood be on us and on our children!' (Matthew 27.25), allegedly shouted by a Jewish mob during the implausible hand-washing ceremony. This quotation has been used century after century to justify attacks by Christians on Jews.

12. The fate of Nero's aunt Lepida (see Chapter Three).

13. No. 10 of the 114 'sayings of Jesus' in the non-canonical Gospel of Thomas (translated by Thomas O. Lambdin), in James M. Robinson (ed.), *The Nag Hammadi Library in English* (2nd edn, Leiden, 1984).

14. The quest for the historical Jesus has had three main phases in the twentieth century. The first fizzled out before the First World War after Albert Schweitzer revealed Jesus as a prophet who mistakenly announced that the Kingdom of God was about to arrive (Mark 1.15). 'Schweitzer realized . . . that people who go around declaring "The End is near" tend to be regarded as crackpots', M.A. Powell, *The Jesus Debate*, p. 23. The so-called 'New Questers', emerging in the 1950s, emphasized Jesus' teachings rather than his actions, and interpreted symbolically his prophecies about the coming Kingdom of God, thereby distancing him from beliefs current in first-century Judaism. 'Third Questers', over the past twenty years, tend to identify him as an eschatological prophet immersed in first-century Judaism.

15. In particular, a case can be made out for Mark's gospel to have been based on evidence from St Peter himself.

16. Matthew 7.6, 15.27; Mark 7.27–9.

17. Acts 2.46–7.

18. cf. Paul in II Corinthians 11.22: 'Are they Hebrews? So am I. Are they Israelites? So am I. Are they the seed of Abraham? So am I.'

19. John 1.1–5.

20. Luke 23.47.

21. Suetonius, *Nero*, 16.

22. A typical gnostic belief was that Jesus was not human (or, at least, not fully human) and that because of his heavenly powers he did not really suffer on the cross. Some believed that God was female. Later Christians persecuted them as heretics. For a readable modern analysis of gnostic beliefs based on the Nag Hammadi discoveries, see Elaine Pagels, *The Gnostic Gospels* (New York, 1980).

23. St Peter was succeeded as leader of the church at Jerusalem by James, the brother of Jesus. It was James and his 'elders' who persuaded Paul to enter the Temple openly and 'purify' himself, the action that led to his arrest and imprisonment, and ultimately his appeal to Nero (Acts 21.17–26). The Temple at Jerusalem 'remained the favourite locus of public prayer

and cultic activity among the adherents of the Jesus movement at least until AD 58' – the date of Paul's arrest there – '. . . and probably until the destruction of the sanctuary in AD 70', Geza Vermes, *The Changing Faces of Jesus* (London, 2000). James was thrown to his death from the Temple roof in 62 on the orders of the chief priest.

24. Acts 18.2.

25. Its short-lived name was Aelia Capitolina. For the Jerusalem massacre, see Epilogue, below.

26. Some examples are given in the Epilogue and associated notes.

27. Petronius, *Satyricon*, 111–12.

28. Matthew 27.57–61.

29. Tacitus, *Annals*, 15.44.

30. Suetonius, *Nero*, 16, 19.

31. 'It may well be that some of the Christians in Rome, seeing the conflagration already raging, felt it was their pious duty to make it rage more fiercely still', Michael Grant, *The Jews in the Roman World* (London, 1973), p. 180.

32. Juvenal, *Satires*, 1.115.

33. Younger Pliny, *Letters*, to Trajan, 10.96.

34. Revelation 13.18.

Chapter Twelve

1. Tacitus, *Annals*, 14.65.

2. Ibid., 15.48.

3. Ibid., 15.60.

4. Little more than 200 words survive of a life of Lucan, attributed to Suetonius. It preserves a half-line of verse by Nero: '*Sub terris tonuisse putes*' ('You might think it was thundering under the earth'). Lucan shouted these words when relieving himself noisily in a communal lavatory; those seated on either side of him fled, for fear of being associated with his hostility to the Emperor. Nero's phrase (or Lucan's use of it) is ingenious: *putes*, in addition to meaning 'you might think', as part of the verb *puto*, can also mean 'You stink!', as part of a different verb, *puteo*. Suetonius, *Lives of Illustrious Men: Lucan*.

5. Tacius, *Annals*, 15.49. W.R. Johnson, a modern admirer of Lucan's works, says that what little we know of him 'depicts the sort of unstable compound of high spirits, raw nerves and gross vanity which is not uncommon in poets', Johnson, *Momentary Monsters: Lucan and his Heroes* (Cornell UP, 1987), p. 21n.

6. Lucan, *Pharsalia*, 1.33–66.

7. Suetonius, *Lives of Illustrious Men: Lucan*.

8. The story of the conspiracy and its aftermath is told in detail in Tacitus, *Annals*, 15.48–74; Dio, *Histories*, 8.129–35.

9. Tacitus, *Annals*, 15.62.

10. Ibid., 15.67.

11. Nero tempered justice with mercy. Tacitus confirms that exiles who returned to Rome after his death admitted they had plotted to kill him; such action against a head of state has been a capital offence in almost every society before the twentieth century. Those who survived owed it to his exercise of *clementia*. It is impossible to credit a report by Suetonius (*Nero*, 36), referring either to the Pisonian plot

or one led by Vinicius the following year, stating that children of the condemned men were exiled, poisoned or starved to death. He does not specify which plot he means, or name any individuals, but he adds the suggestive detail that some children were poisoned along with their teachers and servants. That must surely refer to a particular case of inadvertent food poisoning (far from uncommon in Rome), which Suetonius has inflated into a general accusation of child murder, as part of the *damnatio memoriae* of Nero.

12. Acts 18.12–16.
13. Tacitus, *Annals*, 16.18–19; Suetonius, *Nero*, 35.
14. Tacitus, *Annals*, 16.21–35 (from this point, the rest of the Tacitus' *Annals* are lost); Suetonius, *Nero*, 37; Dio, *Histories*, 8.131.
15. Suetonius, *Nero*, 35; Tacitus, *Annals*, 16.6; Dio, *Histories*, 8.135.
16. Tacitus, *Annals*, 16.7.
17. Dio records (*Histories*, 8.135) that on one occasion Poppaea, catching sight of herself in a mirror, exclaimed that she hoped to die before she became old and faded. Her name lived on not only in artistic works, notably Monteverdi's opera *The Coronation of Poppaea*, but because of a face cream she invented and which was still being used in the century after her death.

Chapter Thirteen

1. Suetonius, *Nero*, 32.
2. D.W. Rathbone doubts the economic explanation for 'devaluing' the currency. 'Nero was probably trying to reform the whole monetary system for a mixture of administrative and aesthetic reasons', Rathbone, 'The Imperial Finances', in *Cambridge Ancient History*, Vol. 10 (1996), p. 319.
3. Elder Pliny, *Natural History*, 35.5; Suetonius, *Nero*, 31.
4. Tacitus, *Annals*, 15.42.
5. The essential modern guidebook for site visits is: Amanda Claridge, *Rome* (Oxford Archaeological Guides, 1998).
6. The beautiful illustrations in the new official guidebook are a great help: E. Segala and I. Sciortino, *Domus Aurea* (Rome, 1999).
7. Axel Boethius and J.B. Ward-Perkins, *Etruscan and Roman Architecture* (London, 1970), p. 248.
8. Tacitus, *Annals*, 15.42.
9. The distinguished French archaeologist Gilbert Charles-Picard says the project 'may recall the pastoral follies of Marie Antoinette at Versailles', but it is the only instance 'in European history of a sovereign claiming for his exclusive use such an enormous area in the very heart of an overcrowded and expanding metropolis', Charles-Picard, *Augustus and Nero* (London, 1966), p. 100.
10. Suetonius, *Nero*, 31.
11. Tacitus, *Annals*, 15.1–18, 24–30.
12. Dio, *Histories*, 8.139–47; Suetonius, *Nero*, 30.
13. Suetonius, *Nero*, 35. Tacitus

credits the Elder Pliny as his source for the supposed involvement of Antonia in the Pisonian plot; as the widow of Faustus Sulla, whom Nero had killed, she would certainly have had a motive. Tacitus, *Annals*, 15.53.

14. 'Turning people into sex-objects is one of the specialities of our species . . . A sex-object is ritual form imposed on nature', Camille Paglia, *Sexual Personae* (Yale UP, 1990).

15. Suetonius, *Nero*, 28.

16. Anthony Storr, *The Dynamics of Creation* (London, 1972), p. 109.

17. Dio, *Histories*, 8.157. Under Agrippina's orders, Helius poisoned Nero's cousin Marcus Junius Silanus at the start of his reign. See Chapter Four.

18. Dio, *Histories*, 8.149.

19. Suetonius, *Nero*, 36.

20. Dio, *Histories*, 8.165.

21. Ibid., 8.139.

22. Dio, *Histories*, 8.151–5; Suetonius, *Nero*, 12, 21.

23. Dio, *Histories*, 8.161; Suetonius, *Nero*, 40.

Chapter Fourteen

1. Suetonius, *Nero*, 22.

2. Ibid., 24; Dio, *Histories*, 8.161.

3. e.g., cricket, whose fascination resides in its rituals. That is why it does not matter overmuch if a match of five or six days ends in a draw. Modern emphasis on winning is partly a function of mass-media attention, especially television 'highlights'. If television cameras had been at the 67 Olympics, we would have had to endure endless action replays of Nero falling out of his chariot; participatory rituals would have been ignored.

4. Suetonius, *Nero*, 23.

5. For the Greek tour as a whole, see Dio, *Histories*, 8.149–67; Suetonius, *Nero*, 19, 23–4; Pausanius (who is chiefly interested in objects that Nero either purloined or donated), 2.17, 37; 5.12, 25–6; 7.17; 9.27; 10.7, 19; Philostratus, *Life of Apollonius*, 5.7–8. Apollonius of Rhodes was a wandering miracle worker, who visited Rome during Nero's reign but happened to be in southern Spain at the time of the Emperor's Greek tour. Philostratus reports that when news of Nero's 'Olympic victory' reached Spain, some of the less sophisticated locals thought he had beaten the 'Olympians' in war.

6. The Jewish revolt of 66 is covered in (often horrific) detail in Book 2 of Josephus' *Jewish War*, which includes coverage of various localized massacres of or by Jews in Alexandria, Caesarea and elsewhere.

7. Josephus, *Jewish War*, 3.1–8; Dio, *Histories*, 8.173.

8. Josephus' account of his own hair-raising adventures reaches a climax in *Jewish Wars* 3.204–407.

9. Dio, *Histories*, 8.163; Suetonius, *Nero*, 19, 23.

10. Josephus, *Jewish War*, 3.522–40. The sea of Galilee was reported to be red with the blood of the slain.

11. *Don Juan*, 86.3: 'The mountains look down on Marathon –

And Marathon looks on the sea;
And musing there an hour alone,
I dreamed that Greece might still
　　be free.'
12. Nero's speech is preserved in
an inscription found at Acraephiae
(Dittenberger, *Sylloge Inscriptionum
Graecarum*, 3.814). His peroration
reads: 'Others have freed cities –
only Nero has freed a province.' A.
Momigliano says the speech
mingles 'genuine love of Hellas'
with 'the most naive self-praise',
Momigliano, 'Nero', in *Cambridge
Ancient History*, Vol. 10 (1934),
p. 735.
13. Dio, *Histories*, 8.167, names as
victims Sulpicius Camerinus and
his son.
14. Dio, *Histories*, 8.169–71;
Suetonius, *Nero*, 25.
15. Vindex's revolt raises problems
of interpretation too complicated to
discuss here. The chief sources are
Dio, *Histories*, 8.173–85;
Suetonius, *Nero*, 40–2; *Galba*,
9–11; Plutarch, *Galba*, 2–7.
16. Suetonius, *Nero*, 43–4.
17. Ibid., 47; Virgil, *Aeneid*,
12.646.
18. For Nero's last night:
Suetonius, *Nero* 47–9; Dio,
Histories, 8.187–93.
19. Homer, *Iliad*, 10.535.
20. Suetonius, *Nero*, 50.

Epilogue

1. Tacitus, *Histories*, 1.4.
2. Ibid., 1.5; Dio, *Histories*,
8.199.
3. Plutarch, *Galba*, 8–14.
4. Tacitus, *Histories*, 1.7.
5. Ibid., 1.6; Suetonius, *Galba*,

12; Dio says (*Histories*, 8.199) that
Galba killed 7,000 of Nero's men
in this clash outside Rome, and
later decimated the survivors, but
that seems rather extreme even for
Galba.
6. The so-called Year of Four
Emperors: successively, Galba,
Otho, Vitellius and Vespasian.
Tacitus' *Histories*, the chief source,
are full of tedious and often
confusing military activity. The
following is a selection covering
points touched on here: 1.12–17:
Rhine legions revolt; adoption of
Piso; 1.18–41: Otho's coup
removes Galba; 2.41–9: Otho's
defeat and suicide; 2.79–81:
Vespasian hailed Emperor;
3.26–34: sack of Cremona;
3.71–86: burning of Capitol, death
of Vitellius. Other accounts: Dio,
Histories, 8.199–257; Suetonius,
Galba, Otho; Plutarch, *Galba*
(notably 8–14 on downfall of
Nymphidius), *Otho*.
7. Tacitus, *Histories*, 1.3.
8. Josephus, *Jewish Wars*,
5.10–7.16: a long, harrowing
account of the siege of Jerusalem.
9. Dio, *Histories*, 8.299;
Suetonius, *Titus*, 8.
10. Dio, *Histories*, 8.237.
11. Suetonius, *Domitian*, 14; Dio,
Histories, 8.351.
12. Tacitus, *Histories*, 2.8.
13. Suetonius, *Nero*, 57.
14. Revelation, 20.15.
15. 'It seems as far from the spirit
of Jesus as it is possible to be, and
yet it provides the conclusion of the
Christian Bible', A.N. Wilson, *Jesus*
(London, 1992), p. 250.
16. Revelation 13.1–8.

17. Ibid., 13.11–18.
18. Ibid., 14.9–11.
19. Ibid., 15 and 16.
20. Plutarch, *Essays*: 'God's Slowness to Punish', 32.
21. Quoted in B.W. Henderson, *The Life and Principate of the Emperor Nero* (London, 1903), p. 420.
22. Ibid., p. 421.
23. 'Letter from Rome', *The Times Literary Supplement*, 28 April 2000, p. 15.

Appendix One

1. 'The fictional speech rather than the authentic document was the hallmark of the ancient historian', Andrew Wallace-Hadrill, *Suetonius: The Scholar and his Caesars* (London, 1983), p. 21.
2. Ronald Mellor, *Tacitus* (New York, 1993), p. 166. In a crowded field, Mellor's eloquent volume is the best introduction to its subject.

SELECT BIBLIOGRAPHY

Rome and Nero

Adam, Jeane-Pierre. *La Construction Romaine: Materiaux et Techniques*, Paris, 1989; English translation: *Roman Building: Materials and Techniques*, London, 1994

Adkins, Lesley and Adkins, Roy A. *Dictionary of Roman Religion*, New York, 1996

d'Ambra, Eve. *Art and Identity in the Roman World*, London, 1998

Ball, Warwick. *Rome in the East*, London/New York, 2000

Balsdon, J.P.V.D. *Roman Women*, London, 1962

Barrett, Anthony A. *Caligula: The Corruption of Power*, London, 1989

——. *Agrippina: Sex, Power and Politics in the Early Empire* (New York, 1996), published in Britain as *Agrippina: Mother of Nero*

Bauman, Richard A. *Women and Politics in Ancient Rome*, London/New York, 1993

Boethius, Axel and Ward-Perkins, J.B. *Etruscan and Roman Architecture*, London, 1970

Bradley, Keith R. *Discovering the Roman Family*, Oxford, 1991

——. *Slavery and Society at Rome*, Cambridge, 1994

Cantarella, Eva. *Secundo Natura*, Rome, 1988; English translation: *Bisexuality in the Ancient World*, New York, 1992

Charles-Picard, Gilbert. *Auguste et Néron*, Paris, 1962; English translation: *Augustus and Nero*, London, 1966

Claridge, Amanda. *Rome*, Oxford Archaeological Guides, 1998

Cunliffe, Barry. *Rome and her Empire*, London, 1978

Dudley, D.R. (ed.). *Neronians and Flavians: Silver Latin I*, London/Boston, 1972

Edwards, Catharine. *The Politics of Immorality in Ancient Rome*, Cambridge, 1993

Elsner, Jás and Masters, Jamie (eds). *Reflections of Nero*, London, 1994

Fantham, Elaine. *Roman Literary Culture: From Cicero to Apuleius*, Johns Hopkins UP, 1996

Ferguson, John, *The Religions of the Roman Empire*, London, 1970

Galinsky, Karl, *Augustan Culture*, Princeton UP, 1996

Garzetti, Albino. *L'Impero da Tiberio agli Antonini*, Rome, 1960; English translation: *From Tiberius to the Antonines*, London, 1974

Grant, Michael. *Nero*, London, 1970

——. *The Roman Forum*, London, 1970

Griffin, Miriam T. *Seneca: A Philosopher in Politics*, Oxford, 1976

——. *Nero: The End of a Dynasty*, London, 1984

Henderson, B.W. *The Life and Principate of the Emperor Nero*, London, 1903

Hopkins, Keith, *Conquerors and Slaves*, Cambridge, 1978

Johnson, W.R. *Momentary Monsters: Lucan and his Heroes*, Cornell UP, 1987

Landels, John G. *Music in Ancient Greece and Rome*, London/New York, 1999

Le Bohec, Yann. *L'Armée Romaine sous le Haut-Empire*, Paris, 1989; English translation: *The Imperial Roman Army*, London, New York, 1994

Levick, Barbara. *The Government of the Roman Empire: A Sourcebook*, London, 1985

——. *Claudius*, London, 1990

——. *Vespasian*, London/New York, 1999

Lintott, Andrew. *Imperium Romanum: Politics and Administration*, London/New York, 1993

Long, A.A. and Sedley, D.N. *The Hellenistic Philosophers*, Cambridge, 1987

Luttwak, Edward. *The Grand Strategy of the Roman Empire*, Johns Hopkins UP, 1976

Mellor, Ronald. *Tacitus*, New York, 1993

Millar, Fergus. *A Study of Cassius Dio*, Oxford, 1964

Momigliano, A. 'Nero', in *Cambridge Ancient History*, Vol. 10 (1934)

Peddie, John. *Conquest: The Invasion of Roman Britain*, Stroud, 1988

——. *The Roman War Machine*, Stroud, 1994

Ramage, Nancy H. and Ramage, Andrew. *Roman Art: Romulus to Constantine*, 2nd edn, London, 1995

Rawson, Beryl (ed.). *Marriage, Divorce and Children in Ancient Rome*, Oxford, 1991

Rickman, Geoffrey. *The Corn Supply of Ancient Rome*, Oxford, 1980

Salway, Peter. *Roman Britain*, Oxford, 1981

Segala, Elisabeth and Sciortino, Ida. *Domus Aurea*, Rome, 1999; official illustrated guide

Sharples, R.W. *Stoics, Epicureans and Sceptics*, London/New York, 1996

Shotter, David. *Nero*, Lancaster Pamphlet, London/New York, 1997

Sørensen, V. *Humanisten ved Neros Hof*, Denmark, 1976; English translation: *Seneca: The Humanist at the Court of Nero*, Edinburgh/Chicago, 1984

Sullivan, J.P. *Literature and Politics in the Age of Nero*, Cornell UP, 1985

Toner, J.P. *Leisure and Ancient Rome*, Cambridge, 1995

Wallace-Hadrill, A. *Suetonius: The Scholar and his Caesars*, London, 1983

——. 'The Imperial Court', in *Cambridge Ancient History*, Vol. 10 (1996)

Walter, G. *Néron*, Paris, 1955; English translation: *Nero*, London, 1957

Warmington, B.H. *Nero: Reality and Legend*, London, 1969

——. *Suetonius: Nero*, Latin text, introduction and notes, Bristol, 1977

Webster, Graham. *The Roman Imperial Army*, London, 1969

Wells, Colin, *The Roman Empire*, 2nd edn, London, 1992

Wiedemann, T.E.J. 'Tiberius to Nero', in *Cambridge Ancient History*, Vol. 10 (1996)

——. 'From Nero to Vespasian', in *Cambridge Ancient History*, Vol. 10 (1996)

Woodman, A.J. *Tacitus Reviewed*, Oxford, 1998

Wheeler, Mortimer. *Roman Art and Architecture*, London, 1964

Williams, Derek. *Romans and Barbarians*, London, 1998

Wiseman, T.P. *Death of an Emperor*, translation and commentary on Book 19 of Josephus' *Jewish Antiquities*, Exeter, 1991

Zanker, Paul. *Pompeji: Stadbilt und Wohngeschmack*, 1995; English translation: *Pompeii: Public and Private Life*, Harvard, 1998

Palestine and Jesus

Coogan, Michael D. *The Oxford History of the Biblical World*, Oxford, 1998

Grant, Michael. *The Jews in the Roman World*, London, 1973

——. *Jesus*, London, 1977

——. *Saint Peter*, London, 1994

Hopkins, Keith. *A World Full of Gods*, London, 1999

Pagels, Elaine. *The Gnostic Gospels*, New York, 1980

Powell, Mark Allan. *Jesus as a Figure in History*, Louisville, Kentucky, 1998; published in Britain as *The Jesus Debate*, Oxford, 1999

Robinson, James M. (ed.). *The Nag Hammadi Library in English*, 2nd edn, Leiden 1984

Sanders, E.P. *The Historical Figure of Jesus*, London, 1993

Vermes, G. *The Dead Sea Scrolls in English*, London, 1962

——. *The Changing Faces of Jesus*, London, 2000

INDEX